Learn
Java
Now

Stephen R. Davis

Microsoft Press

PUBLISHED BY
Microsoft Press
A Division of Microsoft Corporation
One Microsoft Way
Redmond, Washington 98052-6399

Library of Congress Cataloging-in-Publication Data
Davis, Stephen R., 1956–
    Learn Java now / Stephen R. Davis.
       p.   cm.
    Includes index.
    ISBN 1-57231-428-1
    1. Java (Computer program language)   I. Title.
QA76.73.J38D38   1996
005.13'3--dc20   96-22052
                                         CIP

Printed and bound in the United States of America.

1 2 3 4 5 6 7 8 9 QMQM 1 0 9 8 7 6

Distributed to the book trade in Canada by Macmillan of Canada, a division of
Canada Publishing Corporation.

A CIP catalogue record for this book is available from the British Library.

Microsoft Press books are available through booksellers and distributors worldwide.
For further information about international editions, contact your local Microsoft
Corporation office. Or contact Microsoft Press International directly at fax
(206) 936-7329.

Acquisitions Editor: Eric Stroo
Project Editor: Ina Chang
Technical Editor: Jim Fuchs

This book could not have been completed
without the loving support and patience of
my biggest fans, my wife Jenny and son Kinsey.

Contents at a Glance

Table of Contents

Table of Contents

Table of Contents

Table of Contents

Table of Contents

Table of Contents

Table of Contents

Acknowledgments

The fact that my name is the only name that appears on the binding of this book is misleading in the extreme. A small army of editors, technical reviewers, and production people are necessary to produce any book, and this one was certainly no exception. First and foremost I would like to thank my editors, Ina Chang and Jim Fuchs. I would also like to thank Ted Chiang, Sara Tulli, and Stephen Horne for their patient technical input. This book would never have made it off the launch pad without the ground-work of my agent, Claudette Moore, and acquisitions editor Eric Stroo. Finally, I would like to thank Michael Victor, the graphic artist responsible for the neat graphics in Chapter 16.

Readers of some of my other books know that I cannot write without the continuing presence of the family pets outside my window. I am sad to report that Beavis and Butthead, the rabbits who regularly frequented our front yard, have passed on to Greater Pastures, and Marley the cat suc-cumbed to kitty leukemia last winter. However, on a happier note, Bob (also a cat) bore a litter of five healthy, happy, and curious kitties last win-ter. In addition, the original members of the Davis animal family, Trude and Scooter the dogs, are still going strong, although Scooter has grown too old to chase cars if no one's watching. Finally, I would like to intro-duce the newest member of our barnyard clan, Penny the apartment pig. (It seems that Penny's apartment manager quite understandably didn't see the wisdom of keeping a pig in an apartment, so we were asked to inherit Penny on extremely short notice—before the manager could return with a butcher.)

If any errors slipped through despite the hard work of my editors and the encouragement of my animals (certainly not in the same class), I bear full responsibility.

Introduction

The World Wide Web has taken the world by storm. Notice how often you see ads on television with the advertiser's home-page address listed at the end. Even such white-shirt, black-tie programs as CNN's *Nightly Business Report* invite their audiences to join them on the Web as if families all across America drop in on the Web in the same way they might make a phone call to Grandma.

Web pages have been springing up at a frantic pace, each one screaming "Look at me!" to the public. This competition for audience share has forced Web-page designers to be more and more clever in how they design their pages. More competition, better product. That's how it's supposed to work. But there's only so much you can do with a static HTML (Hypertext Markup Language) page. Programmers being who they are (programmers, of course), they immediately start wondering if there isn't a way to design their Web pages to be interactive—that is, make the pages smart.

At first glance, this doesn't seem like too much of a problem. People can write programs in their favorite language (be it C, C++, Visual Basic, or whatever), compile them, and store the executable file on the server along with the HTML page. A minor addition to the HTML language would allow the Web browser to automatically load the program from the server and execute it on the client's computer. The program could open windows, pop up dialog boxes, sing, dance, whatever. *Voila*—smart Web pages.

This plan has several problems, however. First, conventional programming languages are not designed to execute over the Web. They don't have the features needed to perform even the most common operations. The programmer would have to write his own functions to perform even the most basic operations, such as loading an image file from the server to be displayed on the client machine. Web programming in a conventional, non-Web language would quickly become quite a chore. In addition, all this reinventing the wheel would undoubtedly lead to a lot of different solutions to the same problem. This would complicate programmers' lives as they try to read and understand each other's programs.

In addition, conventional programs generate rather large executables. Of course, large is a relative term. 500 KB is nothing to get excited about when you're executing a program from your own hard drive. A program like that can be loaded from disk and ready to execute almost before you've lifted your finger from the mouse button. Even with a 28.8-kilobits-per second (Kbps) modem, however, loading that same program over the phone lines takes more than two minutes, and that's assuming no communication delays due to crowded lines.

Then there's the issue of security. Do you really want your browser executing conventional programs over the Net without your control? Once that Visual Basic program has been downloaded to the client machine and begins executing, it can do anything it wants. That's not a problem in a conventional environment—if I write a program to wipe out my hard disk and then execute it and (guess what) it wipes out my hard disk, who can I blame but myself? (Maybe I can sue the compiler manufacturer?) On the other hand, if I happen to take a peek at some kid's home page and that home page downloads a program onto my computer that wipes out the hard disk, I think I have a legitimate gripe.

The browser could prompt me before going ahead with the operation, with something like: "About to download potentially dangerous program that might wipe out your computer. Browser takes no responsibility for what happens. Should I continue?" What would you answer? Faced with that kind of a threat, hardly anyone would dare execute one of these clever over-the-Net programs.

Finally, there's the problem of different computing environments. There are all different types of computers attached to the Web. These executables that we create—which computer should they support? Granted, the majority of the home computers attached to the Net are undoubtedly PCs, but there are still lots of Macintoshes, UNIX boxes, and the like. Surely we could devise a scheme by which the browser could identify the host computer type to the server. If the client is a PC, send this executable; if it's a Mac, send this one over here. But even that's not enough. Even in the PC world, people are executing Microsoft Windows 3.1, Microsoft Windows 95, Microsoft Windows NT, and OS/2. And who knows what operating systems will come along to replace these someday? This multiple-executable solution puts an unfair burden on the Web programmer to support all possible client environments.

What Is It About Java?

The Java language was designed to solve all these problems and a host of others as well. Java contains built-in support for the Web, freeing the programmer from the burden of coming up with ad hoc solutions to common Web problems. Java generates extremely small executables to facilitate faster loading over potentially slow communications lines. Java enforces tight security—a Java program cannot access anything to which the client computer does not specifically give it access. Java is machine independent. The same program can be executed on a PC, a Mac, or even a UNIX machine (as long as there is a browser on the machine that supports Java— more on this later).

Beyond that, Java is a simple, powerful language in its own right. Java is object oriented. Its syntax encourages the programmer to generate modular, maintainable programs. To the novice, Java looks a lot like that other object-oriented language, C++. There's no doubt that Java was heavily influenced by its powerful predecessor. However, Java differs from C++ in some fundamental ways.

One of the major goals of C++ was backward compatibility with the C language, which isn't object oriented at all. While it ensured the language's acceptance by supporting legacy code, this decision has exacted a high price. The C++ language is extremely complex. As it bends and twists to remain compatible with a language designed almost 30 years ago, C++ gets caught up in some syntactic morasses.

The designers of Java decided to drop backward compatibility with C in favor of simplicity. This has allowed the Java language to adopt a much simpler, more consistent style, somewhat reminiscent of Smalltalk. (If you are not familiar with C++ or Smalltalk, don't worry—it's not a requirement for this book.) It is a good all-around language with or without the Web.

Who This Book Is For

This is not a book about authoring World Wide Web home pages. I assume that you know how to access and use the Web. All this really means is that you know which is the working end of your browser. I don't assume that you know anything much about HTML. (I will teach you the very minimum you'll need to get your Java applet installed in an HTML page and executing.)

I will teach you about Java programming using Microsoft's Visual J++ development environment. I assume that you are familiar with the concepts of programming, but I don't assume that your background is in a particular language. I welcome C, C++, and Visual Basic programmers alike. We'll even make room for an assembler programmer or two.

Conventions Used in This Book

I have found that adopting a standard coding style makes programs easier to understand and, therefore, easier to write. I have pretty much adopted the Microsoft Hungarian naming convention in my programming style, as shown in Table I-1.

Convention	Example
Class names start with a capital letter.	`public class Student;`
Objects start with a lowercase letter; they tend to use the name of the class or some part of it, if possible.	`Student student;`

Primitive types start with a letter indicating their type. (The only exception to this rule seems to be the age-old practice of using *I* and *J* for loop indexes.)	`Boolean bFlag;`
	`byte yField;`
	`char cOneChar;`
	`int nValue;`
	`long lValue;`
	`float fValue;`
	`double dValue;`

Data members are preceded by *m_*.	`int m_nAnIntMember;`
Functions start with an uppercase letter and are not preceded by a type character.	`public void AFunction();` `public int SomeOtherFunction();`
Names of objects tend to be multiword. Each word after the first one starts with a capital letter.	`char cOneChat;`

Braces are used after every control structure even if only one statement is enclosed. The brace follows the control structure. (Neither of these is required by Java.)	`if (nA > nB)`
	`{`
	`    nA = nB;`
	`}`

Member functions precede data members (just a convenient way to find things).	not applicable
Class (static) members precede object (nonstatic) members (again, just a convenient way to find things).	not applicable

Table I-1. *Coding conventions.*

Table I-2 shows the typographical conventions used in this book.

Convention	Description
monospace	All code examples are in a monospace font.
italics	Code examples (such as variable or function names) are italic when they appear within the text.
bold	New terms are in boldface when they appear for the first time.
NOTE	This icon indicates an aside or a particular note that you might already be aware of.
C/ C++	This icon indicates a section of particular importance to readers who know C/C++.

Table I-2. *Typographical conventions.*

C/ C++ Many readers will be familiar with the C and C++ languages. Certainly Java is a different language, but the similarities are obvious. You'll see the C/C++ icon when I compare and contrast Java to these predecessor languages. I do this only when it is helpful in understanding Java.

The Parts of This Book

Java can generate two types of programs. A stand-alone, Web-independent program is called a Java application, or an **app** in Java parlance. For writing apps, Java is simply a neat object-oriented language. Java really starts to shine when you use it to generate programs designed to execute as part of a Web page. These programs are called **applets**. The Visual J++ Applet-Wizard makes generating powerful applets a breeze.

Of course, everyone will want to jump straight to the applets. But you have to walk before you can run, so this book is divided into two parts. Part 1, "Decaf Java: Writing Java Apps," covers the fundamentals of the Java language, including variable types, control structures, Java classes, constructors, inheritance, object-oriented programming in Java, exceptions, and file I/O.

Part 2, "Instant Java: Using the AppletWizard," shows you how to create nifty applets using the Visual J++ AppletWizard. Subjects here include handling events, reading parameters out of the HTML page, multi-threading, animation, and audio. The final chapter in this part explains how to use the Abstract Window Toolkit (AWT), a set of Java classes that you can use to generate sophisticated, platform-independent forms such as dialog boxes and menus.

At the back of this book, you'll find two appendixes. Appendix A contains installation instructions that will help get you up and running. Appendix B contains several interesting programs from Sun Microsystems, Inc., the originators of the Java language.

Other Sources of Information

The best source of Java information is, of course, the Web. The Web sites shown in Table I-3 are useful starting places.

Site	Resources
//www.javasoft.com	This site is run by the originators of the Java language and is full of generic Java information.
//www.microsoft.com/visualj/	This site is run by the Visual J++ developers and is the best source for Visual J++–specific information.
//www.gamelan.com	Gamelan is a clearing house for Java information. Basically, these guys maintain a list of links to other Java sites.

Table I-3. *Java information on the Web.*

Decaf Java: Writing Java Apps

Your First Java Program

Java is an object-oriented programming language in the same programming family as C++. Like C++, its functional programming roots are unmistakable. But unlike C++, Java is not a functional language with object-oriented features grafted on. This makes Java a simpler language with a more consistent syntax. In addition, Java is a secure language.

Hello, World

It's almost mandatory that the first program that you write in a new language print "Hello, world" to the screen. The Java equivalent appears as follows:

```
public class App1_1
{
    public static void main(String args[])
    {
        System.out.println("Hello, world");
    }
}
```

To create this program, choose the New command from the File menu. In the New dialog box, select Text File and then click OK. This opens a blank window in which you can enter the source code above. (You might want to first create a subdirectory in which to place your first program.) For now, enter what you see above exactly as it appears—I'll explain what it does as soon as you've compiled it and seen it execute.

After you finish entering the code, save it to a file called App1_1.java.

 OTE It's important that the name of the file match the name of the class and that the extension be *.java*.

To compile the program, choose Compile from the Build menu. Microsoft Visual J++ requires a project before it can compile your file. (A **project** is a container of files that combine to make a program.) Since you do not have a project, Visual J++ asks you whether you want a default project built. You should select Yes. (If you don't, Visual J++ refuses to go any further.) Visual J++ obligingly builds a project called App1_1 in the current directory and puts the single file App1_1 into it.

To execute the program, choose Execute from the Build menu.

The first time you execute the program, Visual J++ will not know whether App1_1 is an application or an applet. An **application**, or **app**, is a program designed to execute on the host machine like a conventional program. A Java app executes like any other program. The alternative is an **applet**, which is a program designed to execute as part of an HTML (Hypertext Markup Language) Web page. All of the programs we build in Part 1 of this book will be apps. We'll do applets in Part 2.

Select the Run Class As Application option button, and then click OK. Your window should look like Figure 1-1.

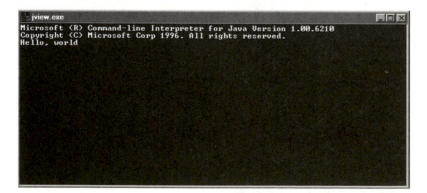

Figure 1-1. *The first time you execute your program, you must tell Visual J++ that it is an app. Visual J++ should then open the output window and present the expected "Hello, world" message.*

OTE The version number that you see on screen when you run an application will be different from the one shown in the figures in this book.

What Does That Do?

Let's go back over that to understand exactly what happens. The first statement in the program above defines our initial class. We'll cover classes in detail in Chapter 3, but for now let's just say that every program has to have one, it has to be marked public, and its name has to be the same as the name of the .java source file.

The following statement defines the first (and in this case, only) function in the program:

```
public static void main(String args[])
{
}
```

Execution always starts with the function *main,* which must be defined exactly as shown. The opening and closing braces contain the code. In this case, our function includes a single Java statement:

```
System.out.println("Hello, world");
```

System is an object that refers to the system in which the program is executing. *out* is the default output object.

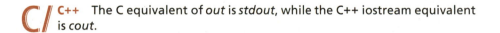 **C++** The C equivalent of *out* is *stdout,* while the C++ iostream equivalent is *cout.*

The function *println* simply prints its *String* argument to the output device followed by a new line.

What Does Visual J++ Do?

The example "Hello, world" program seems pretty straightforward, but it's interesting to look at what Visual J++ does with your program.

When you ask Visual J++ to compile your program, it does not generate a program like you are used to seeing. Rather than generate an executable full of 80x86 machine instructions, the Visual J++ compiler outputs what are known as **Java byte codes**. Java byte codes are instructions written for some virtual Java machine that doesn't really exist. To execute your program you must have a Java byte code interpreter to execute the byte codes, which means you are in effect emulating the **Java virtual machine** (JVM) on whatever computer and operating system you happen to be using. You don't normally notice this, since Visual J++ does this automatically when you execute your app within the Visual J++ Interactive Development Environment (IDE).

When you execute an applet over the Web, it's up to the browser to implement the Java byte codes. (Microsoft Internet Explorer version 3.0 and later and Netscape Navigator version 2.0 and later, among others, implement the Java byte code interpreter on the PC.) This is shown in Figure 1-2.

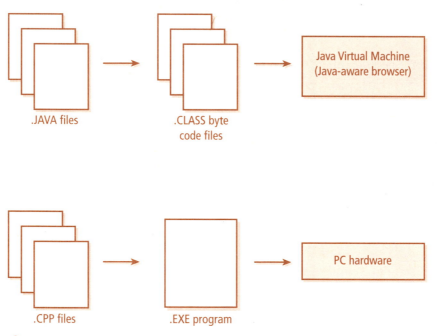

Figure 1-2. *Compiling .java source files produces .class output files containing the Java byte code instructions. These instructions must be downloaded and executed by a Java-aware browser.*

Going through the Java virtual machine serves three purposes:

■ **Machine independence.** There is only one JVM. (Actually, there aren't any—that's what makes it virtual.) There is a different JVM emulator for each different type of PC. This is what gives Java its machine independence.

■ **Security.** Experience has shown how difficult it is to achieve any reasonable level of software security. As long as programs execute on the CPU in native mode, any flaw in the operating system or browser can be exploited by hackers who are looking for a way into the client machine. Java programs do not have this flexibility. The Java program executes within the Java virtual machine created by the browser. As the program executes, the browser is always present, watching over the program's shoulder, so to speak, to make sure that the program does not get into any mischief.

■ **Reduced applet size.** JVM programs are much smaller than conventional programs. This is because the built-in Java library functions that your program calls are resident in the browser rather than linked to your program. This significantly reduces the size of the Java applets that must be downloaded, and thereby reduces download time. Java further reduces the download time by downloading only what it needs. (The byte codes generated for a given class are not downloaded until they are needed by the program.)

Just-in-Time Compilation

There is a downside to interpreting Java byte codes in the browser—decreased performance. Java byte code programs don't execute as fast as normal, native code programs. To address this problem, Microsoft Internet Explorer supports a facility called **Just-in-Time compilation**, or JIT. When Internet Explorer receives a Java applet the first time, if JIT is enabled it converts the Java byte code into a native program, which it saves to disk. Internet Explorer then executes this native program rather than the original Java byte codes. In effect, the JIT looks at the Java byte code as a source language, which it then compiles into a local machine language program.

JIT retains many of the advantages of Java byte codes. Since it doesn't change the Java byte codes generated by Visual J++ in any way, the resulting program is still secure and machine independent, and the download times are still minimized. The JIT-compiled program executes several times faster than even the best Java byte code emulators.

Conclusion

So far Java looks a lot like an interpreted C or C++. Let's step back and go over the primitives of the language before we try to write any more Java applications.

Can I Make a Simple Statement?

Java is an object-oriented language. This means classes—and lots of them. (A class is a user-defined type—never mind if you don't know what that is right now; you'll find out soon enough.) Before we get into object-oriented programming concepts and the Java class, however, let's go over the basic building blocks of Java. We'll start by examining the intrinsic data types. From there we'll move right through operators and into the flow control statements, including user-defined functions. We'll wrap up this chapter with a simple example program so you can see some of these basic features in action.

Java Expressions

A Java statement can be a comment, a block, a declaration, an expression, or a control statement. Most statements end in a semicolon in Java. (Blocks and comments are about the only holdouts.) Spaces, tabs, and new lines are largely ignored. The programmer is free to sprinkle this so-called **white space** into the program at will, to enhance readability. About the only restriction is that you can't put white space in the middle of an operator or an identifier.

> **C/** **C++** C and C++ programmers will find this chapter a pretty quick read because Java borrows much of its syntax from these languages. However, you should skim over the chapter anyway, paying particular attention to the C/C++ notes—there are a few gotchas.

Comments

Three types of comments are defined in Java. The most common is the so-called C++-style comment of two slashes (//) in a row. This type of comment continues from the // to the end of the line.

The second style is the so-called C-style comment, with a /* used to signify the beginning of the comment and a */ used to terminate the comment. New lines are ignored in this type of comment.

Comments are not nested; however, one style of comment can be wholly contained within another. Most often this means that a single /* */ pair can comment out large blocks of code even if that code contains // comments:

```
/* the entire block of code that follows, including
   the // comments, has been commented out:

// these comments occur within some function along
// with a lot of code
if (nA > nB)
{
    nA = nB;
}
*/
```

Java defines a third type of comment that is used only for documentation:

```
/** occurs immediately before a declaration */
int nSomeVariable;
```

This comment can be extracted by automatic document generators. It is used to describe the variable, class, or function that immediately follows the comment. This type of comment is treated like a normal /* */ style comment in Visual J++.

Declaring Variables

All local variables must be declared before they can be used. (A **local variable** is a variable declared within a function; its scope is limited to that function.) Such declarations can appear anywhere within the function. A local variable declaration consists of the type, followed by the name of the variable, optionally followed by the assignment operator (=) and an expression representing the initial value of the variable.

```
int nAnInt;             // declare a variable
int nASecondInt = 10;   // declare another variable and
                        // give it an initial value
```

Intrinsic Data Types

Table 2-1 shows the variable types that are intrinsic to Java. To enhance portability, the size of each type in Java is specified by the language. In addition, all variables are initialized when declared. If you don't initialize them explicitly, they are given the value shown in Table 2-1. All of the numeric types shown in the table are signed. Java does not support unsigned integer numerics.

Notice that *boolean* is not a numeric type. It can have only the values *true* or *false*. It cannot be converted into or from an integer.

Data type	Size (bits)	Default value
boolean	8	false
byte	8	0
char	16	'x0'
short	16	0
int	32	0
long	64	0
float	32	0.0F
double	64	0.0D

Table 2-1. *The size of Java intrinsic types.*

OTE Java specifies the size of a variable type for calculation purposes only; however, it does not necessarily follow (although it is highly likely) that the size of the type in memory is the same. Thus, it is legal for a compiler to use a full 32 bits to store a short if it truncates the short down to 16 bits when using it in a calculation.

A character is considered an integer type. The characters in Java are a full 16 bits and are assumed to be Unicode. (**Unicode** is a superset of ASCII. The first 128 characters are the same as ASCII; after that, Unicode associates other values with accented characters, umlauts, ideographic characters, and so on.)

C/ **C++** This is a welcome change from the messed-up situation of mixed 8-bit ASCII and 16-bit Unicode characters prevalent in C.

This Lady, Could You Identifier?

A variable name can be any valid Java identifier. Identifiers must start with a letter of the alphabet, an underscore (_), or a dollar sign ($). Subsequent characters can include the numeric digits (0 through 9). The letters of the alphabet include:

- *a* through *z*

- *A* through *Z*

- The Unicode character set. Thus, *Männer* and *garçon* are both valid identifiers.

It is best not to begin an identifier with either an underscore or a dollar sign, even though both are allowed. In fact, it's a good idea not to use these characters at all because most programmers assume that variables beginning with an underscore or containing dollar signs are system variables.

Literals

Normal integer literals are 32-bit signed decimal numbers. Literals that begin with 0 are octal, while those that begin with 0x or 0X are hexadecimal. The characters *A* through *F* in a hexadecimal number can be either uppercase or lowercase. Thus, the following numbers have the same value:

```
255, 0377, 0xff, 0xFF, 0XFF
```

Literals greater than 0x7FFFFFFF (2,147,483,647 decimal) are automatically assumed to be long. You can force any integer literal to be *long* by following it with *l* or *L.*

A numeric literal containing either an exponent or a decimal point is assumed to be a floating-point number. By default, floating points are assumed to be of type *double.* Thus, the following are all considered to be of type *double:*

```
3.14159, 0.1, 1.0, 1.602E-19
```

F or *f* can be appended to a literal to explicitly force the literal to be a *float.* Thus, the following are all float literals:

```
3.14159F, 0.1F, 1.0F, 2.997e8F, 1.602E-19F, 1F
```

In addition, *D* or *d* can be appended to a literal to force it to be a *double:*

```
3.14159D, 1.602E-19D, 1D
```

Two *Boolean* literals, *true* and *false,* are true literal constants and do not need to be defined within the program. In addition, *true* and *false* are not numeric values and cannot be cast to an integer.

Character literals are enclosed in a single quote; for example, ' ' is a space. In addition, you can define a character literal using '\x*NN*', where *NN* is the Unicode value of the character. Thus, '\x20' is also a space. Certain nonprintable characters that appear often are given their own special labels. These are shown in Table 2-2.

The special cases for single quote and double quote are necessary to avoid confusing Java. Thus, '\' ' is the single character single quote. The literal '\\' represents a backslash character.

Description	Literal	Description	Literal
New line	\n	Form feed	\f
Horizontal tab	\t	Single quote	\'
Backspace	\b	Double quote	\"
Carriage return	\r	Backslash	\\

Table 2-2. *Special character literals.*

String literals are any number of characters contained within double quotes. String literals are implemented with the class *String*. For example, in the following snippet, *"Hello, world"* is a string literal:

```
System.out.println("Hello, world");
```

 C++ A Java string literal is not implemented as a null-terminated array of characters (often called an ASCIIZ string) as it is in C and C++. It is possible to declare an array of characters, but this array and a literal string have little to do with each other in Java.

Casting About

In general, Java can automatically convert from one numeric type to a larger type; however, you will normally want to use a cast. A **cast** is an explicit conversion of a value from its current type to another. The cast appears as the desired type enclosed in parentheses before the value to be converted, as in the following:

```
// convert the float to an integer
int nIntValue = (int)fFloatValue;
```

Java supports implicit casts from smaller types to larger types (so-called **promoting**), but it complains when the cast might lose significant digits. Thus, the following:

```
int nIntValue;
long lLongValue;
lLongValue = (long)nIntValue; // this is preferred but...
lLongValue = nIntValue;       // ...this is allowed

nIntValue = lLongValue;       // this is not allowed; it
                              // generates a compiler error
nIntValue = (int)lLongValue;  // this is okay
```

The assignment of *nIntValue* to *lLongValue* without a cast is allowed since Java figures no harm can come from it, even though the explicit cast is preferable. However, Java does not allow the assignment of *lLongValue* to *nIntValue* without a cast because digits might be lost. With the cast, however, Java lets it go by.

Smooth Operators

Table 2-3 shows the Java operators. The numbers in the first column indicate the precedence, with 1 being the highest precedence and 15 being the lowest precedence. **Precedence** refers to the order in which operations are carried out. For example, multiplication (*) is performed before addition (+) in the same expression. Operators with the same precedence are executed from left to right. This leads to the following:

```
int nResult;
nResult = 2 + 3 * 4;    // the result is 14, not 20
                        // (* has higher precedence than +)
nResult = 18 - 6 + 2;   // the result is 14, not 10
                        // (left to right within same precedence)
```

You can always override the order of evaluation using parentheses:

```
int nResult;
nResult = (2 + 3) * 4;  // the result is 20
nResult = 18 - (6 + 2); // the result is 10
```

C/ **C++** Most of the Java operators work pretty much the same as their C equivalents except for the addition of two new operators (>>> and ^) and the way the logical operators work when applied to *booleans.* Even the precedence is the same.

Precedence	Operators	Precedence	Operators
1	. [] ()	9	^
2	++ -- ! ~ instanceof	10	|
3	* / %	11	&&
4	+ -	12	||
5	<< >> >>>	13	?:
6	< > <= >=	14	= op=
7	== !=	15	,
8	&		

Table 2-3. *Operator precedence in Java.*

The most important operator is the assignment operator (=). (This is not to be confused with the equality operator, ==.) The assignment operator takes the value on its right and stores it in the object on its left.

In a successful assignment, the type of the expression on the right of the assignment operator must be the same as the type on the left. If it is not cast already, Java will try to cast it for you, but only if that cast can be performed without a loss of information.

The value and type of the assignment operator is the resulting value and type of the lefthand object. Thus, the following is legal:

```
int nA;
int nB;
nB = (nA = 4) / 2;
```

This says: Assign the value 4 to *nA*. Then take the resulting value, which is the integer 4, divide it by 2, and then assign it to *nB*.

Operations on Integers

Operations on integers fall into two categories: unary and binary. Unary operations take one argument, which is usually on the right side of the operator. Binary operations take two arguments, which are on either side of the operator.

 OTE The ternary ?: is also an operator, but it's so strange that I prefer to discuss it separately. See the section titled "Special Operators" later in this chapter.

Unary operations

The unary operations involve a single argument. Java doesn't like to deal with arguments smaller than an *int*. Therefore, if the argument to a unary operation is a *byte, char,* or *short,* the result is an *int*. Otherwise, the result is the same type as the argument. (That is, *int* begets *int, long* begets *long.*)

The unary operators are - (negation), ~ (bitwise complement), ++ (increment), and -- (decrement).

The increment and decrement operators increment and decrement the argument by one, respectively. The value of an expression using these operators is the value of the argument. The question is, which do you want, the value before the argument is incremented or decremented, or the value after? You have your choice.

Both the increment and decrement operators come in two flavors: pre-increment and postincrement. For example, the preincrement increments the argument first, returning the result after it is incremented. The post-increment first evaluates the argument and then increments it.

This is best explained by an example:

```
int nA;
int nB;
int nC;
nA = 1;
nB = ++nA;    // preincrement - nB now equals 2, nA equals 2
nA = 1;
nC = nA++;    // postincrement - nC now equals 1, nA equals 2
```

In both cases, *nA* is assigned the value 1 and then incremented to 2; however, in the first case *nB* receives the value 2 (the value after incrementing *nA*), whereas in the second case *nC* receives the value 1 (the value before incrementing *nA*).

Binary operations

The binary operations involve two arguments on either side of the operator. If both arguments are *int,* the operation is performed in *int* precision. If either argument is *long,* the other argument is converted to *long* and the result is *long*. If the resulting value of an expression is greater than what can be contained in the current precision, the upper bits are lopped off. No overflow indication is generated.

In most cases, Java automatically promotes *byte, char,* and *short* values to *int* before performing the operation. This leads to the following apparent paradox:

```
byte b1 = 2;
byte b2 = 3;
byte b3;
b3 = b1 * b2;    // this is an error
```

The expression *b3 = b1 * b2* generates a compiler error even though all three arguments are of the same type. This is because *b1* and *b2* are promoted to *int* before the multiplication is performed. Java then refuses to downcast the *int* result into a *byte* to be stored in *b3* (without a cast) because this might result in loss of data. Adding a cast avoids the error:

```
b3 = (byte)(b1 * b2);   // this is okay
```

The binary operators +, -, *, and / provide the normal integer addition, subtraction, multiplication, and division operations. Integer division always rounds off toward 0, irrespective of the sign of the arguments. Division by 0 generates an *ArithmeticException.* (More on exceptions in Chapter 9.) Overflow does not generate an exception of any kind.

% acts as a modulo, returning the remainder after division. Thus, 7 % 3 returns the value 1. (The nearest multiple of 3 less than 7 is 6, and 7-6 is 1.) Modulo and division have the following relationship:

```
(a / b) * b + a % b = a;   // for all a and b
```

C/ **C++** It might seem obvious, but this relationship is not part of the C or C++ standards.

The operators &, |, and ^ perform bitwise AND, OR, and EXCLUSIVE OR on their two arguments.

The << operator left-shifts the lefthand argument the number of bits indicated by the righthand argument. Zero bits are shifted into the righthand side. Bits shifted out the lefthand side are lost. The >> operator performs a signed right-shift. Bits shifted out the righthand side are lost. The sign bit is duplicated and shifted into the lefthand side. A second right shift operator, >>>, is provided to perform an unsigned right shift. In this case, 0's are shifted into the lefthand side irrespective of the sign bit.

The comparison operators >, <, >=, <=, ==, and != return a *Boolean true* if the lefthand argument is greater than, less than, greater than or equal to, less than or equal to, equal to, or not equal to the righthand argument, respectively.

C/ **C++** The comparison operators do not return an integer value of any kind.

Operations on Floats

The same operators that work on integers can also be applied to floating-point values. For example, ++ adds 1.0 when applied to a floating-point variable. Even the modulo operation works on floating-point values, generating the remainder after integer division. Operations involving only *float* are evaluated completely in single precision. If either argument is *double,* the other argument is promoted to *double,* and the operation is carried out in double precision. (If either argument is an integer type, it is promoted to the appropriate floating-point type as well.)

Java follows the rules of IEEE Standard 754 for floating-point calculations. For example, no exceptions are generated from floating-point arithmetic. Overflow generates either a positive or a negative infinity. Thus, 1.0/0.0 generates a positive infinity (+Inf). Operations that cannot generate a meaningful result (such as the square root of -1) produce Not A Number (NaN). The standard also defines the rules for mathematical operations on these special numbers. For example, NaN * x equals 0 if x is 0 or Inf if x is Inf; otherwise it generates NaN. (It makes sense when you think about it.) There are lots of other rules in 754 that are interesting but are not relevant to Java programming.

Operations on Booleans

Some of the operations that can be applied to numbers can be applied to *Boolean* values. The logical operators &, |, and ^ can be applied to *Boolean* arguments to perform logical AND, OR, and EXCLUSIVE OR operations, respectively. Note that both lefthand and righthand arguments are evaluated for the & and | operators even when they don't need to be. Consider the following:

```
public void fn1(int nA, int nB)
{
    // OR without short-circuit evaluation
    if ((nA > nB) | fn2(nA))
    {
        // ...perform some operation
    }
}
```

If *nA* is greater than *nB,* there is no reason to call *fn2* because the result will always be *true.* (*true* | *x* is *true* whether *x* is *true* or *false.*) However, *fn2* is called anyway because it might have some desired side effect.

Not calling *fn2* in the above situation is called **short-circuit evaluation**, since the call to *fn2* is said to be "short-circuited." Two special operators, && and | |, are provided to perform the same AND and OR operations as & and | but with short-circuit evaluation. Thus, in the following example *fn2* is not called if *nA* is greater than *nB*:

```java
public void fn1(int nA, int nB)
{
    // OR with short-circuit evaluation
    if ((nA > nB) || fn2(nA))
    {
        // ...perform some operation
    }
}
```

C/C++   The net effect of the above is that the *Boolean* operators work the same as in C/C++.

Operations on Strings

The only operator (besides assignment) that is defined for strings is addition. If either argument to the plus operator is of class *String,* the other argument is converted into a string and the two strings are concatenated. This greatly simplifies generating lengthy output, as in the following example.

```java
int i = 1;
int j = 2;
Systems.out.println("i = " + i + ", j = " + j + '\n');
```

This produces the following output:

```
i = 1, j = 2
```

Special Operators

Several operators warrant at least an honorable mention in the strangeness category. The first is a set of operators that combine a binary operator and the assignment operator into one. If *op* is a conventional binary operator, the following *op=* exists:

```
a op= b;        // is equivalent to a = a op b
```

This works for all binary operators.

What makes this set of operators particularly strange is that they work without a cast even for arguments smaller than *int*. Thus, the following is allowed:

```
byte b1 = 2;
byte b2 = 3;
b1 *= b2;        // allowed even though b1 = b1 * b2 is not allowed
                 // (at least not without a cast)
```

Another strange operator is the comma operator. The comma operator separates two expressions. The right expression is evaluated first, and then the left expression is evaluated. The comma operator is allowed only in the *for* loop, as demonstrated in the following example:

```
// the following function reverses the elements of nArray, making
// the first element the last and the last element the first
int nTemp;
int i, j;
for (i = 0, j = 100; i < j; i++, j--)
{
    nTemp = nArray[i];
    nArray[i] = nArray[j];
    nArray[j] = nTemp;
}
```

As you will see in the next section, the *for* loop allows only for a single expression in initialization position and the increment position. The comma operator allows two expressions to be combined into one.

The strangest of all operators is the ternary operator. (**Ternary** means three and refers to the fact that this operator has three arguments.) This operator is used as follows:

```
(boolexpr) ? expr1 : expr2;
```

First, the *Boolean* expression *boolexpr* is evaluated. If the result is *true,* the value of the operator is the value of *expr1;* otherwise, it is the value of *expr2.* The type of the expression is a type that is compatible with both *expr1* and *expr2.* Thus, if *expr1* is an *int* and *expr2* is a *long,* the result is a *long* whether *expr1* is evaluated or *expr2* is evaluated.

Flow Control

Java provides a full set of flow control statements:

- *if* statement
- *for* loop
- *while* loop
- *switch* statement

These flow controls are statements, not expressions, meaning that they do not have a value or a type.

The *if* Statement

The simplest flow control statement is the lowly *if* statement:

```
if (boolexpr)
{
    // ...any number of statements
}
else
{
    // ...any number of statements
}
```

First the *Boolean* expression is evaluated. If it is *true,* the statements contained in the first block are executed. If not, the statements contained in the else block are executed. Of course, the else clause is optional.

(In this and all of the following examples, if a block contains a single statement, the braces can be omitted; however, the style used in this book is to retain the braces in all cases.)

The *while* Loop

The easiest of the Java loop structures is the *while* loop. The *while* loop comes in two variations:

```
while (boolexpr)
{
    // ...any number of statements
}
```

and

```
do
{
    // ...any number of statements
} while (boolexpr);
```

In the first case, the *Boolean* expression *boolexpr* is evaluated. If it is *true,* the Java statements within the block are executed. If not, control jumps to the first statement after the closed brace. After all of the statements within the brace have been executed, control loops back up to the top of the *while* loop and the *Boolean* expression is reevaluated, thereby starting the whole process over again.

The *do...while* is similar except that the *Boolean* expression isn't evaluated until after the Java statements within the block have been executed. If the expression is *true,* control passes up to the top of the block; if the expression is *false,* control passes to the statement immediately following the *while*.

The keywords *break* and *continue* allow the program to abort execution of the statements from within the loop. The unlabeled break statement passes control outside of the loop immediately.

```
// divide each element of nArray by the corresponding
// member of nDenom
int i = 0;       // start at the beginning
while (i < nARRAY_SIZE)
{
    // if the denominator is zero...
    if (nDenom[i] == 0)
    {
        // ...exit the loop immediately
        break;
    }
    // divide the element of the array by the denominator
    nArray[i] /= nDenom[i];

    // increment to the next element
    i++;
}
```

Here each element of *nArray* is divided by the corresponding member of *nDenom*. If any element of *nDenom* is equal to 0, however, the *break* is executed, which exits the loop.

The break statement can also be labeled to allow control to pass out of multiple loops at one time, as in the following example:

```
// divide each element of nMatrix by the corresponding
// member of nDenom
int i = 0
outaHere:
while (i < nROW_SIZE)
{
    int j = 0;
    while (j < nCOL_SIZE)
    {
        // if the denominator is zero...
        if (nDenom[i] == 0)
        {
            // ...exit both loops immediately
            break outaHere;
        }

        // divide the element of the matrix by the denominator
        nMatrix[i][j] /= nDenom[i];

        // increment to the next column
        j++;
    }

    // increment to the next row
    i++;
}
```

The statement *break outaHere* does not pass control to the label. Rather, it passes control outside of the loop labeled *outaHere*.

 OTE   The labeled break addresses the primary reason that programmers say they need a "goto." This controlled exit is about as close as Java comes to a "goto" statement.

In some cases, you don't really want to break out of the loop. All you really want to do is go to the next case and try again. The *continue* statement passes control immediately to the closing brace, causing control to pass directly to the conditional expression. The *continue* statement can also carry a label, in which case control passes to the closing brace of the labeled loop.

OTE Many books use the labels *inner* and *outer* in their examples when demonstrating *break* and *continue*. Although the compiler allows this, you should not follow this practice because both *inner* and *outer* have been flagged as potential keywords in future versions of the Java language.

The *for* Loop

The most common of the loops is the *for* loop. This has the following appearance:

```
for (expr1; boolexpr2; expr3)
{
    // ...any number of Java statements
}
```

The *for* loop is executed in the following steps:

1. *expr1* is evaluated.

2. *boolexpr2* is evaluated. If the result is *true*, the body of the *for* loop is executed. If not, control passes to the first statement after the closing brace.

3. *expr3* is evaluated.

4. Go to step 2.

expr1 is used to initialize the index variable. *expr1* can also be a declaration. Any variable declared in *expr1* is only defined within the scope of the *for* loop. Once the *for* loop is exited, the variable name is no longer defined and can be reused.

 C++ This behavior of variables differs from C++, in which a variable declared in the initialization clause of a *for* loop remains visible after the *for* loop is exited.

expr3 is used to increment the index variable. *boolexpr2* is used to test for the termination condition.

The short example shown on the next page makes this clear.

```
// initialize array to 0
for (int i = 0; i < nARRAY_SIZE; i++)
{
    nArray[i] = 0;
}
```

Here *i* is declared and initialized to 0. It is then compared to n*ARRAY-_SIZE,* which presumably has been defined somewhere earlier. If *i* is less than n*ARRAY_SIZE, nArray[i]* is zeroed. At this point, *i* is incremented, it is compared to n*ARRAY_SIZE* again, and then the loop starts over.

The *switch* Statement

The *switch* statement is useful when selecting from a number of alternatives:

```
switch(expr)
{
    case cexpr1:
        // Java statements
        break;
    case cexpr2:
        // more Java statements
        break;
    default:
        // even more Java statements
}
```

First, the expression *expr* is evaluated. Its value is then compared to each of the constant integer expressions listed after the case statements. (A **constant expression** is an expression whose value can be computed at compile time.) Control passes to the case whose value matches *expr.* If none of the cases matches, control passes to the optional default case. If no default case is provided, no case is selected and control passes to the first statement after the closed brace.

Notice that the *break* at the end of each case is not required; however, without it control passes straight through to the next case. This can be useful, as in the following:

```
// count the number of digit and nondigit characters
// in the String s passed in from above
int nNumberOfDigits = 0; // no. of digits in s
int nNumberOfNonDigits = 0; // guess!
for (int i = 0; i < s.length(); i++)
{
```

```
// look at each character in the string
switch(s.charAt[i])
{
    case '0':
    case '1':
    case '2':
    case '3':
    case '4':
    case '5':
    case '6':
    case '7':
    case '8':
    case '9':
        nNumberOfDigits++;
        break;
    default:
        nNumberOfNonDigits++;
}
}
```

This code section loops through the characters that make up the string *s*. (*s.length* returns the length of the string in characters.) Each character in the string is examined in the *switch* statement. (*s.charAt[i]* returns the *i*th character in the string *s*.) If the value of this character is 0, control branches to the *case* labeled 0. If the value is 1, control branches to the 1 case, and so forth. Each of the cases 0 through 9 falls through to the postincrement, which increments the variable *nNumberOfDigits* before encountering the *break*. Executing the *break* throws control outside of the *switch* statement, which returns control to the *for* loop. If the character does not match any of the characters 0 through 9, control passes to the *default* case where *nNumberOfNonDigits* is incremented.

Of course, the case statements don't have to be aligned vertically as in the above example.

Example Program: App1_2

Before leaving this chapter, I feel obliged to show you a simple program using some of the features you have learned so far. This program can't go very far with what we've covered, but it's a bit more complicated than "Hello, world."

The following application, App1_2.java, takes as input the date in the form of month, day, and year. From this, it calculates the number of days since the beginning of the year. The month is assumed to be a number starting with 1 for January, 2 for February, and so forth.

```java
// this statement includes the java I/O libraries
// (more on this later)
import java.io.*;

// this program calculates the number of days from a given
// date to the beginning of the year
class App1_2
{
    // execution starts here
    public static void main(String args[])
    {
        // read in the month, day, and year
        int nMonth = Integer.parseInt(args[0]);
        int nDay   = Integer.parseInt(args[1]);
        int nYear  = Integer.parseInt(args[2]);

        // initialize accumulator to zero
        int nDayInYear = 0;

        // now loop through the months, adding
        // in the number of days in each month
        for (int nM = 1; nM < nMonth; nM++)
        {
            switch(nM)
            {
                // the following months have 30 days
                case 4: case  6: case  9: case 11:
                    nDayInYear += 30;
                    break;

                // in February, gotta consider leap year
                case 2:
                    nDayInYear += 28;

                    // if it's a leap year...
                    if (((nYear % 4) == 0) && ((nYear % 100) != 0))
                    {
                        // ...kick in an extra day
                        nDayInYear++;
                    }
                    break;
```

```
                    // all the rest have 31 days
                    default:
                    nDayInYear += 31;
            }
      }

      // now add in the day of the current month
      nDayInYear += nDay;

      // print out the result
      // print out the results
      System.out.print  (nMonth + "-" + nDay + "-" + nYear);
      System.out.println(" is day number "
                              + nDayInYear
                              + " in the year");
    }
}
```

Just as with App1_1, this program begins execution with *main*. The argument *args* is an array of strings containing the arguments to the program. (When executing this program under the IDE, use the Build/Settings/ Debug tab menu option to set the program arguments.) The arguments are assumed to be month, day, and year (in that order), with all numbers separated by a space. Thus, 2 1 1997 would be February 1, 1997.

The program first converts these strings into the equivalent integers. If this conversion is not possible, as would be the case if you forgot one of the arguments, you are greeted with an unpleasant run-time error message.

After the date has been converted into three integers, the program calculates the date into the day of the year. It does this by looping through the months, accumulating the number of days in each month. A switch statement works for most months. A few extra calculations are necessary to handle a leap year. (The rule is that a leap year is any year that is evenly divisible by 4 but not divisible by 100.) Finally, the program adds in the number of days in the current month and outputs the result.

To compile and execute this program, follow the same steps you used for App1_1 in Chapter 1. Be sure to name the source file *App1_2.java*. In addition, make sure that you execute this (and all other programs in Part 1 of this book) as an application and not as an applet.

The result of executing this program appears in Figure 2-1.

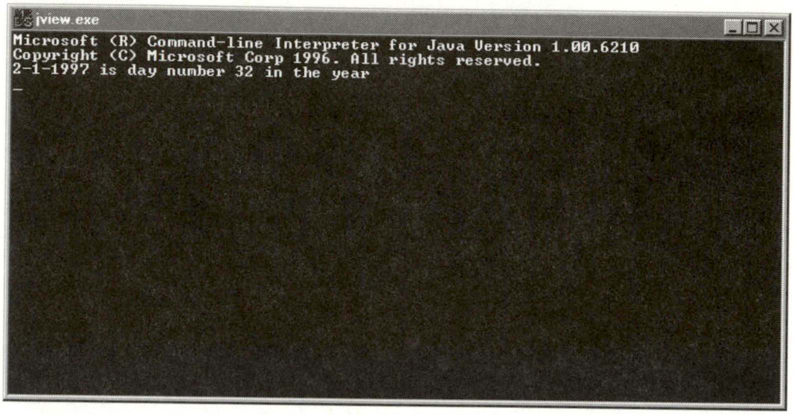

Figure 2-1. *An example run from executing App1_2.*

Conclusion

Java is a complete language that borrows heavily from C and C++. It has a full set of intrinsic types, and it has all the operators you might want, all the logical comparison operators you could ask for, and a full set of flow control statements. In the next few chapters, you will learn about the object-oriented features of the Java language.

Introduction to Java Classes

In this chapter, you will see how to create a class, providing it with both data members and member functions (known as *methods*). You'll also see how to declare and use objects. But even more important, you'll learn the role of a class in the Java program and you'll come to understand why Java is a first-rate object-oriented programming language (whatever that means!).

Defining a Class

In addition to the intrinsic variable types, users can define their own types using the keyword *class*.

C/ C++ The class is the only way that Java provides to create a new type. Java has no equivalent to *typedef, struct,* or *enum* (enumerated types).

A user type definition takes the following form:

```
class MyClass
{
    // the members of the class go here
}
```

The keyword *class* is preceded by the access type. For now we will assume the default access type. (Access types are discussed in Chapter 4.) The *class* keyword is followed by the class name, which must be a valid Java identifier. (The same rules that apply to variables apply to class names.) The brace-delimited class body contains any number of member definitions. The members of the class can appear in any order within the class body.

A class has two types of members: data members and member functions. These are described in the next two sections.

Defining Data Members

Data members are used to describe the data properties of the class. They are declared using the same rules as local variables except that it is a common convention to begin the names of data members with *m_*.

Consider the following *BankAccount* class:

```
class BankAccount
{
    // the following defines the data properties:

    // current balance
    double m_dCurrentBalance;

    // account id
    int m_nId;
}
```

Clearly the current balance is an important property of a bank account. In addition, the account ID is pretty important in uniquely identifying the bank account. Defining *m_dCurrentBalance* gives the class a place to retain the account balance information.

 OTE The name *m_dCurrentBalance* breaks down as follows: *m_* identifies the variable as a data member, *d* means double (the intrinsic type of the object), and *CurrentBalance* describes the object.

Defining Member Functions

Members of a Java class can also be functions.

 OTE All functions in Java must be members of some class.

A **member function** definition appears as follows:

```
class BankAccount
{
    // current balance
    double m_dCurrentBalance;

    // classes can also have member functions:
    // Deposit - make a deposit
    void Deposit(double dAmount)
    {
        if (dAmount >= 0.0)
        {
            m_dCurrentBalance += dAmount;
        }
    }

    // Withdrawal - make a withdrawal
    void Withdrawal(double dAmount)
    {
        if (dAmount >= 0.0 && dAmount < m_dCurrentBalance)
        {
            m_dCurrentBalance -= dAmount;
        }
    }
}
```

> **NOTE** Member functions are also called methods of the class or simply methods. Even though this term makes sense in some other object-oriented languages, most notably Smalltalk, it doesn't relate to anything concrete in Java. Nevertheless, the term is easier to say than *member function* and it seems to have stuck, so I will use it here.

A method definition begins with the return type—the type of the object that the method returns. If the method returns no object, the return type is *void*.

The return type is followed by the method's name, which can be any valid Java identifier. The convention is to begin method names with an upper-case letter.

The name of the method is followed by parentheses containing the parameter list. The **parameter list** is a comma-separated list of declarations of the arguments to the method. If the method takes no arguments, the argument list should be empty.

It is illegal for any of the arguments to have the same name as a variable declared locally within the method. Thus, the following generates a compile-time error:

```
void fn(int i, int nSize, int nArray[])
{
    // i in the following loop hides the argument i;
    // that's not kosher
    for (int i = 0; i < j; i++)
    {
        nArray[i] = 0;
    }
}
```

The braces following the argument list contain the body of the method.

When the method is called, control passes to the open brace of the method. The programmer can exit from any point with the keyword *return*. In the absence of encountering a *return* statement, the method exits upon reaching the closed brace.

If the method returns something other than *void,* a *return* followed by an expression indicating the value to return is required. This is demonstrated in the following *Balance* method, which returns the balance of the current account:

```
class BankAccount
{
    // current balance
    double m_dCurrentBalance;

    // ...other members as before...

    // Balance - return the current balance
    double Balance()
```

```
    {
        return m_dCurrentBalance;
    }
}
```

A method that has a return type other than *void* must exit via the *return* statement because the closed brace returns no value.

 NOTE Even if a method returns a value other than *void*, the caller is free to ignore the returned value. Thus, the following is legal:

```
maxInt(nI, nJ);    // call maxInt() and ignore the result
```

Methods define the active properties of the class. For example, bank accounts receive deposits, withdrawals, and balance inquiries. These active properties are represented by the functions *Deposit, Withdrawal,* and *Balance* in this example *BankAccount* class.

But What Is a Class?

Before we get any further into the details of creating and using classes, let's take a step back and look at the class from more of a philosophical standpoint. What is a class? Where does it fit in the object-oriented programming paradigm? What is the object-oriented programming paradigm? What's a paradigm? (When will I ever stop with the questions?)

Object-Oriented Programming and the Television

To understand Java's concept of the class, you need to understand something about object-oriented programming. Object-oriented programming is more of a programming philosophy than a set of structures or keywords in the Java language. (You'll quickly find that object-oriented types have a special word for almost everything. They call your programming philosophy your paradigm—pronounced "pair-a-dime," as in 20 cents.)

By way of explanation, let me describe an everyday experience. When I decide I've done enough writing for the day, I ease onto my couch, feign exhaustion, and reach for the TV remote. After a quick glance at the program guide, I punch a few buttons on the remote and I'm off channel-surfing. This is not a lot different from what 99 percent of my fellow Americans do every day.

Not too exciting, but think for a second what I don't do:

- I don't take the back off the set and start fiddling with the insides to get it to work. I expect my TV to have a well-defined, complete interface (usually called an API—an application programming interface). To me, my remote represents the only API available to the TV. If I can't do something using that remote, I can't do it at all. It's not that I'm completely ignorant of how a TV works. But I would wager that even TV mechanics don't think too much about video orthicon tubes and the like when they're watching The Big Game.

- I don't puzzle over where the TV starts and stops. The TV is a well-defined concept. That is, I understand the concept of a TV apart from anything else that might be in my living room. Even when I attach a VCR to it, I can still understand the TV by itself. I have trouble dealing with things that I can't conceptualize.

- I expect my TV to be reasonably complete. That is, I don't have to provide a tuner in order for it to work. If any external requirements are necessary, like power or an antenna connection, I expect these to be well documented and standardized.

- I don't expect the TV to crash (not this new TV, anyway). I expect it to be robust.

Java Classes

Java classes are like TVs and other everyday appliances. A Java class should fulfill the following four conditions:

- The class should provide a well-defined API. This API should provide external software with the ability to perform any operation the class supports. In other words, "If it ain't in the interface, the class don't do it!"

- The class should represent a concept in the problem domain. That is, it should stand for something tangible. This concept doesn't have to be physical, but it should be something that you can easily conceptualize. If saying the name of the class out loud does not immediately conjure up a concept in your mind, you probably need to rethink the class.

■ The class should be as complete as possible. If one class does rely on another class to provide something extra, it should be clearly documented what that something is.

■ Finally, the class should be robust. It's okay if the class rejects illegal input. If I attempt to select channel 99 on my remote, my TV ignores the request. (It would be really neat if the class generated a reasonable error message.) It's not okay if the class rolls over in the water and heads for the bottom. For example, I think I would have a legitimate gripe if selecting channel 99 on my television caused it to go up in flames.

Functional TVs

This discussion of TVs and object-oriented programming might not seem all that earth-shattering, but it's not the way software was written in the decades prior to object-oriented programming. In the functional programming paradigm, there is no such concept as a class. Thus, in the functional living room it is typically difficult to find a single entity that one can point to and call a TV. Sure, there's a picture tube over here and a detector circuit over there and pieces of a remote scattered all over, but there's no single entity you can call a TV.

With TV parts strewn all over the living room, there's nothing to keep me from playing with the different parts. In fact, if as an application I have to pass data back and forth among the parts, I am more or less required to get inside the set.

Since there's no concept of a unified TV, it doesn't even make sense to talk about the external requirements of the TV. The picture tube has a set of rather sophisticated input requirements that are satisfied by the detector, which in turn has input requirements that are satisfied by the tuner—and so the story goes. In theory, this is not all that different than in the object-oriented TV. After all, the object-oriented TV has a picture tube, a detector, and a tuner. The difference is that the object-oriented TV handles the connections among these components itself, without interference from or even the knowledge of the user. All too often the functional TV leaves it up to the application to pass the appropriate data back and forth among its parts.

Finally, it's difficult to make such a TV set robust. Maybe you could build a picture tube that could handle any type of signal you threw at it. Without a tough enclosure, however, you would be forced to put the same types of checks at the input to each of the other internal components. In theory this is possible, but in practice the overhead plus the programming burden means that it never happens.

Why Is This Important?

Why is it important that Java support object-oriented programming? People live in a world of TVs, bank accounts, telephones, cars, trees, birds, and other objects. We think in terms of these abstractions. We learn in infancy how to classify and deal with these concepts. This colors the way we think about problems.

Consider for a minute the process that a programmer goes through in solving any nontrivial programming problem:

- Problem formulation—determining the problem to be solved.

- Analysis—analyzing the problem to find the important concepts in the problem. Restating the problem based on these concepts.

- Design—designing a solution to the problem based on the concepts discovered during analysis.

- Coding—implementing the design in code (writing the program).

Take, for example, the problem of establishing a bank account. Usually the problem is given to you. In this case, let's say the problem is to write a program to implement a simple savings account. This savings account should allow deposits and withdrawals, it should charge a $5.00 monthly maintenance fee, and it should pay a fixed rate of interest.

As you look at this problem, concepts such as bank account, deposit, withdrawal, and balance are sure to arise. The statement of the very problem includes these words. The design for our bank account is much easier to understand if it includes these concepts as well.

A programming language like Java that supports object-oriented programming allows the programmer to take these concepts through the coding step as well. The programmer uses the Java class to define and implement a class such as *BankAccount.* This *BankAccount* class can be outfitted with passive properties such as account number and balance, along with active properties such as *Deposit* and *Withdrawal,* in keeping with our design concept of a bank account.

This makes for a much more direct mapping between the design and the code. It makes the code easier to read and understand, and it reduces maintenance costs. Since the code is easier to understand, it also reduces development costs.

Object-oriented programming offers one further advantage—reuse. The concept of a bank account can be understood by the programmer apart from any other concept within the problem. (Remember, I understand my TV even when it isn't in the living room.) This allows the programmer to implement a relatively autonomous *BankAccount* class, one that is independent of the remainder of the problem in which it resides. A sufficiently general *BankAccount* class will undoubtedly find use in other financial problems.

Objects

People sometimes get fast and loose with the terms *class* and *object.* You should be careful not to confuse these two terms. A **class** describes a type of thing. A TV is a device representable by the *TV* class. (Sometimes people use the terms *class* and *type* interchangeably—that's okay.)

On the other hand, any particular TV (say, for instance, my TV) is an **object**. This might be described by a variable *mytv,* declared as follows:

```
TV mytv = new TV();  // accept this pro forma;
                     // the new keyword is explained in Ch. 5
```

In object-oriented-speak, we say that the object *mytv* is a reference to an **instance** of the class *TV*. (More about references and the *new* keyword in Chapter 5.)

A single class can be instanced any number of times. While it makes sense to talk about creating an object, it does not make sense to speak of creating a class (unless you mean the act of writing the Java code that implements the class).

Accessing Members of an Object

The members of an object are accessed using the dot (.) operator, as follows:

```
class TV
{
    // current channel number
    int m_nChannel;

    // Channel(int) - change the channel
    int Channel(int nNewChannel)
    {
        // first make sure that it's in range
        if (nNewChannel > 1 && nNewChannel < 70)
        {
            m_nChannel = nNewChannel;
        }
        return m_nChannel;
    }
}

void SomeFunction()
{
    // get a TV
    TV mytv = new TV();

    // tune it to the Cowboys station
    mytv.Channel(8);

    // output the channel number (just to make sure)
    System.out.println("TV tuned to channel " + mytv.m_nChannel);
}
```

The statement *mytv.m_nChannel* accesses the *m_nChannel* member of the *mytv* object. That's straightforward enough. In a similar vein, *mytv-.Channel(int)* calls the *Channel(int)* method of *mytv*. Said in a slightly different way, this statement invokes the *Channel(int)* operation of the *TV* class on *mytv*. (Said in yet a third way, it changes the stupid channel.)

Example: A Simple Bank Account

Now that you've seen how classes are created and used, let's take a look at a class in action. The following file, BankAccount.java, implements a simple bank account like one you might find at your local financial institution.

```
// BankAccount - implement a bank account like
//                one you would see at your friendly neighborhood
//                financial institution
//
class BankAccount
{
    // let's start with the data members
    // interest rate
    double m_dCurrentInterestRate;

    // balance - the current account's balance
    double m_dBalance;

    // now the member functions
    // CurrentRate/SetRate - inquire or set interest rate
    public double CurrentRate()
    {
        return m_dCurrentInterestRate;
    }
    public void SetRate(double dNewRate)
    {
        // first a sanity check
        if (dNewRate > 0.0 && dNewRate < 20.0)
        {
            m_dCurrentInterestRate = dNewRate;
        }
    }

    // Deposit - add something to the account
    void Deposit(double dAmount)
    {
        // no negative deposits!
        if (dAmount > 0.0)
        {
            m_dBalance += dAmount;
        }
    }

    // Withdrawal - take something out
    void Withdrawal(double dAmount)
    {
        // negative withdrawals are a sneaky way
        // of adding money to the account
        if (dAmount >= 0.0)
        {
            // don't let him withdraw more than he has
            if (dAmount <= m_dBalance)
```

(continued)

```
        {
            m_dBalance -= dAmount;
        }
    }
}


// Balance - return the current balance rounded off to
//           the nearest cent
double Balance()
{
    int nCents = (int)(m_dBalance * 100 + 0.5);
    return nCents / 100.0;
}


// Monthly - each month rack up interest and service
//           fees
void Monthly()
{
    Fee();      // fee first! (reduces interest we pay)
    Interest();
}


// Fee - rack up the monthly fee
void Fee()
{
    m_dBalance -= 5.0;    // $5.00 per month
}


// Interest - tack on monthly interest
void Interest()
{
    // 1200 because interest is normally expressed
    // in numbers like 20%, meaning .2, and because
    // we are accumulating interest monthly
    m_dBalance += m_dBalance *
            (m_dCurrentInterestRate / 1200.0);
}
}
```

The first data member in the *BankAccount* class is *m_dCurrentInterestRate*. The interest rate is set using the *SetRate* method. The *CurrentRate* method returns the current interest rate setting. Notice how the *CurrentRate* method first performs a sanity check, not allowing the application to set a negative interest rate (which would have catastrophic results) or a usurious rate (which would land us in jail in every state except Delaware).

The *m_dBalance* is the current account's balance. This is clearly an object member, since every account has a different balance. The balance is manipulated with the *Deposit* and *Withdrawal* functions shown earlier.

 OTE Both of these methods ignore illegal input. They should probably raise some type of red flag. You'll see what that red flag is in Chapter 9.

Finally, the *Monthly* method performs the monthly account maintenance, such as collecting fees (which are set at a fixed $5.00 per month) and accumulating interest.

The following class, *App1_3,* uses the *BankAccount* class to calculate how much money I can accumulate by being diligent in my saving (which I never am):

```
// App1_3 - test out the BankAcount class.
//          the program expects two inputs: the monthly
//          deposit and the interest rate, as in App1_3 100 8,
//          meaning $100 per month at 8% interest. (to keep
//          things simple, both are assumed to be integers.)
//          the program calculates the bank balance at the end
//          of each month for 10 years.
import java.io.*;   // this includes the println function

public class App1_3
{
    public static void main(String args[])
    {
        // first argument is the deposit per month
        double dPerMonth = (double)Integer.parseInt(args[0]);

        // second argument is the interest rate
        double dInterest = (double)Integer.parseInt(args[1]);

        // create a BankAccount object
        BankAccount baMyAccount = new BankAccount();

        // set the interest rate
        baMyAccount.SetRate(dInterest);

        // make a deposit each month and
        // watch my account grow for 10 years!
        System.out.println("Depositing " +
                         dPerMonth +
```

(continued)

```
                            " per month at " +
                            baMyAccount.CurrentRate() +
                            " percent interest");
        System.out.println("Watch my account grow!");
        for (int nYear = 0; nYear < 10; nYear++)
        {
            System.out.print(nYear + " - ");
            for (int nMonth = 0; nMonth < 12; nMonth++)
            {
                // make my deposit
                baMyAccount.Deposit(dPerMonth);

                // now take monthly fees and interest
                baMyAccount.Monthly();
                System.out.print(baMyAccount.Balance() + ", ");
            }
            System.out.println();
        }
    }
}
```

As before, *App1_3* should be contained in a file called *App1_3.java.* You'll have to accept the *public* in front of the *class* keyword and the *public static* in front of the *main* method for now. I will explain these in the next chapter.

When you execute the program, Java sets up a few things and then calls *main,* which starts by reading in the monthly deposit and the interest rate. (To keep things simple, I used integer conversion, which limits the program to integer interest rates. *BankAccount* has no such limitation, and as soon as I've discussed class wrappers I can relieve this restriction.) The program creates a *BankAccount* object in which to accumulate the monthly balance. It then calls *SetRate* to set the interest rate for my account.

At this point, the program enters a loop of 10 years within which there's a loop for the 12 months of the year. For each month, the program calls *Deposit* to make a deposit and *Monthly* to accumulate interest and fees. The program then outputs the account balance to see how we're doing.

The output from executing this program is shown in Figure 3-1. The information's all there, even though the format might be pretty ugly. Since we haven't seen how to gussy up the output yet, I'll leave it that way for now.

```
iview.exe                                                    _ □ ×
Microsoft (R) Command-line Interpreter for Java Version 1.00.6210
Copyright (C) Microsoft Corp 1996. All rights reserved.
Depositing 100 per month at 8 per cent interest
Watch my account grow!
0 - 95.63, 191.9, 288.82, 386.38, 484.58, 583.45, 682.97, 783.16, 884.01, 985.54
, 1087.74, 1190.63,
1 - 1294.2, 1398.46, 1503.42, 1609.07, 1715.43, 1822.5, 1930.29, 2038.79, 2148.0
1, 2257.97, 2368.65, 2480.08,
2 - 2592.24, 2705.16, 2818.83, 2933.25, 3048.44, 3164.4, 3281.13, 3398.63, 3516.
93, 3636, 3755.88, 3876.55,
3 - 3998.03, 4120.31, 4243.42, 4367.34, 4492.09, 4617.67, 4744.09, 4871.35, 4999
.46, 5128.42, 5258.24, 5388.93,
4 - 5520.49, 5652.93, 5786.25, 5920.45, 6055.56, 6191.56, 6328.47, 6466.29, 6605
.04, 6744.7, 6885.3, 7026.84,
5 - 7169.32, 7312.74, 7457.13, 7602.48, 7748.79, 7896.09, 8044.36, 8193.62, 8343
.88, 8495.14, 8647.41, 8800.69,
6 - 8954.99, 9110.33, 9266.7, 9424.11, 9582.57, 9742.08, 9902.67, 10064.3, 10227
, 10390.9, 10555.8, 10721.8,
7 - 10888.9, 11057.1, 11226.5, 11396.9, 11568.5, 11741.3, 11915.2, 12090.3, 1226
6.5, 12443.9, 12622.5, 12802.3,
8 - 12983.3, 13165.5, 13348.9, 13533.5, 13719.4, 13906.5, 14094.8, 14284.4, 1447
5.3, 14667.4, 14860.8, 15055.5,
9 - 15251.5, 15448.8, 15647.5, 15847.4, 16048.7, 16251.3, 16455.3, 16660.6, 1686
7.3, 17075.4, 17284.9, 17495.7,
```

Figure 3-1. *Output from a sample run of the App1_3 program to exercise the* BankAccount *class.*

Conclusion

In this chapter, you've seen how to declare and use a basic class. Just as important, you've learned about the role of the class in a Java program. Finally, you've seen what you've learned in action in a simple program.

In the next chapter and beyond, I will demonstrate some of the more advanced features of the class.

Java Classes: The Sequel

This chapter explores class features beyond the basic features demonstrated in Chapter 3. Here you will see slightly more advanced features such as method overloading, static members, and access control. The chapter wraps up with an expanded version of the *BankAccount* example from the previous chapter.

Overloading Methods

Java differentiates methods by more than just their names. Java uses what's called the fully qualified method name. A method's **fully qualified name** includes its name, its class, and its arguments. Two methods can have the same name as long as their fully qualified names are different.

Same Name Between Classes

Thus, even though I have a method *ChangeChannel* in the class *TV*, I can still have a separate method *ChangeChannel* in the class *Radio*. The two don't cause confusion:

```java
void fn(TV mytv, Radio myradio)
{
    mytv.ChangeChannel();      // tune the TV
    myradio.ChangeChannel();   // tune the radio
}
```

This is just like people. I know a Jim Voss and a Jim Gibson who both work in the same lab. The fact that they have the same first name doesn't cause that much confusion. We in the lab simply refer to them by their full names.

An unqualified reference to a method from within either class is assumed to be to the method of the same class. Thus, the following:

```java
class TV
{
    void ChangeChannel()
    {
        // ...whatever it does...
    }
    void SomeFunc()
    {
        ChangeChannel();
    }
}
```

Because the *SomeFunc* method is within the class *TV,* the call to *Change-Channel* is assumed to be to the one within *TV* and not to the *Radio* method of the same name.

This is also like people. At Jim Gibson's home, I seriously doubt that they refer to him by his full name. Within a family, unqualified references are assumed to be to members of the same family. Thus, when Jim Gibson's wife calls for Jim, we all know which one she means.

Same Name Within a Class

Even within a class, two methods can have the same name as long as they can be discriminated on the basis of their arguments. (This is not one of those "This is my brother Bill, and this is my other brother Bill" routines.)

Thus, the following is legal:

```java
class BankAccount
{
    // the account's interest rate
    double m_dCurrentInterestRate;

    // Rate - returns or sets the current rate
    double Rate()
    {
        return m_dCurrentInterestRate;
    }
    double Rate(double dNewRate)
    {
```

```
        if (dNewRate > 0.0 && dNewRate < 20.0)
        {
            m_dCurrentInterestRate = dNewRate;
        }
        return m_dCurrentInterestRate;
    }

    // ...and so on like before...
}
```

The *Rate* method has been overloaded to perform two related operations. *Rate* returns the current interest rate, whereas the method *Rate(double)* sets the current interest rate. In practice, it's easy to differentiate between them:

```
double Fn(BankAccount baMyAccount)
{
    baMyAccount.Rate(8.0);    // sets the rate
    return baMyAccount.Rate(); // queries the rate
}
```

> **NOTE** Creating two methods with the same name but different arguments is called **function overloading**.

It is not possible to differentiate two methods on the basis of their return type, however. This is because it is often impossible to determine the return type solely from the way the method is used. Suppose, for example, that the following is allowed:

```
class RealNumber
{
    // convert current RealImaginary number to a double
    double Convert();

    // convert current RealImaginary number to an int
    int Convert();
}

// gives rise to the following problem:
void Fn(RealNumber rn)
{
    rn.Convert();    // which one?
}
```

It is legal to ignore the value returned from a method, but doing so deprives the compiler of a way to determine which *Convert* method the caller is attempting to invoke. To avoid this situation, Java simply excludes the return type from the fully qualified name. Thus, the second definition of *cRealNumber.Convert* generates a compiler error.

 OTE Method overloading is a commonly used feature. It allows sets of methods with very similar purpose to be given the same name.

What Is *this?*

I have a question. Look very carefully at the *Balance* method in the class *BankAccount* shown in the previous chapter. The relevant portions are repeated here:

```
class BankAccount
{
    // balance - the current account's balance
    double m_dBalance;

    // Balance - return the current balance rounded off to
    //           the nearest cent
    double Balance()
    {
        int nCents = (int)(m_dBalance * 100 + 0.5);
        return nCents / 100.0;
    }
}
```

How did *Balance* know which balance to return? At first that seems like a silly question. After all, there's only one balance. But is there really? Consider the following code snippet:

```
void SomeMethod()
{
    // open my account
    BankAccount baMine = new BankAccount();

    // put some money in it
    baMine.Deposit(100.0);

    // now open an account for my son
    BankAccount baSon = new BankAccount();

    // put some money in it as well
    baSon.Deposit(50.0);
```

```
    // now print out the balances
    System.out.println("My balance is " + baMine.Balance());
    System.out.println("My son's balance is " + baSon.Balance());
}
```

Balance is called twice. The first time it returns my balance, and the second time my son's balance. But when you look at the code for *Balance,* there is no explicit reference to either account. How did *Balance* know for which object I wanted the balance? Said another way, which *m_dBalance* was referenced?

Upon reflection, it's clear that a reference to the *BankAccount* object must be getting passed along to the method. In fact, this is true. The object reference is passed as a hidden first argument:

```
baMine.Balance() == is equivalent to ==> Balance(baMine)
```

(It's not that Java will accept the latter, it's just that this is a rough equivalence.)

When *Balance* refers to a *m_dBalance,* it is the *m_dBalance* member of the *BankAccount* object that is passed as the hidden first argument to the function.

Even though this first argument is hidden, it has a name that you can reference from within the method. It's called (brace yourself) **this**, as in "this object." You are allowed to refer to *this* explicitly any time you like. Thus, the following definition of *Balance* with its explicit use of *this* is exactly equivalent to the earlier definition:

```
class BankAccount
{
    // balance - the current account's balance
    double m_dBalance;

    // Balance - return the current balance rounded off to
    //           the nearest cent
    double Balance()
    {
        // I have added the explicit reference to this
        int nCents = (int)(this.m_dBalance * 100 + 0.5);
        return nCents / 100.0;
    }
}
```

Now the *Balance* method explicity refers to *this* object; however, the addition does not change the method in any way. If I leave *this* off of the reference to *m_dBalance,* it is assumed.

 OTE   Any time that a method makes an unqualified reference to another member of the same class, there is an implicit reference to *this* tacked onto the front.

Class Members

Most properties, like the balance in my bank account, are unique to the object. Thus, *baMine* and *baSon* maintain separate balances. But some properties are shared among all objects of a given class. For example, the current interest rate is a property shared by all accounts in the same bank. (There might be special accounts or accounts with different rules, but we'll get into that later.)

Since such properties are shared by every object of a given class, they are called **class members**. (Members that are not shared among objects are called **object members**.) Class members are defined using the keyword *static*. For this reason, class members are also called **static members**, with object members being left with the somewhat less descriptive name **nonstatic members**.

Will Anything Take the *static* Out of My Data Members?

I could have declared the current interest rate, *m_dCurrentInterestRate,* to be static:

```
class BankAccount
{
    // make interest rate static
    static double m_dCurrentInterestRate;

    // Rate - returns the current rate
    double Rate()
    {
        return m_dCurrentInterestRate;
    }
    double Rate(double dNewRate)
    {
        if (dNewRate > 0.0 && dNewRate < 20.0)
        {
            m_dCurrentInterestRate = dNewRate;
```

```
    }
    return m_dCurrentInterestRate;
}

// ...and so on like before...
}
```

If I now change the interest rate with one object, it will stay changed even when viewed from a different object:

```
void SomeFunc()
{
    BankAccount baMine = new BankAccount();
    BankAccount baSon = new BankAccount();

    // now set the interest rate
    baMine.Rate(10);

    //query it from the other object - outputs as 10%
    System.out.println("Son's interest rate = " baSon.Rate());
}
```

This is because the interest rate is shared among all *BankAccount* objects.

How do you store static? In a Leyden jar?

Static data members are not stored inside the object. (If they were, the immediate question would arise: Which object, since all objects share the same statics?) Instead, all of the static members of a class are kept in a single place. Thus, for every class you define, Java creates a single entry in memory to hold the static members of that class. When you create an instance of the class, Java allocates enough storage to hold just the non-static, object data members of the class. This is shown pictorially in Figure 4-1.

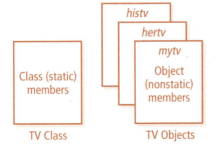

Figure 4-1. *All class members of a given class are kept in one place. Each object keeps its own object members.*

Static Methods

Methods can also be declared static. In fact, consider either of the *Rate* methods. Now that *m_dCurrentInterestRate* has been declared static, to which object do these methods refer? The answer is none. (Or one could equally say that they refer to all objects of class *BankAccount*.)

The following version of *BankAccount* shows the *Rate* and *Rate(double)* functions declared static:

```java
class BankAccount
{
    // make interest rate static
    static double m_dCurrentInterestRate;

    // Rate - returns the current rate
    static double Rate()
    {
        return m_dCurrentInterestRate;
    }
    static double Rate(double dNewRate)
    {
        if (dNewRate > 0.0 && dNewRate < 20.0)
        {
            m_dCurrentInterestRate = dNewRate;
        }
        return m_dCurrentInterestRate;
    }

    // ...and so on like before...
}
```

A *static* method is one that is shared among all objects. That is, a static method is one that does not operate on a single object. Just between you and me, that means it has no *this* pointer.

Calling a static method

How do you call a static method? In the earlier example, when the *Rate* methods were declared nonstatic, they were called using an object, as follows:

```java
void SomeFunc()
{
    BankAccount baMine = new BankAccount();
    baMine.Rate(10);

    // ...other stuff...
}
```

Now that they have been declared static, however, the *Rate* methods have no need of an object. Thus, Java allows the programmer to call a static method using the name of the class rather than an object name:

```
void SomeFunc()
{
    BankAccount.Rate(10);

    // ...other stuff...
}
```

You can still call a static method using an object rather than a class name, but the object is not passed to the static function.

C/C++   Unlike in C++, in Java the object expression is evaluated.

Why bother?

Even as nonstatics, the *Rate* methods were allowed to access the static member *m_dCurrentInterestRate.* Then why bother declaring them static? There are several reasons.

First, it doesn't say so, but writing *Rate* as a nonstatic method implies to the reader that the interest rate is a property of the object rather than a property of the class. Thus, it is not obvious that setting *baMine.Rate(10)* also changes the value returned by *baSon.Rate.*

From a purely pragmatic point of view, it also means that a reference to *baMine* is passed to the method unnecessarily. Worse, if I want to set the interest rate for all bank accounts, and I don't have a *BankAccount* object already, I have to create a new *BankAccount* object, which *Rate(double)* doesn't even use, just to make the call!

Are there any restrictions on static methods?

If static methods are more efficient to call, why not declare all methods static? That's easy: because static methods do not refer to any particular object.

Suppose, for example, that I try to convert one of the other *BankAccount* methods to be static:

```
class BankAccount
{
    // balance - the current account's balance
    double m_dBalance;

    // Deposit - add something to the account
    static void Deposit(double dAmount)
    {
        // no negative deposits!
        if (dAmount > 0.0)
        {
            m_dBalance += dAmount;
        }
    }
    // ...all else the same...
}
```

When I try to call *Deposit,* Java is truly confused:

```
BankAccount ba = new BankAccout(); // open an account
ba.Deposit(100.00);                // make a deposit
                                   // in which account??
```

The call to *Deposit* attempts to make a deposit to the bank account *ba.* Remember, however, that *ba* is not passed to the static method. Thus, *Deposit* has no object to look at when the program gets there.

Said another way, the following conversion is not allowed because there is no *this* pointer:

```
class BankAccount
{
    // balance - the current account's balance
    double m_dBalance;

    // Deposit - add something to the account
    static void Deposit(double dAmount)
    {
        // no negative deposits!
        if (dAmount > 0.0)
        {
            // following not allowed since there is no this
            // pointer within a static method
            this.m_dBalance += dAmount;
        }
```

```
    }
    // ...all else the same...
}
```

Without a *this* pointer, *Deposit* doesn't know which *m_dBalance* it should reference.

Final Members

It is possible to define a data member as **final**, meaning that its value is not subject to change:

```
class MyClass
{
    final int m_nMY_AGE = 29; // not subject to change
}
void fn(MyClass mc)
{
    mc.m_nMY_AGE++;    // reached 30th birthday?
                       // NO WAY - compiler error
}
```

The rules for naming final data members are the same as those for naming any other data members, although some programmers prefer to use all caps for the actual name. It is illegal to attempt to modify a final data member, and doing so generates a compiler error.

Final statics

Static data members can also be declared final. This is commonly used to declare constant properties of the class. For example, I can code the maximum channel number of a TV as follows:

```
class TV
{
    final static int m_nMAX_CHANNEL_NUMBER = 70;
    // ...so on like before
}
```

A final static data member can be used anywhere that a literal constant can be used (for example, as the case in a *switch* statement or the size of an array).

Access Control

Java allows the programmer to control access to classes and their members via the access specifiers **public** and **private**. (A third access specifier, *protected,* will be covered in Chapter 7 after we've discussed inheritance.) These specifiers, along with short descriptions, are shown in Table 4-1.

Specifier	Meaning
<default> (also known as friendly)	Accessible to other members of the same package.
public	Accessible to all methods in all packages.
private	Accessible only to other members of the same class. (Does not apply to classes.)

Table 4-1. *The Java access specifiers.*

If a member of a class is not otherwise marked, it is said to be **friendly**. Friendly members are directly accessible to other members of the same package. (I will discuss packages in Chapter 8, but for now let's just say that friendly members are accessible to other classes within the same java source file.)

Public classes and members are accessible to all classes in all packages (files). Private members are accessible only to other members of the same class.

Classes can be public or friendly; however, they cannot be private. The java file that contains a public class must have the same name as that of the class. Thus, the file that contains a public class *TV* must be named TV.java.

Why Access Control Is Important

Even without access control, the Java class structure goes a long way toward supporting the object-oriented programming paradigm. Classes can describe tangible concepts. Data members give the class its static properties, while methods provide the active properties. This allows for the creation of classes that are tangible, complete, and autonomous. Access control addresses robustness.

How can the class be held responsible for its own health if any method can reach right into the class and modify anything it wants there? Using our television analogy, how can I hold the manufacturer responsible when my TV catches on fire and burns down my house, if I took the case off and let my children play with the insides? If I'm going to hold the class responsible, I must allow the class to control and limit its interface. Access control provides the case on the TV.

A well-written, robust class has a controlled interface made up of a limited number of public methods of the class. These methods should be as strict as a drill sergeant about letting arguments get through. All arguments should be checked for range and validity.

Private methods are meant as helpers. These are the methods that actually get the work done. Since outside methods cannot call these methods directly, the data has already been checked out and found to be free of infectious diseases prior to reaching the private methods. Therefore, private methods can be a lot more trusting of the arguments they receive.

In addition, the private methods are not part of the public interface that the class must maintain. Suppose, for example, that I decide to rewrite the *TV* class for whatever reason. Unless I want to search for all users of TVs (a fairly large lot, I should think), I am obligated to leave the public interface to the *TV* class unchanged. Since the private members are hidden from view, however, I am free to change them as much as I want.

Finally, reducing the public interface can greatly reduce the number of interactions that need to be considered and tested. Reducing the number of things the programmer must think about at once leads to better software in less time.

 NOTE Suppose, for example, that there are 5 classes with some 5 methods apiece. If any method can call any other method, 600 interactions are possible (25 different methods × 24 methods that each can call). Now assume that only 2 of the methods in each class are public and the other 3 are private. This means that 20 different interactions are possible within each class (5 × 4 methods that each can call within the same class) times 5 classes plus an additional 16 interactions between classes (2 methods per class × 4 other classes × 2 methods in each of those classes) for a total of 106 different interactions. Thus, the number of interactions that must be considered is reduced by a factor of almost 6 to 1. The larger the number of methods involved in your program, the greater the effect.

Thus, the clever object-oriented programmer identifies the classes she will need during the design of the overall program. Also during this design phase, the programmer identifies the public interface that each class must provide to the remainder of the program. She then sets about coding these classes as stand-alone entities, more or less without regard to exactly how they will be used. Thus, while she is coding the *TV* class, the programmer is thinking only of how to implement the *TV* class's public interface in the most efficient way possible. She need not give any thought to where in the house the TV will be placed or to what channels will be used most often or to all those other problems that concern the user of the TV.

Once the programmer completes the *TV* class, she can forget about the internals of the class and proceed with the classes that use the *TV*. While working on these classes, she need worry about only the *TV* class's public interface, since these are the only methods accessible anyway.

Are There No Officer Data Members, or Are They All Privates?

Quick quiz: Given what I've told you so far about access control and TVs, why are all data members declared private? Answer: There is no way that a class can control access to a public data member.

Suppose some external code needs to change one or more of the settings in a class. We've already seen one example: Suppose I need to change the channel setting in my *TV* class (not an unreasonable request, and I think you'll agree). Look back again at how *TV* implements that capability. (I added the access specifiers as necessary.)

```
public class TV
{
    // the largest legal channel number
    final static int m_nMAX_CHANNEL = 70;

    // current channel number
    private int m_nChannel;

    // Channel - return the current channel
    public int Channel()
    {
        return m_nChannel;
    }
```

```
    // Channel(int) - change the channel
    public int Channel(int nNewChannel)
    {
        // first make sure that it's in range
        if (nNewChannel > 1 && nNewChannel < m_nMAX_CHANNEL)
        {
            m_nChannel = nNewChannel;
        }
        return m_nChannel;
    }
}
```

"Look," you say, "the application has direct access to *m_nChannel*. All it has to do is call *Channel(int)* to set it and *Channel* to read it." But that's the point—the application does not have direct access. The application can set *m_nChannel,* but only after *Channel(int)* has examined the new value to make sure it's legal. In addition, *Channel* returns the value of *m_nChannel,* not *m_nChannel* itself. Thus, the application can look at the channel by means of that method but it cannot change the channel setting directly. If the program crashes with an illegal value in *m_nChannel,* we need look no further than the *TV* class itself.

Classes and Files

Java maintains a unique relationship between class names and file-names. As I have already mentioned, each public class must be contained in a java source file of the same name. When you compile a java source file, the compiler generates a separate class output file for each class contained within the file, whether that class is public or not. The class file is not loaded into memory until the first time it is referenced. The *import* statement causes the standard Java class files to be loaded.

An application starts execution at the method *public static int main.* Since more than one class can have such a method, a single program might have more than one entry point. This is useful for debugging purposes, with one entry point provided for debugging and a separate one for normal execution.

Example: A Slightly Expanded BankAccount

Now that you've seen a few of the nicer features of classes, let's expand on the *BankAccount* class of the previous chapter:

```java
// BankAccount - a general bank account class
public class BankAccount
{
    // interest rate
    static private double m_dCurrentInterestRate;

    // balance - the current account's balance
    private double m_dBalance;

    // Rate - inquire or set interest rate
    public static double Rate()
    {
        return m_dCurrentInterestRate;
    }
    public static void Rate(double dNewRate)
    {
        // first a sanity check
        if (dNewRate > 0.0 && dNewRate < 20.0)
        {
            m_dCurrentInterestRate = dNewRate;
        }
    }

    // Deposit - add something to the account
    public void Deposit(double dAmount)
    {
        // no negative deposits!
        if (dAmount > 0.0)
        {
            m_dBalance += dAmount;
        }
    }

    // Withdrawal - take something out
    public void Withdrawal(double dAmount)
    {
        // negative withdrawals are a sneaky way
        // of adding money to the account
        if (dAmount >= 0.0)
        {
            // don't let him withdraw more than he has
            if (dAmount <= m_dBalance)
            {
```

```
                m_dBalance -= dAmount;
            }
        }
    }

    // Balance - return the current balance rounded off to
    //           the nearest cent
    public double Balance()
    {
        int nCents = (int)(m_dBalance * 100 + 0.5);
        return nCents / 100.0;
    }

    // Monthly - each month rack up interest and service fees
    public void Monthly()
    {
        Fee();      // fee first! (reduces interest we pay)
        Interest();
    }

    // Fee - rack up the monthly fee
    public void Fee()
    {
        m_dBalance -= 5.0;    // $5.00 per month
    }

    // Interest - tack on monthly interest
    public void Interest()
    {
        // 1200 because interest is normally expressed
        // in numbers like 20%, meaning .2, and because
        // we are accumulating interest monthly
        m_dBalance += m_dBalance *
                (m_dCurrentInterestRate / 1200.0);
    }
}
```

The *BankAccount* class is marked public to make it available to the entire world. (Of course, this means that the enclosing file must be BankAccount-.java.) The first data member in the class is the *m_dCurrentInterestRate*. It is assumed that all accounts share the same interest rate, so this field is marked static. In addition, it's marked private since we don't want others toying with the interest rate. The *Rate(double)* method that sets the interest rate is marked public, although depending on the application I might have flagged this as friendly, thereby reserving the ability to set the interest rate to bank insiders.

The *m_dBalance* is the current account's balance. This is left as a nonstatic member, since every account has a different balance; however, it is marked private. The balance can be adjusted through the public and controller interfaces *Deposit* and *Withdrawal* and queried using the *Balance* method.

 OTE   Both *Deposit* and *Withdrawal* ignore illegal input. They should probably raise some type of red flag. You'll see what that red flag is in Chapter 9.

The following class, *App1_4,* is a slightly updated version of *App1_3:*

```
// App1_4 - test out the BankAcount class.
//          the program expects two inputs: the monthly
//          deposit and the interest rate, as in App1_4 100 8,
//          meaning $100 per month at 8% interest. (to keep
//          things simple, both are assumed to be integers.)
//          the program calculates the bank balance at the end
//          of each month for 10 years.
import java.io.*;

public class App1_4
{
    public static void main(String args[])
    {
        // first argument is the deposit per month
        double dPerMonth = (double)Integer.parseInt(args[0]);

        // second argument is the interest rate
        double dInterest = (double)Integer.parseInt(args[1]);

        // now set the interest rate
        BankAccount.Rate(dInterest);

        // create a BankAccount object
        BankAccount baMyAccount = new BankAccount();

        // make a deposit each month and
        // watch my account grow for 10 years!
        System.out.println("Depositing " +
                        dPerMonth +
                        " per month at " +
                        BankAccount.Rate() +
                        " percent interest");
        System.out.println("Watch my account grow!");
        for (int nYear = 0; nYear < 10; nYear++)
        {
```

```
System.out.print(nYear + " - ");
for (int nMonth = 0; nMonth < 12; nMonth++)
{
    // make my deposit
    baMyAccount.Deposit(dPerMonth);

    // now take monthly fees and interest
    baMyAccount.Monthly();
    System.out.print(baMyAccount.Balance() + ", ");
}
System.out.println();
    }
}
}
```

App1_4 appears to be virtually identical to *App1_3*, except that it can set and query the current interest rate even before any *BankAccount* objects have been created, since *Rate* is now static. The output from this program appears identical to the output for *App1_3*.

Conclusion

In this chapter, you've seen the difference between a static and a nonstatic member. In addition, you've seen the various forms of access control. Finally, I've shown you how to use these features in a program.

In the next chapter, you'll see how Java makes child's play out of that most vexing of all programming problems, the pointer.

Object References

The concept of pointers can be difficult to grasp. Although they are powerful, pointers can cause a lot of grief, even for the grizzled veteran, and they introduce more than their fair share of bugs. Hardly a C or C++ program exists that doesn't include at least one memory leak that is traceable to pointers.

By comparison, the Java seas are much safer. Java has no explicit pointers. Instead, Java offers references, which provide most of the power of pointers without the nagging memory leaks.

What's a Pointer?

A pointer is not a tip about a good stock to buy. A **pointer** is a variable that contains the address of another variable. Every object that you declare, be it an intrinsic object or a class object, is assigned a piece of memory. You can think of computer memory as a long city street. Each object in memory is like a house on that street. Each house on the street is assigned a unique address. Memory addresses are simply numbers. (There's only one street, after all.) Take a look at the following example:

```
int nMyAge;    // assign a piece of memory
nMyAge = 10;   // store a 40 there
```

(continued)

What's a Pointer? *continued*

The declaration reserves a piece of memory and assigns it the name *nMyAge*. For argument's sake, let's say that the address of that piece of memory is 0x1000. (Addresses are always in hexidecimal format.) The assignment says, "Store a 40 at the memory location whose name is *nAnInt*." Since we know that *nAnInt* is stored at location 0x1000, we could say, "Store a 40 at the memory location whose address is 0x1000."

Some languages, such as C and C++, allow the programmer to access the location of an object. Consider the following C/C++ example:

```
// store the address of nMyAge in pnMyAge
int* pnMyAge = &nMyAge;

// now store a 35 in the location pointed at by pnMyAge
*pnMyAge = 35;
```

The declaration defines a pointer and assigns it the address of *nMyAge* in the object *pnMyAge*. That is, the content of *pnMyAge* in this example is 0x1000. The assignment **pnMyAge = 35* says, "Assign the value 35 to the memory location contained in the pointer variable *pnMyAge*."

Pointers are extremely useful in a variety of ways. As you will see in this chapter, references retain the power of pointer variables but avoid many of the pitfalls.

What Can a Reference Do?

You might have noticed in earlier chapters that a class object is not created the same way an intrinsic object is created.

 OTE Some programmers might reserve the term **object** to refer to an instance of a class; however, I use the term to include both an instance of a class and an intrinsic. Thus, I refer to both *myObj* and *nMyInt* as objects:

```
MyClass myObj = new MyClass();
int nMyInt;
```

When I want to differentiate between the two types of objects, I refer to *myObj* as a **class object** and to *nMyInt* as an **intrinsic object**.

Consider the following declaration:

```
TV mytv = new TV();
```

What's going on? What's *new?* Is it required? The answer to the latter is "no." The following is completely legal:

```
TV mytv;
```

This example declares not a *TV* object but a reference to a *TV* object. That is, the variable *mytv* refers to a *TV* object. Which *TV* object? Since we didn't say, the answer is "none in particular." However, Java is pretty strict about making sure you assign a *TV* object to *mytv* before you use the variable.

 NOTE   You should always try to initialize your references when you declare them. If you don't have anything to initialize them to, initialize them to null. You can't make changes to a null reference—any attempt to use it generates an exception. (More on exceptions in Chapter 9, but suffice it to say, it's an error that can prove fatal—to the program, not to you.) If you don't initialize a reference, Java will initialize it to null anyway.

So what can you do with an uninitialized reference? You can assign it to reference a real object:

```
TV mytv;         // mytv now references the null object
mytv = new TV(); // now mytv references a real TV object
```

This is a new use for the assignment operator. When applied to references, the assignment operator causes the reference on the left to refer to the object on the right of the assignment.

So where did the object on the right come from? The *new* keyword actually creates a new object. It takes the memory that it needs to create the object from a special memory pool that Java controls, called the **heap**. All class objects in Java come from the heap.

It is legal for two references to refer to the same object:

```
TV mytv = new TV();
TV sonstv = mytv;    // sonstv refers to the same TV as mytv
```

In the above example, both *mytv* and *sonstv* refer to the same *TV* object. (Think of having two remotes for a single TV.)

If the program changes one reference, the other is changed as well:

```
TV mytv = new TV();    // create a TV object
TV sonstv = mytv;      // make a second reference to same TV
mytv.channel(8);       // I change the channel with my remote
sonstv.channel(4);     // he changes it with his
mytv.channel();        // my TV is now tuned to channel 4
```

Here the program sets the channel to 8 using the *mytv* reference. It then sets the channel to 4 using the *sonstv* reference. Since both references refer to the same *TV,* when the program asks what channel *mytv* is tuned to, the answer 4 is returned.

So What Is a Reference?

You can think of a reference as a name for an object. I have a dog. The dog is an object. I can name it Trude. Trude is a reference to the dog object. I can give my dog several names: Trude, Fido, Stupid. Each of these references refers to the same animal (object). A reference can be redirected. Thus, I can say to the rest of the family, "From now on, when I say Fido, I'm referring to our new dog." This is similar to assigning a reference to point to a different object.

To make this more concrete, consider the following example:

```
BankAccount myAccount = new BankAccount();
BankAccount myFirstAccount = myAccount;
BankAccount mySavingsAccount = myAccount;
// ...later on...
mySavingsAccount = new BankAccount();
```

The first declaration creates a *BankAccount* object and declares *my-Account* as a reference to that object. It essentially gives that object a name (*myAccount*). When I say *myAccount,* I'm referring to the *BankAccount* object that was created in that statement.

The example then gives the same object two other names, *myFirst-Account* and *mySavingsAccount.* Later, for whatever reason, the program decides to redirect the name *mySavingsAccount* to refer to a new object and not the same object as *myFirstAccount* and *myAccount.*

Today on Oprah: "When Objects Have Objects"

One class can reference another class. Consider the following definition of the class *Car:*

```
class Car
{
    private Motor m_motor;
    public void motor(Motor m)
    {
        m_motor = m;
    }
    // ...other stuff
}
```

The *Car* class has thoughtfully provided a method to allow the user application to assign the *Car* a *Motor:*

```
Car car = new Car();      // car created without a motor
car.motor(new Motor());   // this assigns a motor
```

Using References

You might argue that setting two references to the same object is a silly thing to do. However, this referencing method comes up in at least two common constructs: passing objects to functions and manipulating linked lists.

Passing References to Functions

Consider the *ChannelSurf* method of the following function *TV* class:

```
class TV
{
    static public void ChannelSurf(TV atv, int nNewChannel)
    {
        atv.m_nChannel = nNewChannel;  // tune TV
        nNewChannel++;                 // now go to next channel
                                       // (this doesn't work)
    }

    // ...other stuff the same
}
```

(continued)

```
class SomeOtherClass
{
    static public void SomeFunc()
    {
        TV mytv = new TV();
        int nChannel = 8;

        // surf the electromagnetic waves
        TV.ChannelSurf(mytv, nChannel);
    }
}
```

The *ChannelSurf* method is designed to tune the TV provided and then increment the channel to the next channel number.

Because *ChannelSurf* is a member of the class *TV*, it has access to the private data member *m_nChannel*, so the call to *ChannelSurf* in the *SomeFunc* method should have the desired effect of tuning the object referenced by *mytv*. But does it?

Consider closely the call to *ChannelSurf*. This call says, "Pass the value of *mytv*, which happens to be a reference to a valid *TV* object, and the value of *nChannel*, which happens to be 8, to the function *ChannelSurf*."

In *ChannelSurf*, the first argument is given the name *atv*. Thus, *atv* in *ChannelSurf* and *mytv* back in *SomeFunc* refer to the same object, just as if there had been an assignment *atv* = *mytv* made as part of the call. The assignment *atv.m_nChannel* = *nNewChannel* changes the station on the *mytv* object as well as the *atv* object because both references point to the same object.

But the expression *nNewChannel*++ in *ChannelSurf* doesn't have any effect on *nChannel* in *SomeFunc* because a value was passed rather than a reference to *nChannel*. The function *ChannelSurf* doesn't work as expected—the class object is modified back in the calling function, but the intrinsic object is not affected.

> **NOTE** A class object passed as an argument to a function remains modified in the calling function. However, an intrinsic object does not remain modified when passed as an argument to a function.

OTE Use **class wrappers** to pass intrinsic objects by reference. These are special classes such as *Integer, Byte, Boolean,* and so on. One class is defined per intrinsic type. If you want to pass an integer by reference, simply create an *Integer* class object out of it and pass that. Any changes made to the *Integer* class object will remain modified in the calling function.

Privacy Issues

Java's reference model introduces a couple of privacy concerns. Each is best described by example. Consider our *Car* example again:

```
class Car
{
    private Motor m_motor;
    public void AssignMotor(Motor m)
    {
        m_motor = m;
    }
    public Motor GetMotor()
    {
        return m_motor;
    }

    // ...other members as needed
}

// now from within my class
static void SomeFunc()
{
    // create a car
    Car car = new Car();

    // now give it a motor
    Motor motor = new Motor();
    car.AssignMotor(motor);
    // application still owns a reference to motor
}
```

The *SomeFunc* method creates a *Car* object and passes it a *Motor* object, as it should. The problem, however, is that *SomeFunc* retains a reference to the *Motor* object. Thus, even though *SomeFunc* has no access to the *Motor* object through *car*, the method has direct access to the object through the retained reference *motor*.

(continued)

Privacy Issues, *continued*

The *GetMotor* method represents a different issue. At first glance, *GetMotor* appears to be an access function, like *TV.Channel* or *Bank-Account.Balance*. It simply returns the *Motor* object that the *Car* object is using. The only problem is that *m_motor* is a reference to the *Motor* object. Returning a reference to the *Car* object's *Motor* gives the application direct access to the *Motor*.

Neither of these issues is necessarily a problem. As long as *Motor* has its own access control in place, the application can't take the motor away from the car. However, in the above circumstances, *Car* cannot count on hiding its *Motor* from the application.

Linked Lists

The linked list is another structure that is commonly used for references. A **linked list** is a data structure consisting of a variable number of objects. Each object contains a reference to the next member of the list except for the last object, which references null. Two special members, the *head* and the *tail,* refer to the first and last members of the linked list. Linked lists are popular precisely because they are efficient at storing a dynamic number of objects.

Whether you are familiar with or new to linked lists, seeing a linked list implemented in Java can help you understand how references are used in lieu of pointers.

The following class implements a simple singly linked list class. Since we will use this linked list later in the example program section, this example will be a linked list of *BankAccount* objects.

 C++   Java does not support templates. However, you will see in Chapter 8 why this is not as big a problem in Java as it would be in C++.

```
// LinkedList - create a linked list of pointers to "things"
public class LinkedList
{
    // class data - the head and tail pointers
    private static LinkedList m_head = null;
    private static LinkedList m_tail = null;

    // object data - pointer to next element in linked list
    //                plus the pointer to the object
    private LinkedList m_next;
    private BankAccount m_baObject;

    // Add - add an element to the list
    public static void Add(BankAccount ba)
    {
        // create a new linked list object
        LinkedList ll = new LinkedList();

        // set up our pointers
        ll.m_baObject = ba;
        ll.m_next = null;

        // if the head is null...
        if (m_head == null)
        {
            // ...then we are the only member in list...
            m_head = ll;
            m_tail = ll;
        }
        else
        {
            // ...otherwise, add to the end of the list
            m_tail.m_next = ll;
            m_tail = ll;
        }
    }

    // Next - iterate through the list. If ll is null, return the
    //        first element, otherwise return the element after ll.
    //        Return null when list is exhausted.
    public static LinkedList Next(LinkedList ll)
    {
        if (ll == null)
        {
            return m_head;
        }
        return ll.m_next;
    }
```

(continued)

```
// Data - return the data associated with this node
public BankAccount Data()
{
    return m_baObject;
}
}
```

The static members *m_head* and *m_tail* are references to the beginning and end of the list. Since this class example is designed to keep only one list, these are static elements. Each node in the list contains two references: *m_next,* which points to the next element in the list, and *m_baObject,* which references a *BankAccount* object. Figure 5-1 shows how this appears in memory.

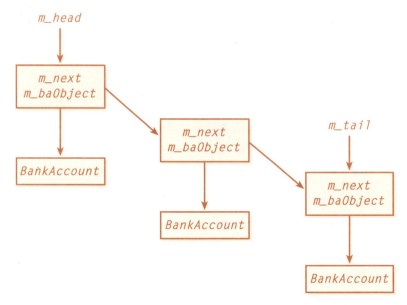

Figure 5-1. *A graphical representation of a singly linked list of* LinkedList *objects in memory.*

To add a new element to the list, the static function *Add* first creates a *LinkedList* node. It then adds the node to the end of the list, setting *m_tail* to point to the node and setting the node's *m_next* pointer to point to null. *Add* sets the node's *m_baObject* reference to point to the *BankAccount* object provided.

In practice, adding a new *BankAccount* object to the linked list appears as follows:

```
// create a new bank account and add it to the list
LinkedList.add(new BankAccount());
```

The *Next* method traverses the list. *Next* expects to receive a node and returns the next node in the list. If the node passed to *Next* is null, *Next* returns the contents of *m_head,* which is the first object in the list. Once the list has been exhausted, *Next* returns null.

Traversing a linked list of *BankAccount*s is accomplished as follows:

```
// setting ll to null causes Next to return the first node
LinkedList ll = null;

// keep fetching linked list nodes until Next returns a null
while ((ll = LinkedList.Next(ll)) != null)
{
    // use the Data method to get the data out of the node
    BankAccount ba = ll.data();

    // process the bank account however you like
}
```

You will see *LinkedList* in action in the example program at the end of the next chapter.

Cleaning Up Lost Objects: Garbage Collection

Objects can get lost. Consider the following code snippet:

```
public static void SomeFunc()
{
    // program allocates a TV...
    TV mytv = new TV();
    // ...does something with it...
    // ...and then exits
}
```

Here the reference *mytv* is local to the function *SomeFunc.* When the function exits, *mytv* goes out of scope. (To **go out of scope** means that the variable is lost and its memory is reclaimed.) But what about the *TV* object to which it refers?

If the *SomeFunc* method is called again, a new *mytv* reference is created and *new* is invoked again to create a new *TV* object. But without a reference to the old *TV* object, that old object is lost. Because the object is no longer accessible, Java is free to reclaim its memory and put it back into the heap for use in building new objects. It does this in a process known as **garbage collection**.

Memory Loss

Loss of memory is a problem for programs as well as programmers. "So what if an object or two gets lost?" you ask. It's no big deal if we're talking only an object or two. But consider programs that lose more than just a couple of objects. The heap manager must periodically ask the operating system for more memory to replace the lost memory. After a while, such programs consume more memory in lost objects than they use for real work. Eventually the operating system memory is depleted, and future requests for memory cannot be granted. The memory-starved application has no choice but to die. (The memory is lost only from the application. Microsoft Windows 95 and Microsoft Windows NT recover any lost memory blocks when the application quits.)

How Does Java Know What It Can Recover?

How does Java know which objects it can return to the heap? Here's how it works. When you allocate an object off the heap, you get more than just the object you asked for. In addition to the object itself, you get room for a reference count. This count is automatically incremented every time the object is assigned to a reference.

Thus, the following statement creates an object with a reference count of 0. (This object is an immediate candidate for the scrap heap.)

```
new TV(); // hey, Java, you can take this back whenever you want
```

The following represents a more normal case:

```
TV mytv = new TV();   // the reference count is 1
TV sonstv;
sonstv = mytv;        // now the reference count is 2
```

Whenever a reference goes out of scope, the reference count of the object that the variable referenced is decremented. Thus, in the above example, as soon as *sonstv* goes out of scope the reference count of the *TV* object is decremented to 1. When *mytv* is lost, the object's reference count is decremented back down to 0. Now the object is lost, and Java can put it back on the heap. (Though popular, the phrase "put it back on the heap" is not completely accurate. Of course, the object doesn't move anywhere. This common phrase means that the memory occupied by the object is made available for other objects to use.)

Any object with a reference count of 0 is a candidate for the scrap pile. Garbage collection is free to return such an object to the heap.

For compound objects, the situation is similar. Whenever an object is lost, Java automatically decrements the reference count of any object to which that object refers. Consider the following example:

```
class Car
{
    private Motor m_motor;
    public void Assignmotor(Motor m)
    {
        m_motor = m;
    }
    // ...other stuff
}
```

In this example, assigning a *Motor* object to the *Car* object increments the *Motor* object's reference count because the *Car* object provides another way of accessing the *Motor* object. However, if the *Car* object is lost, the *Motor* object's reference count is decremented. If the resulting reference count is 0, no further references point to the *Motor* object and it is lost as well.

Likewise, even though no local variable is referencing it, an object contained in a singly linked list has a reference count of 1 since its predecessor still refers to it. The first member of the list is referenced by the head reference. As soon as the head reference is lost, however, the entire list is lost and can be returned to the heap.

Thus, the *Clear* function for our *LinkedList* class is simple:

```
public static void Clear()
{
    m_head = null;
}
```

Removing the reference to the first member of the list decrements that object's reference count to 0, causing it to be lost. This decrements the reference count of the next object in the list to 0, causing it to be lost, and so it goes down the list until the last object in the list is reached. (For a doubly linked list, the same is true; however, the reference count for each object in the list, except the first and last, is 2 because each object is referenced by both neighbors.)

When Does Java Perform Garbage Collection?

Java performs garbage collection under the following circumstances:

- Whenever it needs to. When the amount of memory remaining in the heap falls below some level, the program stops what it's doing and performs garbage collection in an attempt to regain whatever memory it can.

- Whenever you ask. You can force garbage collection by calling *System.gc*.

- Whenever it gets around to it. Java continually executes a background task that looks for things to throw away. This task is low priority so as not to affect the performance of the system; however, Java will eventually get around to picking up any discarded objects left lying about.

C/C++ Doesn't Do It That Way

Those of you who are familiar with C and C++ will note that although both support allocating memory off of the heap, they do not provide anything like garbage collection. Their model for supporting heap memory is based on a "roll your own" philosophy. If you allocate it, you have to return it. If you forget to return it, the memory is lost. This is known as a **memory leak**.

In a perfect application, this is an extremely efficient model. The software knows when it no longer needs a particular block of memory, so there's no need for you to maintain pesky reference counts or for background threads to go sniffing through memory looking for orphaned blocks to clean up. But we all know that no applications are perfect—most have memory leaks.

A small leak seems harmless enough. A lost block here or there doesn't make much difference when you have megabytes to play with. Over time, however, these small leaks can cause a flood when several hours into an edit session or after two hours of downloading that really big file, the application gives up with at best an "Out of Memory" error message (or you get no error message at all). These slow leaks are extremely frustrating and difficult to find.

While Java's approach might involve a little more overhead, it is a price worth paying if it means no more memory leak worries.

Using Arrays

Arrays are objects that are allocated much like any other object. The following declares a reference to an array of integers:

```
int nArray[];
```

The brackets suffixed to *nArray* indicate that this is a reference to an array; however, no number is required (or allowed) within the brackets since the declaration itself does not allocate the space for the array. Interestingly, the brackets can be placed either before or after the reference name. Thus, the following is also allowed (and is more common):

```
int[] nArray;
```

The memory for the array is allocated off the heap using the *new* keyword:

```
nArray = new int[10];    // allocated an array of 10 integers
```

The programmer can use an initialization list when declaring an array of intrinsics:

```
int nArray[] = {0, 1, 2, 3, 4};
```

This statement allocates an array of five integers off the heap (the call to *new* is implicit) and then assigns them the values 0 through 4.

 OTE   You've already seen a similar situation with literal *String* constants:

```
System.out.println("Hello, world");
```

Declaring the string literal *"Hello, world"* causes Java to allocate a *String* object off the heap and assign it the initial value *"Hello, world"*. Here the creation of the *String* object as well as the call to *new* are implicit.

Elements within an array are accessed using brackets as well:

```
// initialize the array to zeros
int[] nArray = new int[10];
for (int i = 0; i < 10; i++)
{
    nArray[i] = 0;
}
```

Java checks the range of every subscript. Thus, if *i* is not in the range 0 through 9, the statement *nArray[i]* generates an *ArrayIndexOutOf-BoundsException* error. (Again, I'll cover exceptions in Chapter 9.)

Since *nArray* is a reference, if it is passed as an argument to a function, the function can permanently change the contents of the array.

Arrays of Objects

You must be careful when allocating arrays of class objects. The following does *not* create an array of 10 *TV* objects:

```
TV[] tvArray = new TV[10];
```

Instead, it creates an array of 10 references to *TV* objects, all of which are assigned the value *null*.

The programmer must use some type of loop to allocate each of the *TV* objects individually:

```
TV[] tvArray = new TV[10];  // allocate 10 references
for (int i = 0; i < 10; i++)
{
    tvArray[i] = new TV();  // make them reference something
}
```

This approach is entirely consistent with the way nonarray intrinsics and objects are declared:

```
int i;      // actually declares an integer
TV mytv;    // declares only a reference;
            // a TV object must be allocated off the heap
```

 NOTE We can see why *main* is declared the way it is:

```
static public void main(String[] args)
```

args is a reference to an array of *String* objects.

Multidimensional Arrays

Java does not directly support higher dimensional arrays, such as matrices. It does support arrays of arrays, however:

```
TV[][] tvMatrix = new TV[2][];
```

This declares a two-element array of references to arrays of *TV* objects. The individual arrays can be populated as follows:

```
// allocate room for the columns
TV[][] tvMatrix = new TV[2][];
for (int i = 0; i < 2; i++)
{
    // allocate room for each row
    tvMatrix[i] = new TV[3];
    for (int j = 0; j < 3; j++)
    {
        // now create an object for each cell
        tvMatrix[i][j] = new TV();
    }
}
```

The two columns need not be the same length because the two columns are allocated separately. I could make one column three elements long and the other six, for example. If the columns are the same length, however, Java allows the following shorthand version of the above:

```
// allocate room for the entire matrix
TV[][] tvMatrix = new TV[2][3];

// now populate it
for (int i = 0; i < 2; i++)
{
    for (int j = 0; j < 3; j++)
    {
        // now create an object for each cell
        tvMatrix[i][j] = new TV();
    }
}
```

In this case, the call to *new* allocates room for an array of two rows of three columns of references.

The Array Class

When I introduced arrays, I stated that arrays are objects. They certainly appear to be objects from their semantics. If arrays are objects, of what class are they an object?

For every class that you create, as well as the intrinsic class types themselves, Java creates a corresponding array class. You can ignore this parallel class universe if you like, but the fact that arrays are classes means that they are outfitted with some useful functions that you might want to use. In particular, every array object has a public data member *length* that you can use to avoid hard coding the array size information (except when the array is allocated):

```
// allocate room for the columns
TV[][] tvMatrix = new TV[2][];
for (int i = 0; i < tvMatrix.length; i++)
{
    // allocate room for each row
    tvMatrix[i] = new TV[3];
    for (int j = 0; j < tvMatrix[i].length; j++)
    {
```

```
        // now create an object for each cell
        tvMatrix[i][j] = new TV();
    }
}
```

Conclusion

Java references offer the power of C and Pascal pointers without much of
the danger. You have seen how to initialize references, how to pass them
to functions, and how to use them to construct containers such as linked
lists. You have also learned how references play a critical role in the allocation of arrays.

One of the only actions that Java references cannot perform is referencing
a function—hardly surprising in a language that is so concerned about
security.

Armed with our understanding of objects and object references, let's return
to some remaining class features. In the next chapter, we'll look at constructors before moving into the uncharted realm of inheritance.

Getting an Object Started Out Right in Life

A **constructor** is a special member function that is used to initialize objects when they are first created. In this chapter, you'll learn how to write and use constructors to start your objects correctly down the path to success and fame.

The Problem

Java tries to start all objects in a known state. For example, if you don't provide an initialization value of some kind, numeric intrinsic variables start with the value 0 (or *false* for *Boolean* variables). Uninitialized references are set to null. Data members of classes start life with their members set using the same rules.

But what if neither 0 nor *null* is a valid setting? Consider the following *BankAccount* class:

```
class BankAccount
{
    private int m_nAccountNumber;
    // ...other members follow...
}
```

Unless I take steps that indicate otherwise, *m_nAccountNumber* will be initialized to 0 when the object is created. Unfortunately, 0 is not a valid number for a bank account.

A Solution: The Initializer

A simple solution to this dilemma is to write a special initialization function. Let's call it *Init*. The application calls this function immediately after creating the object to initialize the data members to some legal value.

Thus, creating a *BankAccount* object looks something like this:

```
// create a BankAccount object
BankAccount myAccount = new BankAccount();

// now initialize its members (including the account number)
myAccount.Init();
```

Looks pretty good, but it can't be that simple. (If it were so easy, the topic wouldn't warrant an entire chapter in this book.)

What's Wrong with This Solution?

The problem with the proposed *Init* function solution is that it violates one of the rules of object-oriented programming—the rule of autonomy. With this solution, the *BankAccount* class must rely on the application to call the *Init* function to put it into a valid state before it can do anything else. But what if the application function doesn't live up to its responsibilities? The bank account is reduced to an invalid state. The *BankAccount* class cannot give up that much control to an outside class.

What is needed is some way to take away the responsibility for calling the *Init* function from the application, which is not trustworthy, and give it to Java, which is. The constructor is the way.

The Constructor and Java Solution

A constructor is a special method that is invoked automatically whenever a class object is created. Its job is to initialize the object to a valid starting state.

Since Java must recognize a constructor in order to call it, the constructor must have a standard name. Java could have called the constructor *Init* or *Start* or anything else, but instead Java's creators decided to use the name of the class for the constructor name. Thus, a simple constructor for class *BankAccount* might appear as follows:

```
class BankAccount
{
    // following static used to allocate each object
    // its own account number
    static private int m_nNextAccountNumber;

    // the account number of this object
    private int m_nAccountNumber;

    // the account balance
    private double m_dBalance;

    BankAccount()
    {
        // allocate this object the next bank account number
        m_nAccountNumber = m_nNextAccountNumber++;

        // zero out initial balance
        m_dBalance = 0.0;
    }
    // ...other members follow...
}
```

When a *BankAccount* object is created, the constructor *BankAccount* allocates the next bank account number to *m_nAccountNumber*:

```
BankAccount myAccount = new BankAccount();
```

There is no need to call an *Init* function—it's built in.

 N **OTE** Notice that a constructor has no return type, not even *void*. A constructor can be declared *public* or *private*; however, if you declare the constructor *private*, no one will be able to create an object of that class.

You call a constructor only as part of creating a new object using the *new* keyword. You cannot call a constructor directly. That is, the following is not legal:

```
BankAccount myAccount = new BankAccount();

// ...use myAccount for something...
// now let's reset myAccount to its initial state
myAccount.BankAccount();   // this call is not allowed
```

A constructor, however, can call other methods. This can reduce the amount of work you need to perform in the constructor. For example, if the class *BankAccount* already includes a *Clear* method, the constructor can use the method to clear out the majority of the data members:

```
public class BankAccount
{
    // following static used to allocate each object
    // its own account number
    static private int m_nNextAccountNumber;

    // the account number of this object
    private int m_nAccountNumber;

    // the account balance
    private double m_dBalance;

    BankAccount()
    {
        // allocate this object the next bank account number
        m_nAccountNumber = m_nNextAccountNumber++;

        // use the clear method to initialize the data members
        Clear();
    }

    // Clear - clear out the BankAccount object
    //         this function is accessible to all
    public void Clear()
    {
        // initialize the members of BankAccount
        m_dBalance = 0.0;
    }
}
```

The application can call *Clear* at any time to reset the object to its original state. Allowing the constructor to call *Clear* simply reduces redundancy and keeps down the size of the constructor. (Of course, the *Clear* function for a real-world class would be considerably larger than this puny example.)

Why Haven't You Seen Constructors So Far?

If a constructor is necessary to create a new class object, why haven't you seen constructors already? After all, the classes in previous chapters created objects using the *new BankAccount* syntax, and they defined no constructors.

But, in fact, constructors were defined. If you do not define a constructor in your class, Java defines a default "do-nothing" constructor for you. I like to call it the "Miranda constructor." (You know, "You have the right to a constructor. If you cannot afford a constructor, a constructor will be provided for you.") It is also called the *default constructor* because you get the constructor by default if you don't define one of your own. The default constructor takes no arguments and does nothing other than initialize all nonstatic members to their 0 states.

What Should a Constructor Do?

A constructor can do anything any other function can do. No restrictions apply. However, a constructor should limit itself to creating an object in good standing with the other objects of its class. That might mean initializing data members, adding the object to a linked list, or incrementing an object count.

Constructors with Arguments

Like any function, a constructor can include arguments. These arguments indicate to the constructor how to set up the object at initialization. For example, normally you are required to open a bank account with some money in it. It might not make sense to create a bank account with no money. (After all, the bank wants to be able to claim its service fee.) In the same way, a better constructor for *BankAccount* might allow an initial balance, as shown on the next page.

```
class BankAccount
{
    // following static used to allocate each object
    // its own account number
    static private int m_nNextAccountNumber;

    // the account number of this object
    private int m_nAccountNumber;

    // the account balance
    private int m_dBalance;

    BankAccount(double dInitialBalance)
    {
        // allocate this object the next bank account number
        m_nAccountNumber = m_nNextAccountNumber++;

        // store the initial balance
        m_dBalance = dInitialBalance;
    }
    // ...other members follow...
}
```

Now the application must provide the bank account with an initial balance when it is created:

```
// open my account with $100.00
BankAccount myAccount = new BankAccount(100.0);
```

 OTE The following is no longer legal:

```
BankAccount myAccount = new BankAccount();
```

Why can't the application use the no argument constructor? Java does not provide a default constructor if the class defines a constructor of its own, whether that constructor takes arguments or not.

Overloading the Constructor

A single class is free to have more than one constructor as long as the constructors have different arguments. For example, the *BankAccount* class might provide two options:

```
class BankAccount
{
    // following static used to allocate each object
    // its own account number
```

```
    static private int m_nNextAccountNumber;

    // the account number of this object
    private int m_nAccountNumber;

    // the account balance
    private double m_dBalance;

    BankAccount()
    {
        // allocate this object the next bank account number
        m_nAccountNumber = m_nNextAccountNumber++;

        // start with an initial balance of 0
        m_dBalance = 0.0;
    }
    BankAccount(double dInitialBalance)
    {
        // allocate this object the next bank account number
        m_nAccountNumber = m_nNextAccountNumber++;

        // start with an initial balance of 0
        m_dBalance = dInitialBalance;
    }
}
```

The first constructor opens an account with a 0 balance, while the second allows an initial balance to be established when the account is opened:

```
// either form is now allowed:
BankAccount emptyAccount = new BankAccount();

BankAccount myAccount = new BankAccount(100.0);
```

The Copy Constructor

The **copy constructor** deserves special mention here. For any class *X* this constructor is defined as *X(X)*. This might seem like an odd fellow indeed, but let's look at a copy constructor in action.

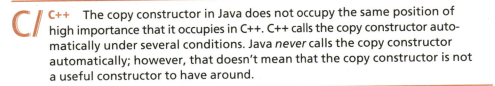

C++   The copy constructor in Java does not occupy the same position of high importance that it occupies in C++. C++ calls the copy constructor automatically under several conditions. Java *never* calls the copy constructor automatically; however, that doesn't mean that the copy constructor is not a useful constructor to have around.

Suppose bank accounts must also be assigned names (the name of the account holder, not the name of the account). The *BankAccount* class might look like the following:

```
class BankAccount
{
    // following static used to allocate each object
    // its own account number
    static private int m_nNextAccountNumber;

    // the account number of this object
    private int m_nAccountNumber;

    // name of the account holder
    String m_sName;

    // the account balance
    private double m_dBalance;

    BankAccount(String sName, double dInitialBalance)
    {
        // save off the name of the account holder
        m_sName = new String(sName);

        // allocate this object the next bank account number
        m_nAccountNumber = m_nNextAccountNumber++;

        m_dBalance = dInitialBalance;
    }
}
```

Here the data member *m_sName* contains the account holder's name. It is initialized in the constructor as follows:

```
m_sName = new String(sName);
```

This statement says, "Go out and allocate a new *String* off the heap, and call the *String(String)* constructor to initialize it." This particular constructor copies the contents of *sName* into the new *String,* thereby making a copy of the original object.

Why do this? Why not simply initialize *m_sName* as follows?

```
m_sName = sName;
```

I could do it this way. But remember that if you don't make a copy of the object's contents in the constructor, the object alone does not own the name. The object shares a reference to the name with whatever function passed it to the constructor (and the same goes for any other objects that the function created with this name). Such a violation of class autonomy is probably okay if the class can be assured that the object won't be changed. By making its own copy, however, the class is now independent of the caller. The calling function can change its name object all it wants—it won't affect the class.

A copy constructor is not difficult to write. Here's an example:

```
class BankAccount
{
    // following static used to allocate each object
    // its own account number
    static private int m_nNextAccountNumber;

    // the account number of this object
    private int m_nAccountNumber;

    // name of the account holder
    String m_sName;

    // the account balance
    private double m_dBalance;

    // make a copy of the object baSource
    BankAccount(BankAccount baSource)
    {
        // in every case, use the corresponding member
        // from the source object
        m_sName = new String(baSource.sName);
        m_nAccountNumber = baSource.m_nAccountNumber;
        m_dBalance = baSource.dInitialBalance;
    }
    // ...other constructors plus any other methods...
}
```

The copy constructor for *BankAccount* uses the source object to supply the information needed to initialize the object. In use, the application does something like the following:

```
public void SomeFunc(BankAccount ba)
{
    // make my own copy of ba
    BankAccount baMyCopy = new BankAccount(ba);
    // ...continue on...
}
```

NOTE   In retrospect, a copy constructor probably isn't a good idea for the *BankAccount* class. Do you really want the application to be able to make copies of a bank account object? This sounds like a good way to embezzle funds. Under similar conditions, you might not want to create copy constructors for all of your classes.

Invoking One Constructor from Another

One constructor can invoke another constructor of the same class using the *this* pointer, as follows:

```java
class BankAccount
{
    // following static used to allocate each object
    // its own account number
    static private int m_nNextAccountNumber;

    // the account number of this object
    private int m_nAccountNumber;

    // the account balance
    private double m_dBalance;

    BankAccount()
    {
        this(0);  // invoke the BankAccount(int) constructor
                  // with a value of 0
    }
    BankAccount(double dInitialBalance)
    {
        // allocate this object the next bank account number
        m_nAccountNumber = m_nNextAccountNumber++;

        m_dBalance = dInitialBalance;
    }
}
```

The call to *this* in the *BankAccount* constructor invokes the *BankAccount-(int)* constructor with the value 0. When one constructor invokes another, the call to *this* should be the constructor's first executable statement.

NOTE   Invoking one constructor from another can result in a considerable reduction in duplicated code. It hardly seems worth the trouble in the above case, but if the constructor performs a lot of operations, the savings are noticeable. This feature is sorely lacking in C++.

What About Static Data?

The constructor is designed to initialize the data members of an object when the object is created. But what about static data? Consider, for example, that *m_nNextAccountNumber* should be initialized to the first legal account number before the first *BankAccount* object is created. An account number of 0 is not legitimate at most banks.

We can't initialize the static *m_nNextAccountNumber* in the constructor since this would reset the static member every time a new object is created. To address this problem, Java allows the programmer to specify an initial value for static data members in the class itself. Thus, the proper solution appears as follows:

```
class BankAccount
{
    // following static used to allocate each object
    // its own account number
    // (100001 is the smallest legal account number)
    static private int m_nNextAccountNumber = 100001;

    // ...all else the same...
}
```

The *m_nNextAccountNumber* data member is now initialized in the class definition itself.nt.

 OTE   Such initialization statements are also allowed for nonstatic members. Java executes them when creating an object prior to invoking the constructor.

The Static Initializer

An initialization statement is fine for a simple case, such as a simple variable. But what about more complicated cases? Consider the following:

```
class TelephoneConnection
{
    // all telephone connections share a fixed number of channels
    // that should be allocated before the first
    // TelephoneConnection is made
    static final int m_nNUMBERCHANNELS = 64;
    static Channel[] m_channel;
    // ...other stuff...
}
```

Here the class *TelephoneConnection* contains a static variable, which is an array of microwave channels. Each time a *TelephoneConnection* object is created, the constructor allocates an unused channel from *m_channel*. This means that the static array of microwave channels must be initialized to valid *Channel* objects before the first *TelephoneConnection* object can be created. But there is no way to initialize *m_channel* using a simple assignment.

To address this, Java defines a constructor of sorts for static members, called the **static initializer**. The static initializer for this class appears as follows:

```java
class TelephoneConnection
{
    // all telephone connections share a fixed number of channels
    // that should be allocated before the first
    // TelephoneConnection is made
    static final int m_nNUMBERCHANNELS = 64;
    static Channel[] m_channel = new
                            Channel[m_nNUMBERCHANNELS];
    static
    {
        for (int i = 0; i < m_nNUMBERCHANNELS; i++)
        {
            m_channel[i] = new Channel(i);
        }
    }

    // ...other stuff...
}
```

Initialization occurs when the class is first loaded into memory. Initializers are executed in the order in which they appear. That is, in this example, *m_nNUMBERCHANNELS* is initialized to 64 first, since it appears first in the class. The *m_channel* array is allocated next, and the static initializer is executed last.

Since it is not truly a function and doesn't have arguments, a static initializer cannot be overloaded; however, a single class can include more than one static initializer. Multiple static initializers are executed in the order in which they occur.

Suppose our *TelephoneConnection* class maintains an array of backup connections as well. The class might appear as follows:

```
class TelephoneConnection
{
    // all telephone connections share a fixed number of channels
    // that should be allocated before the first
    // TelephoneConnection is made

    // primary connections
    static final int m_nNUMBERCHANNELS = 64;
    static Channel[] m_channel =
                            new Channel[m_nNUMBERCHANNELS];
    static
    {
        for (int i = 0; i < m_nNUMBERCHANNELS; i++)
        {
            m_channel[i] = new Channel(i);
        }
    }

    // now the backup connections
    static final int m_nBACKUPCHANNELS = 8;
    static Channel[] m_backup = new Channel[m_nBACKUPCHANNELS];
    static
    {
        for (int i = 0; i < m_nBACKUPCHANNELS; i++)
        {
            m_backup = new Channel(i);
        }
    }

    // ...other stuff...
}
```

Since they appear later in the class definition, the backup connections are allocated after the primary connections.

The Finalizer

Java also allows you to define a function that is automatically called before an object is returned to the heap. Such a function is known as a **finalizer** and is defined with the special name *finalize,* as follows:

```
void finalize()
{
}
```

You must be careful not to rely too heavily on the finalizer. For example, in our *TelephoneConnection* class, you might be tempted to use the *finalize* method to return *Connection* objects to the pool.

The argument in favor of using the *finalize* method is that it makes sense to return the connection as soon as the telephone connection is lost. But this doesn't work, because the *finalize* method is not called when the object is lost but rather when the object is returned to the heap. It might be a long time before garbage collection recovers the object. The valuable *Connection* object might be checked out to an unused *TelephoneConnection* for a needlessly long time. In fact, if the program is terminated before the garbage collector restores the object, the object will not be recovered at all.

A much better use for the *finalize* method is as follows:

```java
class TelephoneConnection
{
    Connect m_connection;

    // constructor allocates a new connection
    TelephoneConnection()
    {
        m_connection = Connect.Allocate();
    }

    // when this object gets returned to the heap, if
    // it still has a telephone connection, generate a
    // warning message and return the connection to the pool
    void finalize()
    {
        if (m_connection != null)
        {
            System.out.println("Lost connection restored");
            m_connection.Restore();
        }
    }

    // provide a disconnect function to be called when
    // call is complete
    void Disconnect()
    {
        m_connection.Restore();
        m_connection = null;
    }
}
```

In use, this class appears as follows:

```
void SomeFunc()
{
    // creating the call object makes the necessary
    // switch connection
    TelephoneConnection call = new TelephoneConnection();

    // now chitchat

    // finally, hang up the phone
    call.Disconnect();
}
```

The constructor *TelephoneConnection* allocates a *Connect* object using the *Allocate* method of that class. Once the call is complete, the application hangs up the phone using the *Disconnect* method. This returns the *Connect* object to the pool immediately to be reused.

If the application fails to return the connection via the *Disconnect* function, the *finalize* method restores the *Connect* object when *finalize* is (eventually) called. This might take a while, but at least the connection is not permanently lost. The *finalize* method also generates a warning message to alert the programmer of a *Connect* leak that might need attention.

 N OTE The Java finalizer should be used only as a last-ditch effort to recover assets before they are lost forever. The finalizer should not be used routinely to restore assets.

The *finalize* Method vs. the C++ Destructor

Most Java classes don't require a *finalize* method. This stands in stark contrast to C++, in which it seems almost every class has a destructor of some sort. The reason for this discrepancy lies with the garbage collector.

In C++ destructors, if the constructor allocates a resource, including memory off the heap, a destructor must be available to return that memory. Consider the C++ *CStudent* class shown on the next page.

(continued)

The *finalize* Method vs. the C++ Destructor, *continued*

```
class CStudent
{
    private:
        String* m_psName;   // student's name
        // ...other data definitions...

    public:
        // create a new CStudent object; give it a name
        CStudent(char* pszName)
        {
            // allocate a String off the heap to hold the name
            m_psName = new String(pszName);
            // ...whatever other stuff...
        }

        // the destructor must return any resources allocated
        // by the constructor
        ~CStudent()
        {
            delete m_psName;
            m_psName = 0;
        }
}
```

(The destructor is the function *~CStudent*.) Since this class allocates memory off the heap (*new String(pszName)*), a destructor must be available to restore the memory to the heap (*delete m_psName*).

The equivalent *Student* class in Java looks similar, except that it needs no *finalize* method:

```
public class Student
{
    private String m_sName;   // student's name
    // ...other data definitions...

    // create a new Student object; give it a name
    public Student(String sName)
    {
        // make our own copy of the student's name
        m_sName = new String(sName);
        // ...whatever other stuff...
    }
}
```

> The heap block to which *m_sName* refers is lost when the *Student* object goes out of scope, causing all of its data members, including *m_sName*, to go out of scope. This memory block is picked up and restored to the heap as soon as the garbage collector finds it.

Conclusion

The constructor allows the programmer to initialize the data members to legal values when the object is created, without relying on the application to call some special function. Similarly, Java allows static data members to be initialized when the class is loaded using the static initializer. Finally, immediately prior to an object being returned to the heap, Java invokes a special *finalize* method to make sure that no assets are being lost.

In the next chapter, we'll build on our knowledge of classes by adding the concept of inheritance.

Expanding on Existing Classes: Inheritance

The class construct we've seen so far seems to be just an organizational tool. Sure, it's nice, but it's nothing to get really excited about. But there's more to it. What gives the class its expressive power is the concept of inheritance. In this chapter, I'll show you how to implement inheritance in Java, and then I'll return to some of the features you've already learned to show you how inheritance affects them. But before I get into that, let's see how inheritance fits into our understanding of real-world objects.

What's Inheritance?

There's one aspect to understanding objects in the real world that I didn't mention in Chapter 3—the idea that an object can receive (inherit) the properties of its parent object. If I grab someone off the street and ask this person to describe a Duck, she is likely to respond with something like "A Duck is a Bird that floats." The details of the answer are not important—ask different people and you'll get different answers—but almost all of the answers will be "A Duck is a Bird that…." Why is that?

Humans are great organizers. They build gigantic taxonomies to describe the relationship of one type of object to another. (Think back to your high school biology days: Every creature has a kingdom, a phylum, a class, an order, a family, a genus, a species, and, usually, a subspecies.) A Duck is a Bird that, a Car is a Vehicle that, a TV is an Appliance that, and so it goes.

Organization helps us drastically reduce the amount of information we must store. For example, if you already know what a Bird is, the relatively compact sentence "A Duck is a Bird that floats" actually imparts a considerable amount of information. It indicates information about the Duck's biology (it's warm blooded), its reproductive cycle (it lays eggs), its seasonal habits (it probably flies south for the winter), and so on. Most of the information we know about class *Bird* can be stored in one place and re-used on the classes *Ducks, Geese, Sparrows, Hawks,* and so on.

The statement also indicates that a Duck can be used wherever a Bird is indicated. Thus, if your friend calls and asks you to bring over your pet Bird and you bring your pet Duck, that friend has no grounds to complain. (Technically you are also within your rights to bring your pet Ostrich, but that's pushing it.)

The relationship between a Duck and a Bird is called the **IS_A** relationship (a Duck IS_A Bird). This relationship and its implications are fundamental to object-oriented programming and are the primary topic of this chapter.

 OTE A Duck IS_A Bird, but the reverse is not true. A Bird is not necessarily a Duck. That is, there might be Birds that do not float.

An Example of Inheritance

One class inherits data members and methods from another class using the *extends* keyword. In practice, this appears as follows:

```
class BankAccount
{
    private double m_dBalance;

    public double Balance()
    {
        return m_dBalance;
    }
    // ...other members of BankAccount...
}

class CheckingAccount extends BankAccount
{
```

```
    public void WriteCheck(double dAmount)
    {
        // ...whatever this function does...
    }
    // ...other members unique to checking account...
}
```

BankAccount is the same class that appeared in Chapter 4. The class *CheckingAccount* is a new class that **inherits** *from* the *BankAccount* class. (There are several ways to express this concept. We can also say that *CheckingAccount* **extends** the class *BankAccount*. We can say that *CheckingAccount* is a **subclass** of *BankAccount* or that *BankAccount* is a **super class** or **base class** of *CheckingAccount*.)

When declared this way, a *CheckingAccount* IS_A *BankAccount*. Thus, the following is legal:

```
class MyClass
{
    public static void SomeFunc()
    {
        CheckingAccount ca = new CheckingAccount();
        ca.Deposit(100.00);  // deposit to checking account
        System.out.println("Checking account balance = " +
                        ca.Balance());
    }
}
```

Balance is not declared within the *CheckingAccount* class. However, *CheckingAccount* inherits the members of *BankAccount,* including *Balance.* When the application calls *ca.Balance,* the *Balance* function within *BankAccount* is invoked. This fits our understanding of inheritance: Since a checking account is a bank account, it has all the rights and privileges of a bank account.

In addition, if a function expects as its argument a *BankAccount* object, we can pass that function a *CheckingAccount* object and it has no grounds for complaint:

```
public MyClass
{
    public static void SomeFunc(BankAccount a)
    {
        // ...whatever it might do...
```

(continued)

107

```
    }
    public static void SomeOtherFunc()
    {
        CheckingAccount ca = new CheckingAccount();
        SomeFunc(ca);    // this call is allowed
    }
}
```

The call to *SomeFunc* is allowed in the above example. Why? All together now: Because a *CheckingAccount* object IS_A *BankAccount* object.

Overriding Super Class Methods

A subclass can override a method in the super class. To **override** a method is to replace an inherited method with a method specific to the subclass. For example, suppose that our checking account accumulates interest differently than other types of accounts. Let's say that a $500 minimum balance is required before the checking account can accumulate interest.

We can implement this method by overriding the *Interest* method in the *CheckingAccount* class as follows:

```
class CheckingAccount extends BankAccount
{
    // Interest - tack on monthly interest
    public void Interest()
    {
        // checking accounts have a $500 minimum
        // before accumulating interest
        if (Balance() >= 500.0)
        {
            // this calculation same as before.
            // Note: m_dBalance and m_dCurrentInterestRate must
            //       be marked public or friendly in the base
            //       class (not private). i'll explain later in
            //       this chapter.
            m_dBalance += m_dBalance *
                    (m_dCurrentInterestRate / 1200.0);
        }
    }
    // ...members unique to checking account...
}
```

Now the class *CheckingAccount* inherits all the methods of *BankAccount* except the *Interest* method for which it provides its own solution.

> **NOTE** An analogous situation exists with our *Bird* class. All birds eat. Thus, all members of class *Bird* include a *feed* method. However, not all birds eat the same way. Thus, an avian subclass *Hawk* might include a *feed* method that is very different from the method defined for the subclass *Hummingbird*.

This raises an interesting problem. Consider once again our generic *Some-Func(BankAccount)* function. Suppose this function is called *Interest*, as in the following:

```
public MyClass
{
    public static void SomeFunc(BankAccount a)
    {
        // accumulate interest
        a.Interest();
    }
    public static void SomeOtherFunc()
    {
        CheckingAccount ca = new CheckingAccount();
        SomeFunc(ca);   // this call is allowed

        BankAccount ba = new BankAccount();
        SomeFunc(ba);   // this call is okay as well
    }
}
```

There seems to be a paradox in the call to *Interest* when *SomeFunc* is called with the *CheckingAccount* object *ca*. When *SomeFunc* calls *a.Interest*, which *Interest* is called?

The function declaration *SomeFunc(BankAccount)* says that the function expects a *BankAccount*, so you might expect the call to invoke *Bank-Account.Interest*. On the other hand, in this case *a* is actually a reference to a *CheckingAccount*, so you might also expect the call to go to *Checking-Account.Interest*. In a case such as this, we say that the **declared type** of *a* is *BankAccount* but the **run-time type** of *a* is *CheckingAccount*. (The declared type of an argument is always the same, but the run-time type is controlled by how the method is called.)

In Java, the call is made based on the run-time type. Thus, even though *a* is declared to be a *BankAccount*, when *SomeFunc* is invoked with the *CheckingAccount* object *ca*, the call to *a.Interest* invokes *Checking-Account.Interest*. The next time that *SomeFunc* is called, it is passed a real *BankAccount* object *ba*. This time, the call *a.Interest* invokes the *BankAccount.Interest* function.

Thus, if a method is overridden in a subclass, Java must decide which method to call at run time based on the run-time class of the object. Java's ability to decide among methods based on run-time type is called **polymorphism**.

Poly-what-ism?

The concept of polymorphism is based on the way people build and use objects in the real world. In the real world, we make assumptions based on facts we know to be true. Certain facts, or methods, apply to all objects of a certain type, and even though the processes by which these facts are applied are varied and complicated, we aren't necessarily concerned with the differences. We know what we need to know.

For example, when I want to watch TV, the first thing I do is switch it on. Like everything else I do to my TV, I do this without regard for what my TV has to do to become operational.

As an electrical appliance, the TV shares this on/off property with other electrical appliances. As a user, I turn on all electrical appliances in about the same way. But each electrical appliance handles this simple command in a different way internally. The internal process that my TV must go through as part of power on is nothing like the process my PC must go through. In object-oriented terms, we would say that the class *Appliance* has an *On* method that is overridden in each of its subclasses. Java controls this process through polymorphism.

Polymorphism greatly increases the level of abstraction in a program, which is a good thing for programmers. In my program I can refer to bank accounts without worrying about including all the different kinds of bank accounts. I simply refer to the *BankAccount* class. The programmer responsible for implementing this class can build the inheritance relationships that are necessary to mimic the real-world relationships among the different account types.

Besides making life easier on the programmer, this increase in abstraction has the side effect of improving application maintenance. The information about the relationship of a checking account to a bank account is isolated in one place: the bank account package. In fact, if the classes are designed properly, the rest of the program has no idea that an object called a checking account even exists or that it has rules that differ from a bank account.

This might not seem like such a big deal until your boss tells you that the rules for checking accounts are about to change. In the functional program, this means searching the entire program for references to checking account rules and changing them appropriately. In the object-oriented Java program, this means simply changing the rules in the single *CheckingAccount* class.

Finally, polymorphism increases your ability to reuse classes. It is often the case that when I look for an existing class to use in my application I find one that is 95 percent correct but not quite there. In a functional world, this means copying the class, giving it a slightly different name, and making the necessary changes. However, this solution is problematic because I now have not one but two classes (and soon three, four, five, and so on) to maintain. A fix to one of these classes must be manually propagated to the other classes, which are likely to have the same bug lurking. (And "manually" means it probably won't happen.)

A better solution is to leave the original class unmodified and inherit information from it. Any methods that the base class doesn't already provide can be added to the subclass, and the methods that aren't quite right can be overridden. This results in minimal duplication of code. In addition, if a bug is found and fixed in the base class, the fix is automatically propagated to all of the subclasses.

In short, polymorphism makes inheritance work.

The Functional Alternative

Consider the functional alternative for a moment. As a functional programmer, I can create some structure *BankAccount* to contain the data members, and to that I can write a function *Interest(BankAccount)* to accumulate interest (using C as an example):

```
void Interest(BankAccount* pBA)
{
    pBA->m_dBalance += pBA->m_dBalance *
                   (pBA->m_dCurrentInterestRate / 1200.0);
}
```

When word of the new account type comes down and it's time to change the interest rules between checking and savings accounts, I can modify *Interest* as follows:

```
void Interest(BankAccount* pBA)
{
    if (pBA->m_nType == CHECKINGACCOUNT)
    {
        // ...checking account rules...
    }
    else
    {
        // ...generic bank account rules...
    }
}
```

That isn't so bad. But then the new rules start coming fast and furious. (As soon as managers find out that computers are programmable, they want to change the rules for everything.) Pretty soon even a simple function like *Interest* looks like the following:

```
void Interest(BankAccount* pBA)
{
    switch(pBA->m_nType)
    {
        case CHECKINGACCOUNT:
        // ...checking account rules...
        case SAVINGSACCOUNT:
        // ...savings account rules...
        case CD:
        // ...CD rules...
        case IRA:
        // ...you guessed it...
        case PASSBOOK:
        // ...and so on...
    }
}
```

It's no longer possible to look at any piece of code without considering every possible kind of bank account.

And, of course, this all assumes that I was smart enough to create a single function *Interest* in the first place. Since that function is only a single line, I would most likely simply insert the single line of code. As a result, pretty soon my program would become a maze of such switch statements that check for each possible account type.

Invoking Super Class Methods

The *CheckingAccount.Interest* method does not truly fulfill its requirement to calculate the interest rate in the same way as any other bank account if the balance exceeds $500. The way the rules currently exist, *Checking-Account.Interest* is written to calculate the interest in the same way that *BankAccount.Interest* currently calculates it.

Suppose, for example, that the rules for calculating interest change. Say the auditors don't approve of our simple divide-by-1200 rule. Of course, *BankAccount.Interest* must change, but will the programmer know to check *CheckingAccount.Interest* and the *Interest* methods of all the other subclasses of *BankAccount*? Wouldn't it be better to be able to make the change in one spot and have it affect everything?

Once *CheckingAccount.Interest* decides that the critical balance has been reached, it would be better to call *BankAccount.Interest* to perform the actual interest calculation rather than repeat the same steps. The following, however, won't work:

```
class CheckingAccount extends BankAccount
{
    // Interest - tack on monthly interest
    public void Interest()
    {
        // checking accounts have a $500 minimum
        // before accumulating interest
        if (Balance() >= 500.0)
        {
            // DOESN'T WORK!
            Interest();
        }
    }
    // ...members unique to checking account...
}
```

Not surprisingly, you can't invoke *Interest* from within *Interest*—the function simply calls itself, resulting in an infinite loop. To get around this problem, Java provides the keyword *super,* which is the same as *this* except that *super*'s run-time type has been changed to that of the immediate super class. Thus, the code shown on the following page works as desired.

```
class CheckingAccount extends BankAccount
{
    // Interest - tack on monthly interest
    public void Interest()
    {
        // checking accounts have a $500 minimum
        // before accumulating interest
        if (Balance() >= 500.0)
        {
            // calculate interest using the
            // BankAccount rules
            super.Interest();
        }
    }
    // ...members unique to checking account...
}
```

The run-time type of *this* is *CheckingAccount*. The run-time type of *super* is *BankAccount*. Thus, the call *super.Interest* is to the method *BankAccount.Interest*, and the function works as expected.

 OTE Calling the overridden method in the super class also avoids duplicating code. The more reuse you can get the better, both in the short term (debugging) and in the long term (maintenance).

Abstract Classes

It is not uncommon in our zeal for organizing to arrive at classes that do not actually exist on their own. Consider the class *Bird*, for example. There is no single bird that is not a member of some subclass of Bird. That is, every Bird is a Duck or Goose or Sparrow or whatever. A class like *Bird* represents more of an abstract concept than a precise physical object that we can point at. Such a class is called an **abstract class**.

 OTE An abstract class cannot be instanced with an object. There are no generic birds—only specific kinds of birds. Thus, there is no instance of class *Bird,* only instances of subclasses of *Bird*. It's not that the concept of a bird isn't useful. Abstract classes represent useful generalizations, and it's something of an irony that the abstract classes are often the most useful.

Show me an abstract class

Suppose that at our bank, accounts come in two flavors, checking accounts and savings accounts, and that the methods for calculating interest for each of the two are completely different. The interest rate for checking accounts might be lower, and savings accounts might use a graduated interest scheme—the more you leave in your account the more you receive back, and so on.

In this environment it is impossible to define *BankAccount.Interest.* We can define *CheckingAccount.Interest* and *SavingsAccount.Interest,* but no rules apply only to bank accounts. We can implement this in Java as follows:

```
abstract public class BankAccount
{
    abstract public void Interest();
    // ...all the other stuff...
}

class CheckingAccount extends BankAccount
{
    public void Interest()
    {
        // ...calculate checking account interest...
    }
}

class SavingsAccount extends BankAccount
{
    public void Interest()
    {
        // ...calculate savings account interest...
    }
}
```

Notice that *BankAccount* is declared using the keyword *abstract.* Declaring a class **abstract** means that the class cannot be instanced. That is, *BankAccount* is a generalization (like *Bird*). There is no *BankAccount* that isn't either a *CheckingAccount* or a *SavingsAccount.* (A class that is not abstract is sometimes called a **concrete class**, as opposed to a *non-abstract class.*)

The *BankAccount.Interest* method is declared abstract as well. Declaring a method *abstract* means that the method cannot be defined. Like the concept of birds and feeding, the method represents an action that is common to all members of the class, but not all members do it the same way.

OTE   An abstract method has no method body—we wouldn't know what to put there even if it did. It is not legal to define an abstract method in a concrete class.

A class that extends an abstract super class can be concrete if it overrides every abstract method of the super class. Said another way, a concrete class cannot inherit an abstract method.

Interest is overridden with a concrete method in both the subclasses *CheckingAccount* and *SavingsAccount;* thus, neither of these classes is abstract.

Since *BankAccount* is abstract, it cannot be instanced:

```
BankAccount ba = new BankAccount();        // this is not allowed
SavingsAccount sa = new SavingsAccount();  // this is okay
```

Someone might try to call *BankAccount*'s *Interest* method, which doesn't exist. Despite this, the following is legal:

```
BankAccount ba = new SavingsAccount();  // this is okay
ba.Interest();                 // calls SavingsAccount.Interest
```

Here I created a reference *ba* to a bank account of some sort. The type of bank account I created is a savings account, however. This assignment is allowed because (here we go again) a savings account IS_A bank account. The call to *ba.Interest* invokes *SavingsAccount.Interest* in keeping with the run-time type of *ba*.

Why bother?

If the method *BankAccount.Interest* doesn't really exist, why declare it? Why can't I leave it off and define *Interest* in both *CheckingAccount* and *SavingsAccount?* The declaration of the *Interest* method in *BankAccount* serves two purposes. First, it tells Java that this property is common to all *BankAccount* objects. Without it, the following is not legal:

```
public class MyClass
{
    public static void SomeFunc(BankAccount ba)
    {
        // the following is not allowed if Interest is
        // not a member of BankAccount
        ba.Interest();
    }
}
```

But is the function really common to all *BankAccount* objects? You bet. Consider the following example:

```
public class MyClass
{
    // EndOfTheMonth - accumulate all interest and all
    //                 fees on all our accounts; the
    //                 accounts are kept in an array of
    //                 type BankAccount
    public static void EndOfMonth(BankAccount[] ba,
                                  int nArrayLength)
    {
        // loop through the members of the array
        for (int i = 0; i < nArrayLength; i++)
        {
            // ask each account to accumulate its interest
            // and fees; these calls are polymorphic
            ba[i].Fee();
            ba[i].Interest();
        }
    }
}
```

Here the bank is keeping its accounts in an array of type *BankAccount*. Remember that we have both *SavingsAccount* and *CheckingAccount* objects in this array. Let's say that the first member of the array happens to be a savings account, but the second member of the array is a checking account. Thus, the first time through the loop, *ba[i].Interest* calls *SavingsAccount.Interest*. On the next pass, however, the very same call, *ba[i].Interest,* invokes *CheckingAccount.Interest*.

The second purpose of the abstract declaration of *Interest* suggests that if the programmer wants to create a new subclass of *BankAccount,* she must define the *Interest* behavior of that subclass. Look at the problem as if you were the programmer of the *BankAccount* class. The boss says, "Look, we need this class called bank account. It has this property and that property and, oh yeah, it accumulates interest."

"How does it accumulate interest?" you ask.

"It depends on what kind of bank account it is. Just implement the remainder of the bank account and leave that part out for now."

By declaring the *BankAccount.Interest* abstract, you alert other programmers that you've done most of the work but that they must provide this missing piece.

Implementation Details

Inheritance has a small effect on some of the concepts that you have already seen. Let's go back now and see what these might be.

Constructors

When you construct an object, the constructor for the super class gets invoked as well:

```
class Base
{
    private int m_nBaseData;

    Base()
    {
        m_nBaseData = 1;
    }
}

class Sub extends Base
{
    private int m_nSubData;

    Sub()
    {
        m_nSubData = 2;
    }
}

class MyClass
{
    public static void SomeFunc()
    {
        Sub sub = new Sub();
    }
}
```

The call to *new Sub* clearly invokes the constructor for the class *Sub*. What isn't so clear is that the call invokes the constructor for *Base* as well.

 OTE   If the constructor for the subclass is not specifically overridden (see below), it automatically calls the no argument constructor of the super class before starting.

Why is this important? Why can't *Sub* just initialize the members of *Base?* The base class should be responsible for initializing itself and should not rely on the subclass.

What if I don't want to invoke the no argument constructor of the base class? Suppose I want to call some other constructor instead? This is allowed using the *super* keyword:

```
class Base
{
    private int m_nBaseData;

    Base(int nB)
    {
        m_nBaseData = nB;
    }
}

class Sub extends Base
{
    private int m_nSubData;

    Sub(int nB, int nS)
    {
        super(nB);         // invoke the base class constructor
        m_nSubData = nS;
    }
}

class MyClass
{
    public static void SomeFunc()
    {
        Sub sub = new Sub(10, 20);
    }
}
```

Here the call *super(nB)* invokes the *Base(int)* constructor to construct the super class portion of the *Sub* object.

NOTE   Invoking *super* from within the constructor of a subclass calls the constructor of the super class, which corresponds to the arguments of *super*. If *super* appears, it must be the first executable statement within the constructor.

Access Control

In Chapter 4, I discussed access control. At that time I presented the *public* and *private* controls. Inheritance introduces another access control specifier: *protected.* Declaring a member **protected** means that it is accessible only to methods of the same class or to any subclass but not to unrelated classes, even if they are from the same package. This is best demonstrated by the following example snippets. First consider the file Super.java:

```
package MainPackage;
class Super
{
    public    void Public(){}
              void Friendly(){}
    protected void Protected(){}
    private   void Private(){}
}

class Subclass extends Super
{
    void a() { Public(); }
    void b() { Friendly(); }
    void c() { Protected(); }
    void d() { Private(); }  // error
}

class OtherclassInSamePackage
{
    super m_object = new Super();
    void e() { m_object.Public(); }
    void f() { m_object.Friendly(); }
    void g() { m_object.Protected(); }  // error
    void h() { m_object.Private(); }    // error
}
```

Subclass has access to all of the methods of *Super* except for *Private.* By comparison, *OtherClassInSamePackage* does not have access to *Protected* because it is not directly related to *Super.*

The situation is even worse for a class contained in a different package, such as the following, ClassInDifferentPackage.java. The classes of one package have access only to the public methods of a class in a different package:

```
package OtherPackage;
import MainPackage.Super;

class ClassInDifferentPackage
{
    Super m_object = new Super();
    void i() { m_object.Public(); }
    void j() { m_object.Friendly(); }    // error
    void k() { m_object.Protected(); }   // error
    void l() { m_object.Private(); }     // error
}
```

Finding Methods

Inheritance can sometimes make it difficult to find a method. For example, the method *available,* which returns the number of bytes remaining to be read from the input file, was used with an object of class *DataInputStream.* However, this method actually appears in the *InputStream* class. *DataInputStream* inherits the method from *DataInputStream.*

Thus, the rule is that when you are searching for a particular method, if you don't find it in the expected class, look in that super class in an iterative fashion until you either find the method or arrive at *Object,* the super class of all classes.

Casting

It is always legal to supply a reference to a subclass when a reference to a base class is required. Thus, assuming that *SubClass* extends *BaseClass,* the following is allowed:

```
class MyClass
{
    public static void SomeFunc(BaseClass bc)
    {
        // ...whatever it does...
    }
    public static void SomeOtherFunc()
    {
        SubClass sc = new SubClass();
        SomeFunc(sc);  // this is allowed
    }
}
```

Casting from a reference to a *SubClass* to a reference to a *BaseClass* is automatic since it relies on the IS_A principle we discussed earlier.

It is also legal to cast from *BaseClass* to *SubClass;* however, an explicit cast is required:

```
class MyClass
{
    public static void SomeFunc(BaseClass bc)
    {
        SubClass sc = (SubClass)bc; // this is checked
        // ...continue on...
    }
    public static void SomeOtherFunc()
    {
        SubClass sc = new SubClass();
        SomeFunc(sc);  // this is allowed
    }
}
```

Thus, *SomeFunc* can attempt to cast *bc* into a *SubClass* object *sc*. The cast is checked, and if *bc* does not actually reference an object of class *SubClass* (or a subclass of *SubClass*), the cast generates a run-time error. (Actually it throws a *ClassCastException*. I'll cover exceptions in Chapter 9.

You can save yourself the embarrassment of Java spitting up your cast by using the *instanceof* operator:

```
class MyClass
{
    public static void SomeFunc(BaseClass bc)
    {
        // check to make sure before performing the
        // cast
        if (bc instanceof SubClass)
        {
            // now that we've checked, the following
            // cast is guaranteed safe
            SubClass sc = (SubClass)bc; // this is checked
            // ...continue on...
        }
        else
        {
            //...non-SubClass case...
        }
    }
```

```
public static void SomeOtherFunc()
{
    SubClass sc = new SubClass();
    SomeFunc(sc);  // this is allowed
}
}
```

The binary operator *instanceof* returns a *Boolean true* if the object to the left of the assignment operator is the same type as the object to the right. (It might be of that type or a subtype.) In this way, the cast is guaranteed safe.

Static Methods

Static methods can be overridden in a subclass. However, since no object is involved, a call to a static method is never polymorphic.

Final Classes and Methods

You have already seen that a data member can be declared *final,* meaning that its value cannot be changed. A class can also be declared final, meaning that it cannot be extended. In addition, a method can be declared final, meaning that it cannot be overridden in a subclass. Since it is not accessible from a subclass, a *private* method is always final.

Interfaces

Java supports a concept similar to the class, called the **interface**. An interface is a collection of abstract methods. An interface can be public or private: All methods within an interface are public and abstract; data members within an interface, if they exist at all, are implicitly final, public, and static. (In other words, they're constants.)

An interface allows the programmer to describe a set of capabilities that a class must implement. For example, consider the following interface definition:

```
interface IPersistent
{
    void Store();
    void Restore();
}
```

A class inherits an interface using the *implements* keyword. Any class that implements *IPersistent* must override both *Store* and *Restore.* Thus, the program is assured that any *IPersistent* object knows how to store and restore.

NOTE Actually, a class that implements an interface does not have to override each of the methods of the interface; however, it will be abstract, and each class that extends it will remain abstract until they have each been overridden.

Why bother with interfaces? The interface represents a lightweight type. The overhead of implementing an interface is not as great as the overhead of inheriting from a class.

NOTE A class that implements an interface is not inheriting anything. It is merely promising to implement the methods defined in the interface. This is the origin of the *implements* keyword.

In particular, Java does not support multiple inheritance. That is, a Java class cannot extend more than one class. However, the programmer can use interfaces to achieve almost the same effect as using multiple inheritances. Consider the following example using the *IPersistent* interface:

```
// the following class is used to model bank transactions
class Transaction
{
}

// this class represents bank transactions, but by
// implementing IPersistent it is also able to
// save itself to and restore itself from disk
class PersistentTransaction extends Transaction
                                implements IPersistent
{
}

class Disk
{
    public void PowerDown(IPersistent obj)
    {
        // we know that obj.Store exists because object
        // is of type IPersistent
        obj.Store();
        // ...anything else that's necessary...
    }
```

```
public void SomeFunc()
{
    PersistentTransaction pt = new PersistentTransaction();
    PowerDown(pt);
}

// ...other methods...
}
```

The class *Transaction* models bank transactions such as deposits and withdrawals to individual accounts. The class *PersistentTransaction* inherits the methods of *Transaction;* however, it also implements the *IPersistent* interface, which means it promises to add the *Store* and *Restore* methods to record and restore transactions to and from disk.

The class *PersistentTransaction* is of type *IPersistent* because it implements the *IPersistent* interface, in the same way that it is of type *Transaction* because it extends the *Transaction* class. This is why *Disk.SomeFunc* can call *PowerDown(IPersistent)*, passing it a *PersistentTransaction* object.

The Final Bank Account Example

Armed with inheritance, let's return to the bank account program one last time to implement a final requirement. Let's say that there are savings accounts and checking accounts at our bank. These two account types are identical except for the following differences:

- Savings accounts are numbered 1*xxxxx*, starting with 100001. Checking accounts are numbered 5*xxxxx*, starting with 500001.

- Savings accounts charge no fee if the balance exceeds $200. Checking accounts pay no interest until the balance exceeds $500.

This can be implemented as follows:

```
// BankAccount - a general bank account class
abstract public class BankAccount
{
    // interest rate
    private static double m_dCurrentInterestRate;

    // balance - the current account's balance
    private double m_dBalance;
```

(continued)

```java
// constructor - open account with a balance
BankAccount(double dInitialBalance)
{
    m_dBalance = dInitialBalance;
}

// AccountNo - return the account number
abstract public int AccountNo();

// Rate - inquire or set interest rate
public static double Rate()
{
    return m_dCurrentInterestRate;
}
public static void Rate(double dNewRate)
{
    // first a sanity check
    if (dNewRate > 0.0 && dNewRate < 20.0)
    {
        m_dCurrentInterestRate = dNewRate;
    }
}

// Deposit - add something to the account
public void Deposit(double dAmount)
{
    // no negative deposits!
    if (dAmount > 0.0)
    {
        m_dBalance += dAmount;
    }
}

// Withdrawal - take something out
public void Withdrawal(double dAmount)
{
    // negative withdrawals are a sneaky way of
    // adding money to the account
    if (dAmount >= 0.0)
    {
        // don't let customer withdraw more than he has
        if (dAmount <= m_dBalance)
        {
            m_dBalance -= dAmount;
        }
    }
}
```

```
    // Balance - return the current balance rounded off to
    //           the nearest cent
    public double Balance()
    {
        int nCents = (int)(m_dBalance * 100 + 0.5);
        return nCents / 100.0;
    }

    // Monthly - each month rack up interest and service
    //           fees
    public void Monthly()
    {
        Fee();      // fee first! (reduces interest we pay)
        Interest();
    }

    // Fee - rack up the monthly fee
    public void Fee()
    {
        m_dBalance -= 5.0;   // $5.00 per month
    }

    // Interest - tack on monthly interest
    public void Interest()
    {
        // 1200 because interest is normally expressed
        // in numbers like 20%, meaning .2, and because
        // we are accumulating interest monthly
        m_dBalance += m_dBalance *
                (m_dCurrentInterestRate / 1200.0);
    }
}

class CheckingAccount extends BankAccount
{
    private static int m_nNextAccountNo = 800001;
    private int nAccountNo;

    // constructor
    CheckingAccount(double dInitialBalance)
    {
        super(dInitialBalance);

        nAccountNo = m_nNextAccountNo++;
    }
```

(continued)

```java
    // AccountNo - return the current account ID
    public int AccountNo()
    {
        return nAccountNo;
    }

    // Interest - don't accumulate interest if balance
    //            under $500
    public void Interest()
    {
        if (Balance() > 500.0)
        {
            super.Interest();
        }
    }
}

class SavingsAccount extends BankAccount
{
    private static int m_nNextAccountNo = 100001;
    private int nAccountNo;

    // constructor
    SavingsAccount(double dInitialBalance)
    {
        super(dInitialBalance);

        nAccountNo = m_nNextAccountNo++;
    }

    // AccountNo - return the current account ID
    public int AccountNo()
    {
        return nAccountNo;
    }

    // Fee - don't charge fee if balance over $200
    public void Fee()
    {
        if (Balance() < 200.0)
        {
            super.Fee();
        }
    }
}
```

The *BankAccount* class appears much as it did in Chapter 4; however, now
it is an abstract class since it does not know how to assign an account ID.

(A rule was given for assigning checking accounts and IDs. A similar rule was given for savings accounts. No rule was given for bank accounts except to specify that they have an account ID.)

The class *SavingsAccount* inherits from the *BankAccount* to provide the account an account ID. This class also overrides the *Fee* method to waive the monthly fee if the balance exceeds $200. Similarly, the class *Checking-Account* inherits from *BankAccount* in order to waive the monthly interest rate if the balance does not exceed $500.

The following simple application demonstrates the results of depositing $100 per month in both a checking account and a savings account at 8-percent interest:

```
// Appl_7 - test out the SavingsAccount and CheckingAccount
//          classes. this version accumulates interest
//          and performs routine withdrawals from both
//          checking and savings.
import java.io.*;    // this includes the println function

public class Appl_7
{
    public static void main(String args[])
    {
        // set the interest rate first - just assume 8%
        BankAccount.Rate(8.0);

        // create a savings account and a checking account
        SavingsAccount sa = new SavingsAccount(0.0);
        CheckingAccount ca = new CheckingAccount(0.0);

        // for 10 months, deposit $100 in each and then
        // accrue monthly interest and fees
        for (int i = 0; i < 10; i++)
        {
            ca.Deposit(100.0);
            sa.Deposit(100.0);

            ca.Monthly();
            sa.Monthly();

            System.out.print (i + " - ");
            System.out.print (ca.AccountNo() + ":" +
                              ca.Balance() + ", ");
```

(continued)

```
                    System.out.println(sa.AccountNo() + ":" +
                                        sa.Balance());
            }
        }
}
```

The results of executing this program are shown in Figure 7-1. Although not very attractive, these results demonstrate the differences between the savings and checking accounts.

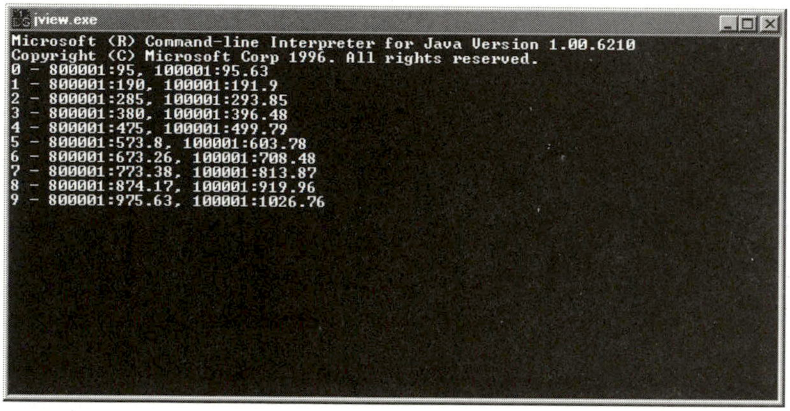

Figure 7-1. *Output from App1_7 demonstrating the result at the end of each month of depositing $100 per month in a checking account and a savings account at 8-percent interest.*

Conclusion

In this chapter, you've learned how inheritance adds to the expressive power of the class to complete the object-oriented paradigm. You've seen how a subclass inherits members from a super class and how the subclass can override the methods of the super class. You've learned how, in the event that the subclass overrides a method of the super class, Java decides which method to invoke on the basis of the object's run-time type rather than its declared type. Finally, you've learned how interfaces give the programmer most of the benefits of multiple inheritance without the extra overhead that inheritance brings.

In the next three chapters, you'll see how to organize classes that inherit from each other and how to inherit from and use the built-in Java classes.

Vacuum-Packed Java: Packages

You've learned how to build and use classes in a program. In this chapter, I'll show you how to combine your classes into packages to better keep track of them.

A **package** is a loose affiliation of classes. The classes within a package don't have to be related, at least not in the way that a subclass is related to its super class. To return to our object-oriented TV analogy, the Home-Furnishings package might contain the different classes that go in a house. HomeFurnishings might include the *TV, Couch, Blender,* and *Rug* classes. These classes are not related (a rug does not share any properties with a TV), but the package is a convenient way to group them together.

Often the classes within a package are designed to work together. For example, the *BankAccount* class might be found in the same Bank package with *Transaction* and *BalanceSheet*. Not only do each of these classes describe different aspects of processing banking transactions, but they also rely on one another, with the methods of one class calling methods of the other classes.

N OTE   Members declared friendly are visible only to other members of the same package because classes within a package are usually designed to work together.

Package names can contain periods. By convention, package names consist of several words, with the first word indicating the name of the organization that developed the package. (This avoids any confusion if one group happens to use some of the same class names as another.)

 NOTE Everything I say about classes in this chapter is also true of interfaces, unless otherwise noted.

Building Packages

Every class belongs to a package. The class is added to the package when it is compiled. The class indicates the package to which it belongs using the *package* keyword:

```
package srd.math;  // add this class to the srd.math package
public class ComplexNumber
{
    // ...whatever stuff you want...
}
```

The *ComplexNumber* class is now a member of the srd.math package. If the srd.math package does not exist, it is created when the source file is compiled the first time.

 NOTE When present, *package* must be the first noncomment, nonblank line in the source file.

If no package is indicated, the class is added to the default package, also known as the **unnamed** package since it has no name.

Using a Package

A class from one package can access a class belonging to another package by preceding the class name with the package name. Consider the following dummy *ComplexNumber* class:

```
package srd.math;

public class ComplexNumber
{
```

```
    private double m_dReal;
    private double m_dImag;

    // constructors
    public ComplexNumber(double dR, double dI)
    {
        m_dReal = dR;
        m_dImag = dI;
    }
    public ComplexNumber(double dR)
    {
        this(dR, 0.0);
    }

    // operators
    public ComplexNumber Add(ComplexNumber cn)
    {
        return new ComplexNumber(m_dReal + cn.m_dReal,
                                 m_dImag + cn.m_dImag);
    }
    // ...other operators follow here...
}
```

To access this class from a *Test* class in the unnamed package, the *Complex-Number* class is referred to as *srd.math.ComplexNumber:*

```
public class Test
{
    public static void main(String[] s)
    {
        srd.math.ComplexNumber c1 =
                    new srd.math.ComplexNumber(1.0, 2.0);
        srd.math.ComplexNumber c2 =
                    new srd.math.ComplexNumber(1.0, 0.0);
        srd.math.ComplexNumber cSumm = c1.Add(c2);
    }
}
```

While this looks simple enough, typing out the package name two or three times per declaration is a bit verbose, even for me. To avoid this, you can use the **import** keyword.

The *import* keyword is followed by the name of a class. Importing a class adds that class to the current file's name space. For example, the *Test* class could have been written as shown on the next page.

```
// include the srd.math.ComplexNumber class in current
// file's name space. this makes the class readily available.
import srd.math.ComplexNumber;

public class Test
{
    public static void main(String[] s)
    {
        // much more reasonable class names
        ComplexNumber c1 = new ComplexNumber(1.0, 2.0);
        ComplexNumber c2 = new ComplexNumber(1.0, 0.0);
        ComplexNumber cSumm = c1.Add(c2);
    }
}
```

The import statement tells Java which *ComplexNumber* class is intended when a class name is used without reference to a package.

 NOTE   The *import* keyword must follow the package statement but must also precede all other noncomment lines of code.

 NOTE   The full method or class name, including the package name, must be used when two imported packages contain a method or class with the same name. For example, suppose that both the srd.math and srd.psychology packages contain a class named *Complex.* If a single applet wants to import both packages, it must refer to the two classes as *srd.math.Complex* and *srd.psychology.Complex.*

An asterisk can be used in lieu of a class name to import all of the classes in a package:

```
// include all of the classes in the srd.math package.
import srd.math.*;

public class Test
{
    public static void main(String[] s)
    {
        // much more reasonable class names
        ComplexNumber c1 = new ComplexNumber(1.0, 2.0);
        ComplexNumber c2 = new ComplexNumber(1.0, 0.0);
        ComplexNumber cSumm = c1.Add(c2);
    }
}
```

This is the form of the *import* statement that you've seen in some of the example programs used in this book. Using this form of the *import* statement is easy, since you don't generally have to worry about importing each class that you intend to use. On the other hand, this form might slow down compilations a little, since it forces Java to import all of the classes in the package whether it needs them all or not.

 NOTE   It is not necessary to import your own package. A class automatically has access to the other classes in its package even without an *import* statement. In addition, it is not necessary to import the java.lang package because these classes are so fundamental that no application can execute without them.

Packages and the File System

Java packages were conceived in part to hide the file system of the operating system on which the Java program is executing. (Remember that Java is designed to be as independent as possible from any one environment.) Nevertheless, a direct mapping occurs between Java packages and Windows directories (folders).

First, remember that the name of the Java source file must be the same as the public class contained in the file. In addition, during compilation, each class in the source file generates its own class output file containing the Java byte codes. (Again, the name of the class file is identical to the name of the class it contains.)

Java places each package in its own directory. The name of the directory is the same as the name of the package, with the periods replaced by backslashes. Thus, the srd.math package is placed in the srd\math directory. When I reference the *ComplexNumber* class of the srd.math package, for example, Java knows to look in the file srd\math\ComplexNumber.class for the byte codes.

This path doesn't have to start in the root; and, in fact, it normally doesn't. Instead, Java looks in the CLASSPATH environment string to determine where to start looking for the file. CLASSPATH consists of a set of directory names, each separated from its neighbor by a semicolon. The special symbols . for the current directory and .. for the parent directory are allowed.

 OTE From the Visual J++ IDE, choose the Options command from the Tools menu. In the Options dialog box, click the Directories tab, and then in the Show Directories For drop-down list box select the Class Files option. From here you can edit the CLASSPATH list.

Thus, if CLASSPATH is set to *.;\msdev\vj\classes*, Java first looks for the file .\srd\math\ComplexNumber.class. If it doesn't find that file, Java looks for \msdev\vj\classes\srd\math\ComplexNumber.class. If it doesn't find the file after searching all the directories contained in CLASSPATH, Java generates an error message.

Java Library Packages

The Java class library is divided into the following packages:

- java.lang includes the most fundamental classes of the Java library. This package is so important that it is imported by default even if you don't import it explicitly. You'll see some of these classes at the end of this chapter.

- java.applet includes the classes needed to create those neat World Wide Web applets. This package will consume our attention for the majority of Part 2 of this book.

- java.awt, the Abstract Window Toolkit, is a machine-independent windowing toolkit. This is discussed in Chapter 17.

- java.io includes the classes that perform file I/O. This package is discussed in Chapter 10.

- java.net includes the classes needed to perform low-level Internet I/O.

- java.util includes a hodgepodge of general utility classes such as *Date*, which is used to manipulate dates in a system-independent fashion.

For the balance of this chapter, I'll explain the most fundamental Java classes.

The *Object* Class

Object is the super class of all classes. Even if you don't specify a super class, your class automatically extends *Object*. Thus, the following two class definitions are completely equivalent:

```
class MyClass1            // extends Object by default
{
}
class MyClass2 extends Object
{
}
```

All classes inherit the methods of *Object*. Some of the more important methods are shown in Table 8-1. Notice that some of these methods, in particular *toString,* are designed to be overloaded in the subclasses of *Object.*

Method	Purpose
protected Object clone	Returns a copy of the object.
public final Class getClass	Returns the *Class* object. The *Class* object describes the current class; in particular, *Class.toString* returns the name of the class.
String toString	Returns a Unicode description of the object. *Object.toString* returns the address of the object; however, other classes overload *toString* to provide a more useful description of the *Class* object.

Table 8-1. *The major methods of* Object.

Java's Equivalent to Templates

Java has no template construct like that found in some languages, most notably C++. By basing all classes on *Object,* Java obviates the need for the template.

Consider the problem of the *LinkedList* class discussed in Chapter 5. This class is built specifically to support lists of *BankAccount* objects. We cannot use *LinkedList* to build a singly linked list of some other type of objects because the object data member is declared as a reference to a *BankAccount* object:

```
// BankAccount version
public class LinkedList
{
    BankAccount m_baObject;

    // Data - return the data associated with this node
    public BankAccount Data()
    {
        return m_baObject;
    }

    // ...remaining members are not BankAccount specific
}
```

But what if we want a *LinkedList* class capable of containing any type of object? In C++ this would mean creating a template class *LinkedList<T>,* where *T* is the class of objects to be contained.

In Java this is unnecessary. If we convert the *LinkedList* class to contain a list of objects of the *Object* class, we are assured that *LinkedList* can contain any type of object we want (other than intrinsics such as *int* and *byte,* which are not subclasses of *Object*):

```
// generic version
public class LinkedList
{
    Object m_object;

    // Data - return the data associated with this node
    public Object Data()
    {
        return m_object;
```

```
    }
    // ...remaining members just like before
}
```

This class, however, might be a bit too generic, as the following code snippet shows:

```
class MyClass
{
    static public void someFunc()
    {
        LinkedList ll(new BankAccount());
                            // add a bank account to list
        LinkedList ba = ll.Data();  // this is not allowed
    }
}
```

It is legal to add a *BankAccount* object to the list since *BankAccount* is an object. On the other hand, it is not okay to assign the object returned by *Data* to a *LinkedList* reference since an object is not necessarily a *BankAccount* object. In this case, a cast is required:

```
class MyClass
{
    static public void someFunc()
    {
        LinkedList ll(new BankAccount());
        LinkedList ba = (BankAccount)ll.Data(); // cast required
    }
}
```

Alternatively, a special subclass of *LinkedList* can be created to perform any necessary casting for you:

```
// this version of the linked list class inherits
// all the members but makes the necessary casts
// to covert the generic Object reference to a reference
// to a BankAccount object
public class BankAccountLL extends LinkedList
{
    BankAccount Data()
    {
        return (BankAccount)super.Data()
    }
}
```

(continued)

Java's Equivalent to Templates, *continued*

> Here the object returned by *LinkedList.Data* is cast into the appropriate object type before being returned to the caller.
>
> Note that, unlike the C++ template, the Java solution is not type safe. That is, it is possible to add an object that isn't a *BankAccount* object to a linked list of *BankAccounts;* however, the cast from *Object* to *BankAccount* will fail if the object recovered from the list is not a *BankAccount* object of some kind. Thus, while Java won't catch the error at compile time, it will detect the problem at run time.

The Class Wrappers

As I mentioned in Chapter 3, intrinsics (such as *byte, short,* and *int*) are not classes. However, for each intrinsic type there is a class type that provides some general functions that are useful in dealing with that numeric type: For example, the *Integer* class defines the *parseInt(String)* method, which converts a Unicode string into an integer, as well as the *toString* method, which converts the *Integer* back into the equivalent *String*. This class is called a **class wrapper** for the intrinsic because it wraps the intrinsic in a class.

The *String* Class

String is the general class used to represent Unicode character strings. The *String* class offers a series of useful methods, such as *concat* to concatenate two strings, *compareTo* to compare strings, and *toUpper* and *toLower* to convert the string to all uppercase and all lowercase, respectively.

The *String* class represents a fixed-length string of characters. The *StringBuffer* class represents a dynamically sizable character array. (In other words, the *StringBuffer* can grow and shrink as characters are added to or removed from the *StringBuffer*.) The *StringBuffer* class is more useful for manipulating character strings. For example, the *StringBuffer* class defines the *append* method to add characters to the end of the *StringBuffer* and the *insert* method to insert characters in the middle.

As an example of the relationship between the *String* and *StringBuffer* classes, consider the *ComplexNumber* class. All classes inherit a *toString* method from the super class *Object*. The *toString* method is called by error handlers and can be called by the user to generate display output from an object. But as you might expect, the *Object* class is so generic that *Object.toString* can't really display much useful information. (It merely outputs the name of the object's class and the address of the object.) Therefore, you are expected to overload the *toString* method for each class that you create.

For the *ComplexNumber* class, this appears as follows:

```
package srd.math;

public class ComplexNumber
{
    // ...other members just like before

    // toString - display a complex as (r,i)
    public String toString()
    {
        // build a StringBuffer into which to build output
        StringBuffer sb = new StringBuffer();

        // put the real part first
        sb.append('(').append(m_dReal).append(',');

        // now add the imaginary part
        sb.append(m_dImag).append(')');

        // convert the result into String
        return sb.toString();
    }
}
```

ComplexNumber.toString outputs a complex number in the format *(r, i)*, where *r* is the real number part and *i* is the imaginary part. The method starts with an empty *StringBuffer sb*. To this it appends an open parenthesis followed by the real part of the complex. The *append* method returns the same *StringBuffer* it was passed in order to allow calls to *append* to be strung together as I have done. In addition, *append* is overloaded for all of the intrinsic types. *ComplexNumber.toString* wraps up by appending the imaginary part to *sb*.

 NOTE   No *StringBuffer.append* methods exist for user-defined classes; however, you can append the *String* returned from *toString* as follows:

```
sb.append(myclassObj.toString());
```

Once *ComplexNumber.toString* finishes building the output string in *sb*, it converts the *StringBuffer* into a fixed-length string by calling *sb.toString()*. It then returns the fixed-length string.

In use, *Complex.toString* has a natural appearance:

```
import srd.math.*;

public class Test
{
    public static void main(String[] s)
    {
        // create two complex numbers and add them together
        ComplexNumber c1 = new ComplexNumber(1.0, 2.0);
        ComplexNumber c2 = new ComplexNumber(1.0, 0.0);
        ComplexNumber cSumm = c1.Add(c2);

        // ComplexNumber.toString converts complex into String
        System.out.println(c1.toString() + " + " +
                           c2.toString() + " = " +
                           cSumm.toString());

    }
}
```

The output of executing this program is shown in Figure 8-1.

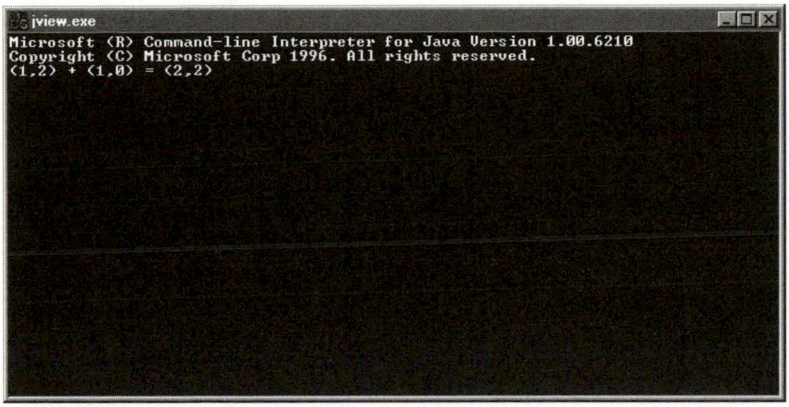

Figure 8-1. *The result of executing the simple test program, showing the output from* ComplexNumber.toString.

Conclusion

Classes are combined in loose affiliations known as packages. If you don't specify a package for your Java class, it is placed in the generic, unnamed package. Java maps the package concept on the file directory structure of the operating system in a system-independent fashion.

Java provides a series of packages that combine to form the Java class library. The most fundamental member of the Java class library is the *Object* class from which all other classes inherit. Basing all classes on *Object* has some distinct advantages, including obviating the need for templates.

In the next chapter, we'll look at how to use the Java exception mechanism to handle any errors that might pop up unexpectedly in your programs.

Handling Errors Using Exceptions

The exception mechanism is Java's way of detecting and reporting errors. In this chapter, you'll learn how (and why) to use exceptions. You'll also learn what to do when you're not prepared to handle an exception.

Why Use Exceptions?

Why bother with exceptions? What's wrong with good ol' error returns? After all, if it was good enough for Dijkstra, it's good enough for me. Right?

The Problem with Error Returns

The theory behind using error returns is simple: Every function should return an error indication. In addition, every function should check the error indications returned by the function it calls. At least that's the way I learned it.

But the practice is a lot more complicated than that. Using simple error returns to detect and handle errors results in the following problems:

■ Complex logic. Returning an error indication when an erroneous situation occurs is not typically a problem. For example, before you perform a division, you check the denominator. If it's 0 you return an error indication. The problem arises, however, when the caller has to check that error return and take action. Usually, the error is returned to its caller, who must check the return, and so on. Pretty soon the amount of logic devoted to checking error returns and taking action is greater than the amount of code devoted to getting the work done. Worse yet, eventually the error logic starts to obscure the main logic flow.

- **Limited information.** A limited amount of information can be encoded in a single error return value. (Error returns are almost always integers.) Thus, I might say that returning a 1 means "divide by 0," 2 means "latitude out of range," and so on. This conversion information has to be coded somewhere. In addition, some other function shouldn't use these same values since a single function might call both. Even if I do keep the various return values separate, a return value of 2 doesn't tell me which latitude was out of range or what its value was. Nor does it tell me where in the program the problem was detected. All of this information could be useful for decoding the output of an errant program.

- **Used-up returns.** An error return can get in the way of a function that returns its own nonerror value. A common rule to avoid this problem is to use positive values for data and use negative values for error returns—but what about functions that return both positive and negative data?

- **No returns.** I admit this is not a problem that occurred in my Fortran days, but Java constructors don't return any value. This means there is no way to pass an error return back from a constructor.

The net result of these problems is that we seldom checked and took action on every single error return. We made value judgments: "Oh, that error can't happen." It was almost impossible to prove us wrong in the lab. It wasn't until the program got out of the lab and into the field with real users that the "impossible" errors occurred. Sure we felt guilty about it, but schedule, performance, and memory constraints left us little choice.

OTE There's a reasonable solution to the limited information problem. Rather than return a simple integer, we can return an object of some specially designed class, say, *Error*. The *Error* object can contain a description of the problem, a reference to the object that caused the problem, the location of the problem, and other information. If the function returns a reference to null, we can assume that no error occurred. This solution, however, still doesn't address the other three problems.

The Exceptional Alternative

Java borrows an alternative error reporting mechanism from the Ada programming language: exceptions. An **exception** is an error condition that interrupts the flow of the program. In Java, an exception occurs when the program executes the *throw* keyword. The *throw* statement passes control to an associated **catch block**. If there is no *catch* in the current function, control exits immediately to the calling method without returning a value. Java then looks for a catch block within that method. If Java cannot find a catch block, it passes control to the method that called that method. Control continues to pass up through the call stack until Java finds a catch block capable of handling the error.

Throwing an Exception

The theory of exceptions is all very nice, but how does it look in practice? In practice, the throw appears as follows:

```
package srd.math;
import java.lang.Exception;

class ComplexNumber
{
    private double m_dReal;
    private double m_dImag;

    // constructors
    public ComplexNumber(double dR, double dI)
    {
        m_dReal = dR;
        m_dImag = dI;
    }
    public ComplexNumber(double dR)
    {
```

(continued)

```
        this(dR, 0.0);
    }

    // division operator written to use exceptions
    public ComplexNumber Divide(double d) throws Exception
    {
        if (d == 0.0)
        {
            throw new
Exception("Attempted divide by zero in ComplexNumber.divide");
        }
        return new ComplexNumber(m_dReal / d, m_dImag / d);
    }

    public String toString()
    {
        StringBuffer sb = new StringBuffer();
        sb.append('(').append(m_dReal).append(',');
        sb.append(m_dImag).append(')');
        return sb.toString();
    }
}
```

The new *Divide(double)* method returns a *ComplexNumber,* which is the result of dividing the current object by the real number *d*. Of course, if *d* is 0, the answer is meaningless. Rather than proceed with the division, *Divide* checks for *d* equal to 0.0. In the event that *d* is 0, *Divide* throws an exception containing an error message.

The *throw* keyword is followed by the allocation of an object off the heap. This object must be a subclass of *Throwable*. You always throw an object of class *Exception* or some subclass of *Exception*.

 OTE Another subclass of *Throwable*, *Error*, is reserved for Java's use and should never be thrown by an application.

The constructor for *Exception* accepts a *String* object, which should contain at least a description of the problem.

 OTE The similarity between the *Exception* class and the *Error* class described above is more than accidental. The *Exception* class contains the same type of useful debug information that the *Error* class contains.

148

Since *Divide* does not catch the exception thrown in this case, the exception is guaranteed to return to the caller.

The programmer must alert Java and the caller of the *Divide* method that an exception might be forthcoming by appending the phrase *throws Exception* to the method declaration. (*throws* is a keyword, and *Exception* is the class of object thrown.) Any method that calls *Divide* must either handle the *Exception* itself or indicate that it might throw an *Exception* by appending *throws Exception* to its declaration.

 NOTE   Java and any good programmer both know that run-time exceptions can pop up at any time. Therefore, it is not necessary to include a *throws* descriptor on method declarations for *RuntimeException* or any of its subclasses, including *NullPointerException, ClassCastException, IllegalThreadStateException,* and *ArrayIndexOutOfBoundsException.* However, including a *throws* descriptor for these declarations, especially if you throw one of the exceptions yourself, is probably a good idea.

Catching an Exception

The keyword **catch** is used to introduce the catch block. As described earlier, the catch block is the section of code designed to process a thrown exception. The catch block must immediately follow a try block or another catch block. The try block encloses a sequence of statements from which a throw can originate. This is best described by example:

```
import srd.math.*;
import java.lang.Exception;

public class MyClass
{
    public static void main(String[] s)
    {
        try
        {
            ComplexNumber c = new ComplexNumber(4.0, 2.0);

            System.out.println(c.toString() + " / 2 = "
                        + c.Divide(2.0).toString());

            System.out.println(c.toString() + " / 0 = "
                        + c.Divide(0.0).toString());
```

(continued)

```
            System.out.println(c.toString() + " / 4 = "
                            + c.Divide(4.0).toString());
    }
    catch(Exception e)
    {
        System.out.println("Output from e.toString:");
        System.out.println(e.toString());
        System.out.println("\n");

        System.out.println("Output from e.printStackTrace:");
        e.printStackTrace();              }
    }
}
```

As soon as control enters the try block, this example program creates a *ComplexNumber* object *c*. The example then goes through a series of routine divisions to show off the new *Divide* method; however, the second call attempts to divide by 0. (The 0 in this case is hard coded to be more obvious, but it could just as well be a variable.) As we know, this causes *Divide* to throw an exception.

When the exception is thrown, control returns immediately from *Divide* and passes to the closed brace of the try block. From this point, Java begins looking through the catch blocks for a block that can handle the type of object thrown. Since *Divide* throws an *Exception* object, the one (and only) catch block provided handles the situation nicely.

The catch block can recover from the error in many ways. This particular catch block simply displays the error message saved in the *Exception* object. *Exception.toString* is overloaded to output the name of the *Exception* class followed by the reason for the exception, which was passed into the constructor.

Exception.printStackTrace is provided for debug purposes. This method also identifies where the exception was thrown, followed by where that method was called, followed by where *that* method was called, and so on in reverse order back to the original function that fielded the exception. Since this information is only marginally useful to the user, but is of great use to the programmer, it is common to suppress the stack trace via a debug flag after the application is in use in the field.

The output from this program appears in Figure 9-1.

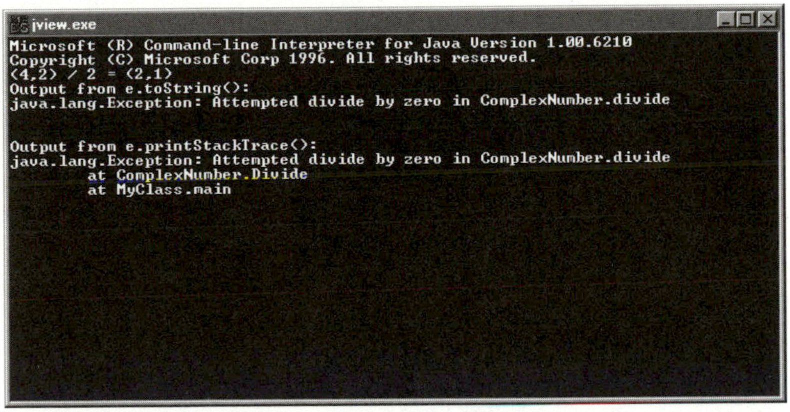

Figure 9-1. *The result of executing a simple throw/catch test program.*

If no error is thrown from within the try block, the catch block is disregarded.

Advantages of Exceptions

Although Java supports the simple error return approach, Java exceptions offer several advantages.

First, exceptions reduce programming complexity. The calling functions do not need to check pesky return values. If the function returns in the normal fashion, the caller is assured that no error occurred. In addition, by encasing multiple calls in a single try block, the error code can be isolated at the bottom of the method, out of the way of the normal logic flow. This makes the resulting code easier to understand and maintain.

Second, exceptions make it impossible to ignore the errors returned from functions. If the caller does not handle the exception, the exception is passed to that function's caller until some function is prepared to handle the problem. If no function handles the exception, Java fields it and outputs a nasty message before terminating the program—but at least the problem won't be ignored.

Just as important, the exception mechanism enables a function to ignore the exception if it can do nothing about the problem. Consider the following function, for example:

```java
import srd.math.*;

public class MyClass
{
    // declare an array of ComplexNumber
    static final int M_NELEMENTS = 10;
    static private ComplexNumber[] complex =
                            new ComplexNumber[M_NELEMENTS];

    static {
        for (int i = 0; i < M_NELEMENTS; i++)
        {
            complex[i] = new ComplexNumber(0, 0);
        }
    }

    // DivideAll - divides all complexes by the same value
    public void DivideAll(double d) throws Exception
    {
        for (int i = 0; i < M_NELEMENTS; i++)
        {
            complex[i] = complex[i].Divide(d);
        }
    }

    // ...other methods follow...
}
```

The *DivideAll(double)* method divides every member of the *complex* array by *d*. If *d* is 0, however, *Divide* throws an exception, as we know. *DivideAll* can catch the exception, but what can it do about the problem? It doesn't know why *d* is 0. The better course of action is to allow the exception to pass back to the method that called *DivideAll* with the bogus denominator in the first place.

 OTE The *throws Exception* keywords are necessary in the declaration of *DivideAll* because even though *DivideAll* does not throw an exception itself, it does not catch an exception thrown by a method that it does call. Thus, *DivideAll* is capable of sending an exception to its caller.

By providing an alternative error return path, the exception mechanism does not get in the way of "good data" that a function might return. Thus, a logarithm function that might return either a positive or a negative double does not have to establish special values to handle such error cases as a negative argument.

Finally, the *Exception* class provides a convenient place to store more information than a single integer return code can hold.

Creating Your Own Exception Class

Quite a few exception classes are already defined; however, you are free to define your own exception classes to fit particular needs. Consider the *BankAccount* class, for example. If a check is written that is larger than the amount of cash in the account, the *Withdrawal* function simply ignores the request. It is more efficient for *Withdrawal* to throw an exception—let's call it the *InsufficientFundsException*. This is shown in the following code fragment:

```
// BankAccount - a general bank account class
public class BankAccount
{
    private static int m_AIds = 0;

    // ID - this is the account ID
    private int m_nAccountId;

    // balance - the current account's balance
    private double m_dBalance;

    // constructor - open account with a balance


    BankAccount(double dInitialBalance)
    {
        m_dBalance = dInitialBalance;
        m_nAccountId = ++m_AIds;
    }
```

(continued)

```
        // Id - return the account ID
        public int Id()
        {
            return m_nAccountId;
        }

        // Balance
        public double Balance()
        {
          return ((int)(m_dBalance * 100.0 + 0.5)) / 100.0;
        }

        // Withdrawal - make a withdrawal
        public void Withdrawal(double dAmount)
                    throws   InsufficientFundsException
        {
            // if there are insufficient funds on hand...
            if (m_dBalance < dAmount)
            {
                // ...throw an exception
                throw new InsufficientFundsException(this, dAmount);
            }

            // otherwise, post the debit
            m_dBalance -= dAmount;
        }
    }

public class InsufficientFundsException extends Exception
{
    private BankAccount m_ba;  // account with problem
    private double m_dWithdrawalAmount;

    InsufficientFundsException(BankAccount ba, double dAmount)
    {
        super("Insufficient funds in account ");
        m_ba = ba;
        m_dWithdrawalAmount = dAmount;
    }
```

```java
    public String toString()
    {
        StringBuffer sb = new StringBuffer();
        sb.append("Insufficient funds in account ");
        sb.append(m_ba.Id());
        sb.append("\nBalance was ");
        sb.append(m_ba.Balance());
        sb.append("\nWithdrawal was ");
        sb.append(m_dWithdrawalAmount);
        return sb.toString();
    }
}
```

The constructor to the *InsufficientFundsException* class accepts a reference to the account causing the trouble and the amount of the withdrawal. The constructor stores this information for use by the *toString* method. *toString* generates a meaningful error message based on the information stored.

The following is a small test program showing how the exception is used:

```java
public class test
{
    public static void main(String[] s)
    {
        try
        {
            // open a bank account with $50 in it
            BankAccount ba = new BankAccount(50.0);

            // now try to take out $100
            ba.Withdrawal(100.0);

            System.out.println("Withdrawal successful!");
        }
        catch(Exception e)
        {
            // output exception's error message
            System.out.println(e.toString());
        }
    }
}
```

The output from executing this example program is shown in Figure 9-2 on the next page.

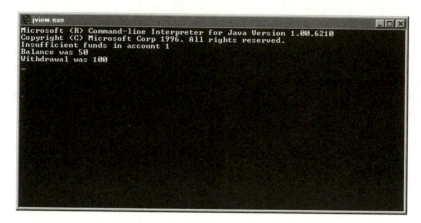

Figure 9-2. *The result of executing the small test program showing the* InsufficientFundsException *in action.*

Handling Multiple Exceptions

A single method can throw more than one exception. For example, consider the following version of *BankAccount* that does everything by account ID:

```java
// BankAccount - a general bank account class
public class BankAccount
{
    // ...other methods the same...

    // Find - look up an account by ID
    public static BankAccount Find(int nAccountId)
                        throws AccountNotFoundException
    {
        // ...goes through some process to find account
        //    by ID; if it doesn't find the account, it
        //    throws an AccountNotFoundException...
    }

    // Withdrawal - make a withdrawal
    public static void Withdrawal(int nAccountId, double dAmount)
    throws AccountNotFoundException, InsufficientFundsException
    {
        BankAccount ba = Find(nAccountId);
        if (ba.m_dBalance < dAmount)
        {
```

```
                throw new InsufficientFundsException(ba, dAmount);
        }
        ba.m_dBalance -= dAmount;
    }
}

public class AccountNotFoundException extends Exception


{

    AccountNotFoundException(int nAccountId)
    {
        super("Account not found " + nAccountId);
    }
}

public class InsufficientFundsException extends Exception
{
    // ... this class same as before...
}
```

Here we see that *Withdrawal* now accepts a bank account ID as well as
an amount. It first looks up the *BankAccount* object by ID using the *Find*
method before attempting the withdrawal. If *Find* can't locate the account,
it throws an *AccountNotFoundException*. Since it is not prepared to field
that exception, *Withdrawal* is actually capable of throwing either bank
account exception. Thus, we see two exception types in its declaration.

The calling program can perform a generic catch as follows:

```
public class test
{
    public static void main(String[] s)
    {
        try
        {
            // withdraw $100 from account #1
            BankAccount.Withdrawal(1, 100.0);
        }
        catch(Exception e)
        {
            System.out.println(e.toString());
        }
    }
}
```

This single catch handles either type of bank account exception. However, if the calling function wants to handle them differently, it can do so as follows:

```java
public class test
{
    public static void main(String[] s)

    {
        try
        {
            BankAccount.Withdrawal(1, 100.0);
        }
        catch(AccountNotFoundException anfe)
        {
            // ...handle "account not found" exception...
        }
        catch(InsufficientFundsException ife)
        {
            // ...handle different exception type here...
        }
        catch(Exception e)
        {
            // ...generic exception handler here...
        }
    }
}
```

Java compares the object thrown with the parameter of each catch block, starting at the first catch block after the try and stopping with the first one that matches. An object matches the catch block parameter if it is of the same type as the parameter or is a subclass of the parameter.

Assume, for example, that the call to *BankAccount.Withdrawal* generates an *InsufficientFundsException*. This exception is first compared to *AccountNotFoundException*. Since *InsufficientFundsException* is not a subclass of *AccountNotFoundException* (they're siblings), there is no match with this first catch block. Java then looks at the next catch block, which contains an exact match in class type, so control passes to this catch block.

Since the search of catch blocks is performed in the order that the catch blocks appear, it is important to put the more generic catch later.

Suppose, for example, that I had ordered the catch blocks as follows:

```
public class test
{
    public static void main(String[] s)
    {
        try
        {
            BankAccount.Withdrawal(1, 100.0);
        }
        // don't do the following - control goes to the
        // Exception case every time no matter what's thrown
        catch(Exception e)
        {
            // ...generic exception handler here...
        }
        catch(AccountNotFoundException anfe)
        {
            // ...handle "account not found" exception...
        }
        catch(InsufficientFundsException ife)
        {
            // ...handle different exception type here...
        }
    }
}
```

Now, suppose an *InsufficientFundsException* is generated. The first block that Java considers is the generic *Exception* block. Since *InsufficientFunds-Exception* is a subclass of *Exception,* control passes to this catch block before Java ever gets a chance to find a closer match further down.

 N **OTE** In fact, Visual J++ won't let you make such a silly mistake as placing a generic *Exception* case before more specific cases. It generates a compiler error to warn you of this situation.

Finally!

Control exits from a try block as soon as the program executes a return or an exception is thrown. However, Java allows the user to define a block of code to be executed before control exits the method, no matter what. This is called the **finally block** because it is defined using the *finally* keyword.

```
public class test
{
    public static void main(String[] s)
    {
        try
        {
            // normal processing here - this processing
            // is aborted as soon as exception is thrown
            // or a return is encountered
        }
        catch(Exception e)
        {
            // this is executed only in the event
            // an error is thrown
        }
        finally
        {
            // this block is executed before control exits
            // the method no matter what, even if
            // the try block includes a return or
            // throws an exception
        }
    }
}
```

The finally block is executed before control exits the method, even if the try block contains a return statement! This makes the finally block an ideal place to release any permanent resources the method might have allocated. For example, you might close any open files in the finally block.

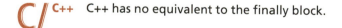 C++ has no equivalent to the finally block.

Conclusion

The Java exception mechanism provides a robust means of handling those pesky error conditions that arise during the execution of a program. Java exceptions allow methods to handle error conditions when they can and to ignore them when they can't. In addition, using exceptions doesn't put an undue burden on the programmer. The Java *finally* clause also ensures that valuable resources are not lost (until garbage collection can pick them back up in the finalizer; see Chapter 5) when an unexpected return or exception is encountered.

File I/O

File I/O in Java follows the same model used by C and C++: It uses no file I/O language primitives. All I/O is provided by classes contained in the java.io package. Java I/O is type safe, which means that it is impossible to perform the wrong I/O operation for the given data type.

C/ **C++** C and C++'s *printf/scanf*–based I/O is not type safe. Just leave off an ampersand in your call to *scanf,* and your program will certainly crash ignominiously. However, C++'s *iostream* I/O is type safe.

Java I/O is layered, which means that Java does not attempt to build too much capability into one class, because not everyone wants all the features all the time. Instead, a programmer can get the features she wants by layering one class over another. For example, the basic input stream class *Input-Stream* is not buffered; however, the class *BufferedInputStream* adds buffering to the *InputStream* class.

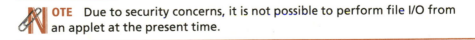 **OTE** Due to security concerns, it is not possible to perform file I/O from an applet at the present time.

Using the Standard I/O Objects

Three static I/O objects have already been created by the time your *main* method gets control. These are defined in Table 10-1. All three of these objects are public static members of the *System* class.

 NOTE The *System* class provides a system-independent interface to certain general functions; however, *in, out,* and *err* are the most useful capabilities *System* provides.

Object	Type	C++ Equivalent	Purpose
System.in	*BufferedInputStream*	*cin*	standard input (usually from the keyboard)
System.out	*PrintStream*	*cout*	standard output (usually to the display)
System.err	*PrintStream*	*cerr*	error output (usually to the display)

Table 10-1. *Standard I/O objects.*

System.in is used for retrieving input from the standard input, which is usually the keyboard, whereas *System.out* is used for sending output to the default display, which is normally the screen. Some operating systems (including MS-DOS) allow the default input and output devices to be re-directed to a file. (MS-DOS uses the symbols < and > to redirect input and output.) *System.err* is normally also connected to the default display; however, some operating systems allow the standard output and standard error streams to be redirected independently.

The following simple IOTest.java program illustrates the use of *in* and *out*:

```java
import java.io.*;

public class IOTest
{
    public static void main(String[] args)
    {
        try
        {
            // let's try reading input from the keyboard
            byte bArray[] = new byte[128];
            System.out.println("Enter something:");

            // the following reads in an array of bytes
            System.in.read(bArray);

            // output the array of bytes - this generates
            // peculiar results
            System.out.print("You entered:");
            System.out.println(bArray);

            // let's investigate
            Class InClass = System.in.getClass();
            Class OutClass= System.out.getClass();
            System.out.println("in is " + InClass.toString());
            System.out.println("out is " + OutClass.toString());
        }
        catch(IOException ioe)
        {
            System.out.println(ioe.toString());
            ioe.printStackTrace();
        }
    }
}
```

The program starts by importing the java.io package in order to access the I/O operations. *main* prompts the user to enter information by calling *System.out.println(String)* and then reads the response by calling *System-.in.read(byte[])*. In this example, the *main* method provided must be prepared to catch the *IOException* that *System.in.read* can generate.

Just on a lark, the program also outputs the class name of the *System.in* and *System.out* objects. It does this by asking each of the objects for its class using the *Object.getClass* method and then asking the class for its name using the *Class.toString* method.

Executing this program generates the rather confusing output shown in Figure 10-1.

```
jview.exe                                                        _ □ X
Microsoft (R) Command-line Interpreter for Java Version 1.00.6210
Copyright (C) Microsoft Corp 1996. All rights reserved.
Enter something:
Hello, world
You entered:[B@422610
in is class java.io.BufferedInputStream
out is class java.io.PrintStream
```

Figure 10-1. *The confusing output generated by our first standard read/write attempt.*

The names of the input and output classes appear properly. However, in response to the prompt *Enter Something Now:* I entered *Learn Java Now,* to which the program responded with some unintelligible gibberish. (If your gibberish is not exactly the same as mine, don't worry—gibberish is gibberish.)

The reason for this confusion stems from the fact that *read(byte[])* is a low-level function that reads input from the keyboard as a stream of bytes.

OTE The gibberish appears when the call to *System.out.println(bArray)* invokes *PrintStream.println(Object),* which displays the address of the object. Thus, what you see is the address of the byte array containing the data.

Unfortunately, the simple *InputStream* doesn't offer anything more sophisticated than *read(bytes[])*. However, we can convert the array of bytes into a *String* and then output that:

```java
import java.io.*;

public class IOTest
{
    public static void main(String[] args)
    {
        try
        {
            // let's try reading input from the keyboard
            byte bArray[] = new byte[128];
            System.out.println("Enter something:");

            // the following reads in an array of bytes
            System.in.read(bArray);

            // convert the array into a String before attempting
            // to output it
            String s = new String(bArray, 0);
            System.out.println(s);
        }
        catch(IOException ioe)
        {
            System.out.println(ioe.toString());
            ioe.printStackTrace();
        }
    }
}
```

This version converts the byte array into a *String* and then uses the *PrintStream.println(String)* method to output to *System.out.* This generates the not very exciting but anticipated results shown in Figure 10-2 on the next page.

Figure 10-2. *The fixed program simply echoes whatever is entered, but at least it works.*

Notice that *PrintStream.println(String)* sends a new line to its stream after the *String*. The similar *PrintStream.print(String)* does not.

> **NOTE** *PrintStream.println(String)* is the *println* function that we've been using throughout the book.

Creating Your Own File I/O Objects

The *FileInputStream* class is used to open a file for input, and the *File-OutputStream* class opens a file for output. The following simple example program expects two filenames when it is executed. The program copies the first file into the second.

```java
public class FileIO
{
    public static void main(String[] args)
    {
        try
        {
            // open args[0] for input
            FileInputStream in = new FileInputStream(args[0]);

            // add buffering to that InputStream
            BufferedInputStream bin =
                                new BufferedInputStream(in);
```

```
        // open args[1] for output and add buffering to
        // it as well
        FileOutputStream out = new FileOutputStream(args[1]);
        BufferedOutputStream bout =
                            new BufferedOutputStream(out);

        // now read as long as there is something to read
        byte bArray[] = new byte[256];
        int nBytesRead;
        while(bin.available() > 0)
        {
            // read up a block - remember how many bytes read
            nBytesRead = bin.read(bArray);

            // write that many bytes back out starting
            // at offset 0 in the array
            bout.write(bArray, 0, nBytesRead);
        }
    }
    catch(IOException ioe)
    {
        System.out.println(ioe.toString());
    }
}
}
```

The program begins by opening the input file (the first argument to the program) with the *FileInputStream* class. If the file does not exist, *FileInputStream* throws a *FileNotFoundException* that is fielded by the catch block. The program then wraps the *FileInputStream* object *in* in a *BufferedFileInputStream* object that it calls *bin*.

> **NOTE** The first time the program reads from *bin,* the *BufferedInputStream* reads a large block from *in,* returning to the caller only the amount of data asked for. *bin* retains the rest of the data read to service future input requests. *bin* does not read from *in* again until the input buffer has been exhausted. This buffering is invisible to the application; however, since the disk is a relatively slow device compared to the CPU, buffering can greatly improve the performance of the program.

The program repeats the process with the second argument to the program for the output file, creating a *bout* object of the class *BufferedOutputFile*.

The program then enters a loop, reading from *bin* as long as *bin.available* returns a nonzero value. (*available* returns the number of remaining bytes to be read from the input file.) For each pass through the loop, the program reads a block of data from *bin* and writes the same block to *bout*. On each read except the last, *bin.read* reads as much data as *bArray* can hold. On the last read, however, the file reaches end-of-file before the array is filled (unless the length of the file just happens to be an integral multiple of the size of *bArray*). Thus, *bout.write* writes only the actual number of bytes read.

 OTE Buffering can cause problems under certain conditions. Consider a bank transaction application. Transactional programs must be written so that an unexpected loss of power or a program crash doesn't cause a bank transaction to be lost. Such programs carefully choreograph how data moves from the program to disk. Until a particular transaction actually gets committed to disk, the program retains extra information in a recovery log in case the power goes.

At certain points, this type of program makes sure that any buffered data is written to disk even if the buffer is not full. This is called flushing the output buffer.

The program can flush a buffered output stream at any time by calling the *flush* method. In addition, most file streams support the *autoflush* method, which forces output to the disk with each and every disk output operation, even if the stream is normally buffered.

More Sophisticated File I/O

The *BufferFileInputStream* and *BufferedFileOutputStream* classes are fine for moving large blocks of data; however, the I/O operations offered by both are relatively crude. Neither understands anything other than bytes.

To perform *println* type output to a file, the user can create a *PrintStream* object. For example, the following program reads a file as before, but its output is in "hex dump" format:

```java
import java.io.*;

public class FileIO
{
    public static void main(String[] args)
    {
```

```
try
{
    // use a normal input stream for bulk input
    FileInputStream in = new FileInputStream(args[0]);
    BufferedInputStream bin =
                        new BufferedInputStream(in);

    // create a buffered print stream for output
    FileOutputStream out = new FileOutputStream(args[1]);
    BufferedOutputStream bout =
                        new BufferedOutputStream(out);
    PrintStream pout = new PrintStream(bout);

    // read 8 bytes at a time
    byte bArray[] = new byte[8];
    int nBytesRead;
    while(bin.available() > 0)
    {
        // first output them as hex numbers
        nBytesRead = bin.read(bArray);
        for (int i = 0; i < nBytesRead; i++)
        {
            int nByte = (int)bArray[i];
            String s = Integer.toString(nByte, 16);
            if (s.length() == 1)
            {
                pout.print(" ");
            }
            pout.print(s + ", ");
        }

        // then if they are printable, output the
        // character (if not, output a ".")
        pout.print("-");
        for (int i = 0; i < nBytesRead; i++)
        {
            char c = (char)bArray[i];
            if (Character.isDigit(c)      ||
                Character.isLowerCase(c) ||
                Character.isUpperCase(c))
            {
                // retain c - do nothing
            }
            else
            {
                c = '.'; // replace with a "."
            }
            pout.print(c);
```

(continued)

169

```
                    }
                    pout.println(" ");
                }
            }
            catch(IOException ioe)
            {
                System.out.println(ioe.toString());
            }
        }
    }
}
```

This program reads from the input file as before (except that now it reads only 8 bytes at a time). On the output side, however, it uses the formatting capabilities of the *print* and *println* functions available with a *PrintStream* to output the characters in both hex and Unicode formats. Figure 10-3 shows an output file created by this program.

Figure 10-3. *A typical output file created by* FileIO *when viewed by Notepad.*

Some programs must be able to read the different intrinsic types (as opposed to simply reading arrays of bytes). The *DataInputStream* class provides methods such as *readInt, readShort, readFloat,* and so on. Similarly, the *DataOutputStream* class provides a write method for each of the intrinsic types (*writeInt, writeShort, writeFloat,* and so on). Use these two classes when you are saving data to disk that you want your program to reread at a later date.

Conclusion

In this chapter, you learned how to open a file either for input or output. You saw how to read and write either in bulk or in byte-sized intrinsic packages. You saw how to enable buffering and when it can cause problems.

In the 10 chapters of Part 1, you learned the Java language the way a student would approach any new programming language. You saw how to declare variables and functions. You saw how to create, use, and inherit classes. Finally, you saw how to use the exception mechanism and how to manipulate files.

But Java is not just a language like any other. What sets Java apart is its ability to easily create neat applets. In Part 2 of this book, you'll learn how to use Java to write applets and how to execute these applets on the World Wide Web.

Instant Java: Using the AppletWizard

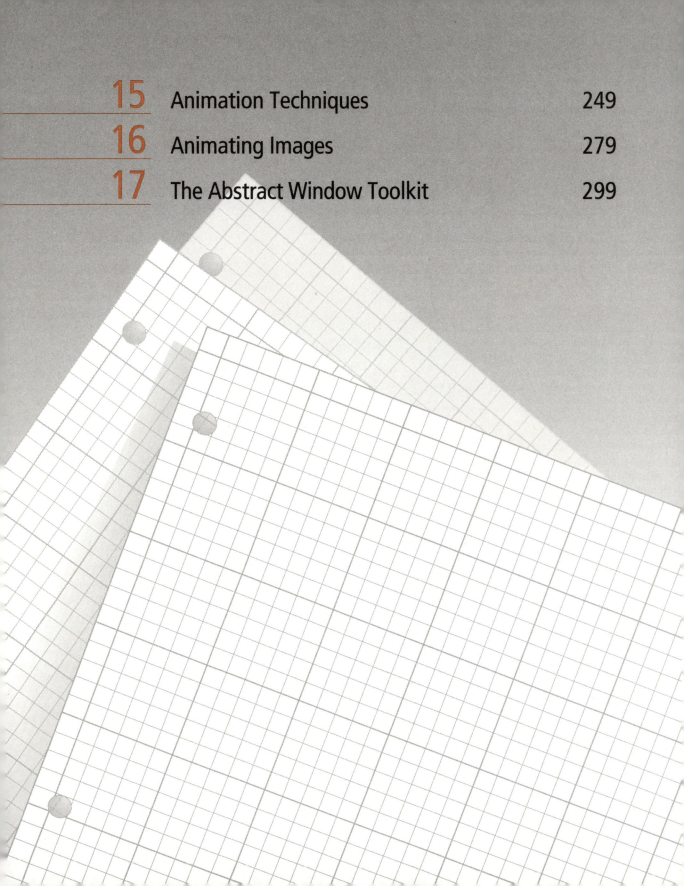

Your First Applet:
Fresh-Ground Java

In Part 1 of this book, you learned the basics of the Java programming language. You saw how Java combines a powerful C++-like syntax with an object-oriented approach into a machine-independent, consistent, and secure programming language.

While all that stuff is great, there are plenty of other powerful object-oriented languages that don't attract as much attention as Java does. What gets people so excited about Java are the neat applets that you can create.

In Part 2, I'll show you how to use the Java language skills you learned in Part 1 to build applets like the ones you've seen on the Web. In just a few more chapters, your home page will be bristling with programmed activity.

In this chapter, you'll write your first Java Web applet. Microsoft Visual J++ provides a slick aid known as the AppletWizard to help you to create applets more easily, but you'll write this first applet by hand so you can better learn the parts of a Java applet and how they interact.

The Applet

An **applet** is a Java program that is designed to be executed by a Web browser. Java applets can be executed only on Web browsers that are specially designed to execute Java .class files. This means that they must be equipped with a Java byte code interpreter.

 OTE   As of this writing, only Microsoft's Internet Explorer 3.0 and later, Netscape's Navigator 2.0 and later, and Sun's HotJava browsers support Java applets.

Java and the Web

Most improvements in computer technology are of the incremental, evolutionary variety. Occasionally, however, a new breakthrough technology appears that shakes up the entire PC industry. The World Wide Web is certainly one of those technologies.

The Web did to the Internet what the telephone did to the telegraph wire. Before the Web, the Internet provided a powerful international communications medium, but it was definitely not easy to use. The Internet user of old had to be familiar with a profusion of inane programs like *ftp, telnet,* and *rlogin,* each with its own commands and its own gotchas to learn.

With its point-and-shoot interface, the Web has brought relative order to this confusion. Through the Web, the user can surf from site to site without worrying about UNIX-like commands. She can look up text information, download files, view images, listen to live music, even order a pizza. But prior to the advent of Java, the one thing that the Web could not do very well was execute a program. It was great at handling static data; with some difficulty, it could even handle forms (the kind of forms where you enter your name, address, and so on), but that's about as far as it went. Of course, before long programmers wanted to execute programs over the Web.

One approach to executing programs remotely is to set up a client-server arrangement. The program executes on the remote server while the PC becomes the local client. The client sends keystrokes and mouse commands to the server, and the server sends back windowing commands to make images appear on the screen. This arrangement works great over very fast communication paths like a small LAN. At today's modem speeds, however, this isn't practical. Even when household ISDN becomes common, the communication bandwidth over long-haul telephone carriers will simply not support the enormous amounts of traffic such a client-server approach would require.

Another approach is to download the program from the server and execute it locally, but who'd want to? First, you'd have to be sure the program was designed to execute on the same type of machine as yours, otherwise the program would be worse than useless. Plus, how could you be sure that the application was benevolent? It's easy to write a program that wipes out the hard disk of any machine that downloads it. Finally, conventional programs take too long to download.

Java was designed to address these problems. It does not require the high-bandwidth connections required by a client-server arrangement. Its byte code executable format is compact to support rapid downloads and machine independence. In addition, Java's security features keep malicious programmers from destroying your precious data. Plus, Java applets are small to allow quick downloading.

The "Hello, World" Applet

Because an applet is a type of program, we'll start off with the mandatory "Hello, world" example. Create a Java Workspace project in the conventional way. (I called my project *HelloMan*.) Into this project insert the following HelloMan.java file. This is the famous "Hello, world" example program from Chapter 1 rewritten as an applet:

```java
import java.applet.Applet;
import java.awt.*;

public class HelloMan extends Applet
{
    public void paint(Graphics g)
    {
        g.drawString("Hello, world", 0, 20);
    }
}
```

Compile this class in the conventional way.

To execute the applet under the Visual J++ IDE, choose Execute HelloMan from the Build menu. This time, however, select Run Class As Applet instead of Run Class As Application. Figure 11-1 shows the results of executing this program as an applet.

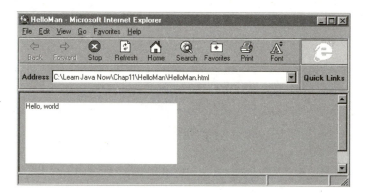

Figure 11-1. *The results of executing the "Hello, world" applet from the Visual J++ IDE.*

Executing "Hello, World" from a Web Browser

To execute the "Hello, world" applet from a Web browser, you need to build a HyperText Markup Language (HTML) page for it. (See page 181 for more information about HTML.) Create the following file with any ASCII text editor. (You can use the Visual J++ editor, if you like.)

```
<HTML>
<HEAD>
<TITLE>Hello World</TITLE>
</HEAD>
<BODY>
<APPLET CODE="HelloMan.class"
            WIDTH=250
            HEIGHT=100>
</APPLET>
</BODY>
</HTML>
```

OTE   The editor built into the Visual J++ IDE works well for simple HTML files because it performs syntax coloring.

Save this to a file called HelloMan.html. (Actually, this time you can use any name you like as long as it ends in *.html;* the name of the HTML page does not have to match that of the class name.)

 OTE   If you are using Microsoft Windows 3.1, use the extension *.htm*.

Now examine this file with your Java-capable Web browser. When you do this, you don't see the above text at all. Instead, a window pops up and the text "Hello, world" appears. This "Hello, world" was written into the window by your applet.

 OTE   Using Internet Explorer, choose the Open command from the File menu and then browse over to HelloMan.html. Using Netscape Navigator, choose the Open File command from the File menu and browse to HelloMan.html.

 OTE   The only reason you don't have to create an HTML page when you execute your applet under the Visual J++ IDE is that the IDE creates one for you automatically.

Executing Your Applet over the Web

If you have your own personal home page with an Internet service provider, you can install the "Hello, world" applet (and any other applet in this book) on your home page. Admittedly, this particular applet is not much to get excited about, but some of the later applets in this book are pretty cool. (Well, at least I think they are.)

To do so, you transfer the HelloMan.html file and the HelloMan.class files to your home page. There are a number of ways to accomplish this.

Several Windows-based shareware and freeware ftp utilities make the job easy. If you do not have a Windows-based ftp utility, you can use the MS-DOS–based ftp program that comes with Microsoft Windows 95 and Microsoft Windows NT.

First establish your Point-to-Point (PPP) connection using the Windows DialUp Networking utility. Then, from an MS-DOS window, connect to your Internet service provider by entering *ftp <service provider>*. At the login prompt, enter your account name and password. Now *cd* to your Web page directory. Set the transfer mode to binary (enter *binary*) and send the files one at a time by entering *send <filename>* for each file. A sample session is shown in Figure 11-2.

```
C:\java\Applets>ftp www.topher.net
Connected to mail.topher.net.
220 mail.topher.net FTP server (Version wu-2.4(2) Wed Jun 7 17:22:02 MDT 1995) ready.
User (mail.topher.net:(none)): srdavis
331 Password required for srdavis.
Password:
230 User srdavis logged in.
ftp> binary
200 Type set to I.
ftp> send HelloMan.html
200 PORT command successful.
150 Opening BINARY mode data connection for HelloMan.html.
226 Transfer complete.
173 bytes sent in 0.11 seconds (1.57 Kbytes/sec)
ftp> send HelloMan.class
200 PORT command successful.
150 Opening BINARY mode data connection for HelloMan.class.
226 Transfer complete.
413 bytes sent in 0.06 seconds (6.88 Kbytes/sec)
ftp> quit
221 Goodbye.

C:\java\Applets>
```

Figure 11-2. *A session log showing the ftp'ing of my HelloMan.html and HelloMan.class files to execute the "Hello, world" applet from my home page.*

To execute your new applet, point your Web browser to *http://<your home page URL>/HelloMan.html.* (With most Web browsers, including both Internet Explorer and Navigator, all you have to do is type the Web address in the little window.)

> ## What's in a Name?
>
> The World Wide Web uses an encoding scheme called **Uniform Resource Locator** (URL) for its filenames. URLs have the following general format:
>
> ```
> service://hostname/pathname
> ```
>
> The service indicates the protocol used to get data from the site. For example, *ftp* is a possible service. By far the most common service for Web browsing is *http* (which stands for HyperText Transport Protocol). This is the service you use when you surf from one site to another on the Web. Use the service *file* when you want the browser to load a file directly from your hard disk rather than from the Web. This is useful when testing applets that you create locally before you upload them to your Web page. The service field is required.
>
> *hostname* indicates the Web address of the site that contains the file. For example, *www.microsoft.com* is Microsoft's home page address. This field is required for all remote services. (*file* is the only local service.)
>
> *pathname* is the name of the file to load. When it is not present, the browser loads the default file, which usually has the name *index.html*. This file is called the site's **home page**.

How Does All That Work?

So what is all this stuff? What's an HTML file and why do I need one to execute my applet? What else can I do with an HTML file? Why doesn't my applet have a *main* method? Let's go over this simple "Hello, world" applet and examine exactly how it works.

How Does the HTML Page Work?

The World Wide Web is designed around a document format called HyperText Markup Language (HTML). HTML gives the Web its power. A complete description of the HTML language is beyond the scope of this book, but you can get pretty far on just a few commands.

OTE For those who are really curious, try *http://www.webcrawler.com/-select/internet.html.html*. It's full of HTML guides, tutorials, and editors.

An HTML document is an ASCII file containing HTML commands. Table 11-1 shows a list of some of the more important browser commands. This is only a small subset. HTML 3.0 defines more than 130 HTML commands and the list is growing all the time; however, this list is sufficient for our purposes.

HTML Command	Purpose
`<HTML>`	Should be the first command in the HTML file.
`<HEAD>`	Introduces the head section.
`<TITLE>title</TITLE>`	Gives the HTML document a title. Different browsers do different things with the title. Most place the title on the title bar when the page is displayed. In addition, this is the name stored if the user adds this page to the Bookmarks.
`</HEAD>`	Concludes the head section.
`<BODY>`	Introduces the body section.
`<P>`	Paragraph break. Places a break between paragraphs.
`<HR>`	Horizontal rule. Places a horizontal line across the page.
`<I>text</I>`	Displays *text* in italics.
`<B>text</B>`	Displays *text* in bold.
`<Hn>text</Hn>`	Makes *text* a level *n* head where *n* is a single digit between 1 and 6.
`<A HREF="urlname">text</A>`	Declares a hot link. *text* appears to the user in a different color. Selecting *text* causes the browser to automatically go to the file *urlname*.

HTML Command	Purpose
`<IMG SRC="urlname" ALT="text">`	Declares a hot link to an image. When the page is loaded, the browser loads and displays the image contained in *urlname*. The ALT *text* is displayed if the browser doesn't have graphics capability (or if graphics is turned off).
`<APPLET CODE = "classname" WIDTH=w HEIGHT=h>`	Begins an applet definition. *classname* is the name of the applet class. *width* and *height* are the initial dimensions of the window in which the applet runs. *classname* is generally relative to the current directory of the current html page. (This can be overridden.)
`<PARAM NAME="paramname" VALUE="paramvalue">`	Defines a parameter to the applet. *paramname* is the name of the parameter and *paramvalue* is its value. This can be repeated as often as you like. We'll cover this in Chapter 14.
`</APPLET>`	Ends the applet definition.
`</BODY>`	Ends the body section.
`</HTML>`	Ends an HTML file.

Table 11-1. *Some of the more common HTML commands.*

We can now analyze HelloMan.html using this information. The following is the same HelloMan.html file as before, but with my italicized comments added. (The italicized comments are not part of the HTML.)

```
<HTML>                              start of HTML file
<HEAD>                              start of head section
<TITLE>Hello world</TITLE>          "Hello, world" title
</HEAD>                             that's it for the head
<BODY>                              now comes the body
<APPLET CODE="HelloMan.class"       load the HelloMan applet...
            WIDTH=250               ...in a 250 by 100 pixel...
            HEIGHT=100>             window
</APPLET>                           end of applet definition
</BODY>                             end of body
</HTML>                             end of HTML
```

Is All That Stuff Really Necessary?

Actually, not all of the fields shown are truly necessary. For example, most browsers don't require the <HTML> and </HTML> commands, nor do they require an explicit head and body section. Thus, the following represents a minimal HTML file that will work on most browsers:

```
<TITLE>Hello world</TITLE>
<APPLET CODE="Hello.class"
            WIDTH=250
            HEIGHT=100>
</APPLET>
```

However, this HTML does not follow the standard and might not be supported by all browsers, today or in the future.

How Does the Applet Work?

The HelloMan.html file contains the Applet command, which tells the browser to open a window and to associate an applet with that window. The initial dimensions of the window are given by the *height* and *width*. The units of these dimensions are not specified, but on a PC the unit is pixels. The Applet command also tells the browser where to find the .class file containing that applet.

The .class file that the browser loads needs no *main* method. The applet contains only the methods necessary to support the window. What do I mean by "support the window"? Read on.

The Windows-based programming model

Java applets support the same graphics-based paradigm used by Windows-based applications. Windows-based applications are designed to execute in an environment where the user can have multiple programs executing simultaneously, each with its own visible window. The user moves back and forth between applications by simply clicking on the window he wants to work in.

In this environment, applications cannot take over sole control of the computer. Each application has an opportunity to process an input, such as a keystroke or a mouse click, and update its window (or windows) as necessary, but then it must return control to the operating system. The next user input might be destined for a different application.

The operating system tells the application when it has something else for it to do by sending it a **message**. Thus, each time I press a key while working on this manuscript, Windows sends my word processor a message with the keystroke in it. The word processor is then responsible for putting the text in the window and formatting it properly (as well as saving the keystroke to disk, of course). Each keystroke is called an **event**.

Other types of events can cause Windows to send a message to the application. For example, if I resize or unhide the word processor's window, Windows sends the program a Paint message that causes the program to redraw the contents of its window.

 OTE This is the programming paradigm used by Visual Basic, Visual C++, Delphi, and all other Windows-based programming languages.

Back to the applet

The Applet command within the HTML file tells the browser to create, position, and size the applet window. It also associates the applet with this window.

 C++ In C-based programs, creating and sizing the application window is the job of the *WinMain* procedure. In Visual Basic and MFC-based C++ programs, this step is done for you.

However, the browser has no idea what to put in the window. The browser must rely on the applet class to draw the contents of the window the first time it is displayed and each time it is redisplayed. It does this by calling the *paint(Graphics)* method.

The *Graphics* object passed to *paint*, commonly called *g*, is a handle to the applet's window. The *Graphics* class defines image manipulation commands, such as *drawString*, the results of which are sent directly to the window. The *Graphics* object also knows information about the window such as its size, its font, its position, and so forth.

C/ **C++** The *Graphics* object is the logical equivalent of the device context in a C or C++ Windows-based program.

Notice that *paint* doesn't write to the screen using a function like *println*. Instead, *paint* draws on the graphics display using the *Graphics.drawString* method. The first argument to *drawString* is a string, while the second and third are the x and y coordinates at which to draw the string, as shown in Figure 11-3. The x offset is in display units from the left edge of the window. Positive x values are to the right. The y offset is in measured units from the top of the window with positive values going down.

C/ **C++** This coordinate system is equivalent to the MM_TEXT mapping mode in a C or C++ Windows-based program. Java does not support the other mapping modes that Windows supports.

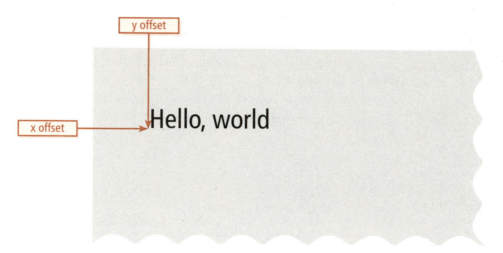

Figure 11-3. *The coordinate system used by the draw functions is measured from the left and top of the display window.*

NOTE It's not that *paint* can't call *println*. It's just that *println* output does not appear in the window. Instead it appears in something called the Java console. This is also where unhandled exception messages appear. For that reason, some browsers, such as Netscape Navigator, allow you to look at the Java console. However, this is certainly not a place that your applet users will think to look for output.

Can you show me the repaints?

As written, it isn't easy to tell that the *paint* method is called every time the window needs redrawing; however, with a slight modification we can make it obvious:

```java
import java.applet.Applet;
import java.awt.*;

public class HelloMan extends Applet
{
    // let's keep track of how often we're called
    // on to redraw the window
    static private int m_nRepaintCount = 0;

    public void paint(Graphics g)
    {
        String s = "Hello, world (" + ++m_nRepaintCount + ")";
        g.drawString(s, 0, 20);
    }
}
```

Now execute the program. When the window first appears, the count is displayed as 1, as expected. Resize the window, however, and the count increments (sometimes rapidly, depending on the browser).

If you are executing the modified applet in a Web browser, go to another Web site and then return using the back button. The count is incremented upon return when the browser repaints the HTML page containing our applet. In fact, you can simply select the reload button. This causes the number to increment as the browser repaints the display.

Conclusion

In this chapter you developed the most basic of all applets, the "Hello, world" applet. You wrote and compiled the applet, and then you wrote a small HTML page to execute it. Finally, you executed the applet both locally and, hopefully, over the Net.

In the next chapter you'll see how the Visual J++ AppletWizard can simplify the job of creating an applet by automating some of the tedious steps you did by hand in this chapter.

The Visual J++ AppletWizard

When you first learn a new programming language, it's important to do things manually so you can understand the steps involved. You also learn to appreciate all the background work that's done by automation tools. After you try the manual approach once or twice, however, I'm all for automation. That's why I'm a big fan of the AppletWizard built into Visual J++. In this chapter, you'll learn how to use the AppletWizard by recreating the basic "Hello, world" example applet.

Starting Up the AppletWizard

The AppletWizard is a utility built into Visual J++ that helps you build new applets. It automates several steps:

- It creates the necessary classes and .java files to support the most common programming options.

- It builds the beginnings of a set of methods to support these options.

- It adds comments to indicate what each of these methods does and to direct you in adding your code.

- It builds an HTML page to execute your applet.

- It builds a project for your applet.

To create the "Hello, world" applet using the AppletWizard, choose the New command from the File menu and select Project Workspace in the New dialog box, as you normally do. This time, select Java AppletWizard from the options in the list box on the left side of the dialog box. For the name of the project, I specified HelloAuto. The dialog box should look similar to Figure 12-1.

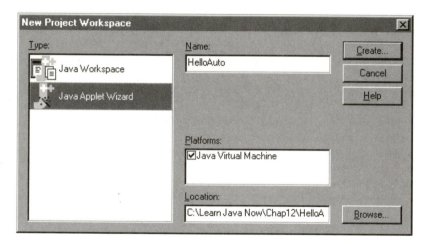

Figure 12-1. *The New Project Workspace dialog box that appears when you create the "Hello, world" applet with the aid of the AppletWizard.*

When you click *Create,* you are presented with the dialog box shown in Figure 12-2. This dialog box asks how you want the applet to execute and whether you want the AppletWizard to add helpful comments. The defaults are okay in this case, so you can simply click Next.

The Step 2 dialog box asks whether you want a sample HTML file and what the initial size of your window should be. The defaults for this window are okay as well, so click Next again to move to the third dialog box.

The Step 3 dialog box asks whether you want your applet to be multi-threaded. Select No. Leave the other buttons unselected. When properly filled out, this dialog box should look like Figure 12-3.

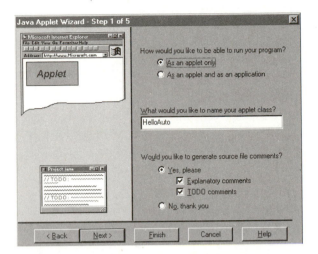

Figure 12-2. *Step 1 in the Java AppletWizard sequence of five dialog boxes.*

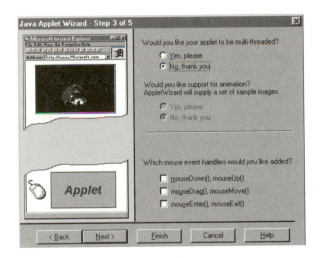

Figure 12-3. *The Step 3 dialog box showing the multithreading option deselected.*

The Step 4 dialog box asks you for any parameters you want to load from the HTML file. This refers to the PARAM HTML command. Since this applet has no parameters, you can leave this dialog box blank.

The Step 5 and final dialog box allows you to fill in whatever string information you like. This information is ignored by the applet but is returned by the *getAppletInfo* method. Figure 12-4 on the next page shows how I fill in my *getAppletInfo* information. You can fill in anything you like.

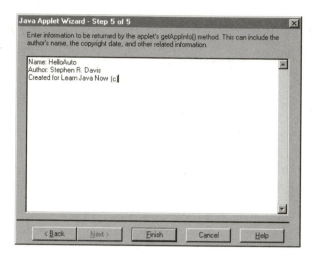

Figure 12-4. *The Step 5 dialog box showing the optional* getAppletInfo
information.

> **NOTE** *getAppletInfo* is somewhat like *toString* in that it's intended to be
> a generic method that the browser can use to get information about the
> applet. In addition, *getAppletInfo* can be used to provide information for
> the applet's About dialog box.

Clicking Finish at this point brings up a summary window that displays a
summary of the options selected. The summary for this applet appears as
shown in Figure 12-5.

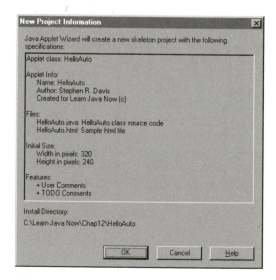

Figure 12-5. *The summary window for the "Hello, world" applet.*

NOTE This summary shows all of the options selected in the AppletWizard. This gives you one last chance to review your selections before creating an applet. For all subsequent applets in this book, I will use this summary window to describe the AppletWizard selections used.

Click OK and the AppletWizard creates a new project and populates it with the *HelloAuto* class. If you make a mistake anywhere along the way, you can back up or cancel and start over.

 NOTE The AppletWizard is a one-time good deal for creating an applet. You cannot edit an existing applet with the AppletWizard. (Of course, you can edit an applet to your heart's content using the IDE editor.) However, if you get all the way to the end and you decide you made a mistake and want to start over again, simply close the project and delete the directory that the AppletWizard created. You can then go back and start over.

The Java Project Window

The Java project window contains three views of your applet. (You can select a view by clicking a tab at the bottom of the project window.) The most useful view is known as the File View. This view shows you the files that go together to make up your applet. There will generally be one HTML file and one or more .java files. You can open any of these files by simply double-clicking on the filename.

The default view is the Class View, which shows the classes that go into your applet. Each of these classes appears as a folder that is similar to the folders in Windows Explorer. Opening a Class View folder shows you the members of the class. The methods are clearly differentiated from the member data. In addition, private members are preceded by a small padlock. You can go straight to the member by double-clicking the member name in the Class View.

The last view is known as the Test View. This view shows the templates that go into your applet.

Coding the "Hello, World" Applet

It's now time to do some Java programming. If the project isn't already visible, display it by choosing the Project Workspace command from the View menu. Display the classes by clicking the ClassView tab and clicking the plus sign in front of the HelloAuto Classes folder. The folder expands to reveal the only class in the project, *HelloAuto*. Now display the members of the *HelloAuto* class by clicking the plus sign in front of it. As you can see in Figure 12-6, this class has a surprising number of methods already.

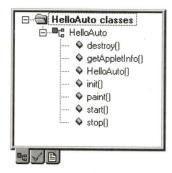

Figure 12-6. *The members of the* HelloAuto *class created by the AppletWizard.*

We know from experience that we'll need to edit the *paint* method. Double-clicking on *paint* opens the HelloAuto.java file and places the cursor in the *paint* method. Add the line *g.drawString("Hello, world", 0, 20);*. The completed HelloAuto.java file appears as follows:

```
//*************************************************************
// HelloAuto.java:     Applet
//
//*************************************************************
import java.applet.*;
import java.awt.*;


//=============================================================
// Main Class for applet HelloAuto
//
//=============================================================
public class HelloAuto extends Applet
{
```

```
// HelloAuto Class Constructor
//-------------------------------------------------------------
public HelloAuto()
{
    // TODO: Add Constructor code here
}

// APPLET INFO SUPPORT:
// The getAppletInfo() method returns a string describing
// the applet's author, copyright date, or miscellaneous
// information.
// HelloAuto information, Author, Copyright, etc.
//-------------------------------------------------------------
public String getAppletInfo()
{
    return "Name: HelloAuto\r\n" +
           "Author: Stephen R. Davis\r\n" +
           "Created for Learn Java Now (c)";
}


// The init() method is called by the AWT when an applet
// is first loaded or reloaded.  Override this method to
// perform whatever initialization your applet needs, such
// as initializing data structures, loading images or fonts,
// creating frame windows, setting the layout manager, or
// adding UI components.
//-------------------------------------------------------------
public void init()
{
    resize(320, 240);

    // TODO: Place Addition Initialization code here
}

// Place additional applet clean up code here.  destroy()
// is called when when your applet is terminating and
// being unloaded.
//-------------------------------------------------------------
public void destroy()
{
    // TODO: Place applet cleanup code here
}
```

(continued)

```
// HelloAuto Paint Handler
//------------------------------------------------------------
public void paint(Graphics g)
{
    g.drawString("Hello, world", 0, 10);
}

// The start() method is called when the page containing the
// applet first appears on the screen. The AppletWizard's
// initial implementation of this method starts execution of
// the applet's thread.
//------------------------------------------------------------
public void start()
{
    // TODO: Place additional applet Start code here
}

// The stop() method is called when the page containing the
// applet is no longer on the screen. The AppletWizard's
// initial implementation of this method stops execution of
// the applet's thread.
//------------------------------------------------------------
public void stop()
{
}

    // TODO: Place additional applet Code here
}
```

The line of code that we had to add to the code created by the Applet-Wizard is shown in bold.

You can now compile and execute the HelloAuto applet just like you did the manual applet in the previous chapter. The results of executing this applet appear identical.

What's the Rest of That Stuff?

Even though it was easier to generate, this automatic version of the "Hello, world" applet seems a lot larger than the manual version we created in the previous chapter. What are all those other methods in *HelloAuto?*

Table 12-1 shows a list of the methods created by the AppletWizard in our simple "Hello, world" applet, along with a brief explanation of their purpose.

Method	Called When...	Common Use
HelloAuto	applet starts	Constructor—used to initialize nonstatic data members in the class.
getAppletInfo	N/A	Returns information about the applet. Can be used to provide information for the About dialog box.
init	applet first starts—called after constructor	Initializes any data structures that *paint* will need. Might also initialize any values that don't change over the life of the applet.
destroy	applet exits	Reverses any steps taken by init.
paint	window needs refreshing	Redraws the contents of the window.
start	browser enters applet window	Starts the applet animation.
stop	browser goes to new HTML page	Stops the applet animation.

Table 12-1. *The methods generated by the AppletWizard for the "Hello world" applet.*

Even though such a simple applet doesn't need any of these methods except *paint,* the AppletWizard doesn't know that. Since these are commonly used methods, the AppletWizard puts in a stub function and adds prompts in the form of comments to remind you what goes in each one.

For example, the following is the *init* function that the AppletWizard generated:

```
// The init() method is called by the AWT when an applet
// is first loaded or reloaded.  Override this method to
// perform whatever initialization your applet needs, such
// as initializing data structures, loading images or fonts,
// creating frame windows, setting the layout manager, or
// adding UI components.
//-------------------------------------------------------------
public void init()
{
    resize(320, 240);

    // TODO: Place Addition Initialization code here
}
```

The lead-in comments explain the *init* method, while the TODO comments serve as prompts.

 N OTE You can turn off either or both of these sets of comments by deselecting these options in the Step 2 dialog box of the AppletWizard. Personally, I find the TODO comments to be extremely helpful even when starting my umpteenth applet.

What Is *init* Again?

The four functions *init, start, stop,* and *destroy* are called in a particular sequence as the user moves into and out of the HTML page containing the applet. The *init* method is invoked the first time the applet is loaded (or whenever it is reloaded) by the browser. The *start* method is called anytime the applet is displayed. The *stop* method is called when the applet is hidden, and the *destroy* method is called when the user abandons the applet.

A typical sequence is as follows. When the user enters the Web page containing the applet, the browser first calls *init* to initialize the applet. It then calls *start* since the window is now visible. Suppose the user clicks on a hot link on this HTML page. Before the browser loads the new Web page, it calls the *stop* method to "stop" the current page. If the current applet is displaying graphical animation, it can use the *stop* method to turn this off to save CPU time. (No one will see the animation anyway because the window isn't visible.)

Now suppose that after some time, the user clicks the back button to re-enter the page. The browser calls *start* again to restart the page. If the user clicks the back button again, the browser calls *stop* to stop the current page, immediately followed by *destroy*. The browser then unloads the applet.

This sequence can be made visible by adding a counter to each of the above methods:

```
//*****************************************************************
// HelloAuto.java:    Applet
//
//*****************************************************************
import java.applet.*;
import java.awt.*;

//================================================================
// Main Class for applet HelloAuto
//
//================================================================
public class HelloAuto extends Applet
{
    // user defined data
    private int m_nInitCnt;
    private int m_nStartCnt;
    private int m_nStopCnt;
    private int m_nDestroyCnt;

    // HelloAuto Class Constructor
    //------------------------------------------------------------
    public HelloAuto()
    {
        m_nInitCnt    = 0;
        m_nStartCnt   = 0;
        m_nStopCnt    = 0;
        m_nDestroyCnt = 0;
    }

    public void init()
    {
        resize(320, 240);

        m_nInitCnt++;
    }
```

(continued)

```
public void destroy()
{
    m_nDestroyCnt++;
}

// HelloAuto Paint Handler
//----------------------------------------------------------------
public void paint(Graphics g)
{
    g.drawString("Hello, world", 0, 10);
    g.drawString("Init count    = " + m_nInitCnt,    0, 20);
    g.drawString("Start count   = " + m_nStartCnt,   0, 30);
    g.drawString("Stop count    = " + m_nStopCnt,    0, 40);
    g.drawString("Destroy count = " + m_nDestroyCnt, 0, 50);
}

public void start()
{
    m_nStartCnt++;
}

public void stop()
{
    m_nStopCnt++;
}
}
```

The results of executing this program are shown in Figure 12-7. (I entered the Web page, moved to a new page, and then returned via the back button several times.)

Figure 12-7. *The result of adding counters to the* init, start, stop, *and* destroy *methods of the* HelloAuto *class.*

Conclusion

While this wasn't much of an applet, the principles you learned in this chapter combined with the knowledge of Java you gained from Part 1 will propel you rapidly into some rather interesting applets.

Chapter 3

Handling Events

All of the applets we've seen so far provide a *paint* method to handle the repaint event. But there are many events besides the repaint event. Events are usually (but not always) associated with external actions such as mouse movement, mouse button clicks, and keystrokes. Sometimes the external actions are more subtle—for example, an event is generated whenever the mouse enters or exits your window.

In this chapter, we'll look at some applets that handle a few of the more common event types. You will be able to apply the principles we discuss here to other event types in your own applets.

Events

All applets inherit the *handleEvent(Event)* method from the *Applet* class. (Actually, *handleEvent* is defined in *Component,* which is a super class of *Applet.*) This method is called whenever an event occurs that needs processing.

The *Event* object passed to *handleEvent* describes the nature of the event that occurred. The *Event* object has the following properties:

■ *id*—a number that identifies the nature of the event.

■ *target*—the object upon which the event occurred. For example, if this is a resize, the object is the window being resized.

- *when*—the time that the event occurred.

- *modifiers*—the modifier state. Includes the state of the Shift, Control, and Alt keys.

- *x,y*—the x and y coordinates of the mouse pointer (for mouse events only).

- *clickCount*—the number of times in a row that the mouse was clicked (mouseDown only).

- *key*—the key that was pressed or released (keyDown and keyUp only).

- *arg*—a second object for some event types (optional).

The default action for most event types is for the applet to ignore the event. To give your applet the capability to handle a particular event, you can overload the *handleEvent(Event evt)* method and test *evt.id*. Fortunately, this isn't usually necessary. The default *handleEvent(Event)* method breaks out the most common events and invokes one of the following methods:

- *mouseEnter*—called when the cursor enters the applet's window.

- *mouseExit*—called when the cursor leaves the applet's window.

- *mouseMove*—called every time the mouse moves, the mouse is within the applet's window, and the mouse button is up.

- *mouseDrag*—called every time the mouse moves, the mouse is within the applet's window, and the mouse button is down.

- *mouseDown*—called when the mouse button is pressed.

- *mouseUp*—called when the mouse button is released.

- *keyDown*—called when a key is pressed on the keyboard and the applet's window has the focus.

- *keyUp*—called when a key is released on the keyboard and the applet's window has the focus.

- *gotFocus*—called when the applet's window gains the focus (becomes the active window).

- *lostFocus*—called when the applet's window loses the focus.

In this chapter, I'll show you a few applets that field some of these events. (One other event type, action events, will be discussed in Chapter 17.)

Mouse Events

The mouse events report three items of particular interest:

- The nature of the event—is it a *mouseMove,* a *mouseClick,* or what?

- The state of the mouse button—is it up or down?

- The location of the mouse. The mouse coordinates are reported in display units from the upper left corner of the window. These are the same units used in the x and y coordinates passed to the graphics draw methods. This simplifies the job of painting with the mouse event information.

 OTE Java does not understand a two-button or three-button mouse, so it does not report the condition of the right or middle buttons.

In the first applet, we'll use the mouse location to place a crosshair on the display. In the second applet, we'll add mouse-click detection. In the third applet, we'll add double-click detection to clear the display.

Mouse Move: The CrossHair Applet

This first applet demonstrates the mouse location by using the *mouseMove* and *mouseDrag* methods to paint a small cross at the current mouse pointer's location. In addition, the applet paints the x and y location numerically in the upper right corner of the window.

Building the CrossHair project

Build the CrossHair project using the AppletWizard. Use the same settings as those used for the "Hello, world" applet, except:

- Disable comments in Step 1 (optional). (I disable them in my applets to reduce the size of the listings for this book. You can leave them on if you like.)

- Set a reasonably sized window in Step 2. I selected 640x480.

- Select mouseDrag/mouseMove interaction in Step 3.

Selecting these options generates the following applet summary:

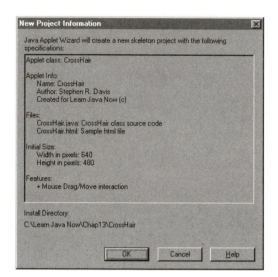

If your options match these, click OK to create the CrossHair project and the boilerplate for your applet.

Filling in the *CrossHair* class

In this initial version, let's paint the cursor location information in the upper left corner of the display. (This is easier.) Once we get that working, we'll move it over to the right side. The completed *CrossHair* class appears as shown below.

 OTE In this and all other applets, I have removed the AppletWizard-generated "do nothing" methods, which I have not modified. This saves book space and allows you to concentrate on the methods that actually do something.

```
//***********************************************************
// CrossHair.java:     Applet
//
//***********************************************************
import java.applet.*;
import java.awt.*;


//===========================================================
// Main Class for applet CrossHair
//
```

```
//================================================================
public class CrossHair extends Applet
{
    // User data here
    private Dimension m_dimCursorLoc;  // location of cursor
    private boolean m_bDrag;     // TRUE->we are currently dragging

    public String getAppletInfo()
    {
        return "Name: CrossHair\r\n" +
                "Author: Stephen R. Davis\r\n" +
                "Created for Learn Java Now (c)";
    }

    public void init()
    {
        resize(640, 480);

    }

    // CrossHair Paint Handler
    //-----------------------------------------------------------
    public void paint(Graphics g)
    {
        // first build a string containing the current cursor
        // location in the format (xx,yy) and output that
        String sCursorLoc = "("
                            + m_dimCursorLoc.width
                            + ","
                            + m_dimCursorLoc.height
                            + ")";
        g.drawString(sCursorLoc, 10, 20);

        // now put an x where the cursor is located
        // (make it red if we are dragging and black if not)
        if (m_bDrag)
        {
            g.setColor(Color.red);
        }
        else
        {
            g.setColor(Color.black);
        }
        int nX = m_dimCursorLoc.width;
        int nY = m_dimCursorLoc.height;
        g.drawLine(nX - 2,    nY, nX + 2,    nY);
        g.drawLine(   nX, nY - 2,    nX, nY + 2);
    }
```

(continued)

205

```
// MOUSE SUPPORT:
//------------------------------------------------------------
public boolean mouseDrag(Event evt, int x, int y)
{

    // set the drag mode to true
    m_bDrag = true;

    // record the mouse location
    m_dimCursorLoc = new Dimension(x, y);

    // now force a repaint - this will repaint the window
    // with the crosshair at the current mouse location
    repaint();

    // returning true indicates that we handled the event
    return true;
}

// MOUSE SUPPORT:
//------------------------------------------------------------
public boolean mouseMove(Event evt, int x, int y)
{

    // same as mouseDrag with drag mode turned off
    m_bDrag = false;
    m_dimCursorLoc = new Dimension(x, y);
    repaint();

    return true;
}
}
```

The first additions to the *CrossHair* class are the data members. The *m_dim-CursorLoc* member is used to store the current location of the mouse cursor. The *m_bDrag* member is set to *true* if this location was reported in a *mouseDrag* event and *false* if it was reported in a *mouseMove* event.

Skipping ahead: The *mouseDrag* method is called with the x and y location of the mouse cursor any time the mouse is moved across the applet's window with the mouse button held down. This method sets the *m_bDrag* member to *true* before storing the mouse location in *m_dimCursorLoc.* It then calls *Applet.repaint,* which causes the browser to refresh the applet's window. *mouseMove* does the same thing, except that it sets the *m_bDrag* member to *false.* The browser repaints the window as soon as it can by calling our *paint* method.

> **N** OTE   Calling *repaint* does NOT cause the browser to call our *paint* method directly. Instead, it tells the browser to repaint the applet's window as soon as it gets around to it.

paint starts by building a string *(x,y)* where *x* is the cursor's x location and *y* is the cursor's y location. This information is taken from *m_dim-CursorLoc,* where either the *mouseDrag* or the *mouseMove* method put it. *paint* outputs this information in the upper left corner of the screen (at location [10,20], to be exact) using the *Graphics.drawString* method.

The CrossHair applet uses the *Graphics.drawLine* method to draw a small cross 3 units across and 3 units high. It does this by drawing a line from the current mouse cursor's x location minus one to the cursor's x location plus one and then repeating the process in the vertical (y) direction. The output from executing this program is shown in Figure 13-1.

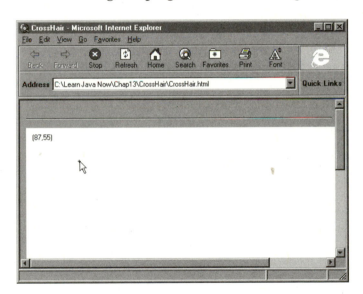

Figure 13-1. *The results of executing the initial CrossHair applet.*

Why not update the window in the *mouseDrag* method?

Why did *mouseDrag* store the mouse pointer location and then force a repaint of the window? Why didn't it just paint the cross itself?

The problem with this "direct" approach is that there are lots of other reasons for repainting a window besides moving the cursor. Suppose, for example, that the applet window is obscured by some other application. When the window is unobscured, the *paint* method is called to restore the window. If the cursor information is not output from the *paint* method, the window remains blank until the *mouseDrag* or *mouseMove* method is invoked.

Of course, we could repaint the window in both the *paint* and *mouseDrag* methods, but that would involve duplicating code. This makes for a maintenance nightmare because changes to one method must be manually transferred to the other. It's much better to leave the painting code in the one method where it must be, *paint,* and invoke it from *mouseDrag* via the *repaint* request.

Using font metrics

This first version of CrossHair is okay, but the original problem was to paint the pointer's x and y location in the upper right corner of the window, not the upper left. For this we will need to know a few things like "How big is the window?" and "How long is our display string?" The following version of CrossHair shows the necessary changes:

```
//**********************************************************
// CrossHair.java:     Applet
//
//**********************************************************
import java.applet.*;
import java.awt.*;

public class CrossHair extends Applet
{
    // User data here
    private Dimension m_dimCursorLoc;  // location of cursor
    private boolean m_bDrag;    // TRUE->we are currently dragging
    private FontMetrics m_fm;  // font metrics

    public void init()
    {
        resize(640, 480);

        // Let's get the font metrics so we know how big our
        // font really is
        Font f = getFont();
        m_fm = getFontMetrics(f);
    }
```

```
// CrossHair Paint Handler
//---------------------------------------------------------------
public void paint(Graphics g)
{
    // first build a string containing the current cursor
    // location in the format (xx,yy)
    String sCursorLoc = "("
                            + m_dimCursorLoc.width
                            + ","
                            + m_dimCursorLoc.height
                            + ")";

    // calculate the y offset of line 2
    // (this is 2 * the height of the font)
    int nY = 2 * m_fm.getHeight();

    // (set x so that the string ends 5 pixels from
    // the right side of the window)
    Dimension dimWinSize = size();     // size of the window
    int nWidth = m_fm.stringWidth(sCursorLoc);
    int nX = dimWinSize.width - (nWidth + 5);

    // now paint the string at that location
    g.drawString(sCursorLoc, nX, nY);

    // now put an x where the cursor is located
    // (make it red if we are dragging and black if not)
    if (m_bDrag)
    {
        g.setColor(Color.red);
    }
    else
    {
        g.setColor(Color.black);
    }
    nX = m_dimCursorLoc.width;
    nY = m_dimCursorLoc.height;
    g.drawLine(nX - 2,      nY, nX + 2,      nY);
    g.drawLine(     nX, nY - 2,      nX, nY + 2);
}

    // ...same for remainder of class...
}
```

The biggest changes to the applet are in *paint*. This new CrossHair applet wants to place the *(x,y)* string two lines from the top and five units from the right edge of the screen.

Did you ever wonder how I knew to use 10 for the y-offset in the "Hello, world" applet? I didn't. I just guessed and hoped that it would be big enough for the font used. A much better approach is to ask the font for its dimensions. This is done by calling *get.FontMetrics*. The *FontMetrics* object returned has information about the height and width of the font characters.

Placing the string on line two means setting the y offset to two times the height of the font. This is the meaning of *2 * m_fm.getHeight*. The *m_fm FontMetrics* member is initialized in the *init* method. (I could request a new *FontMetrics* object on each call to *paint*, but this is unnecessary over-head because the font size will not change.)

Placing the string at the far right is a bit tougher. First the applet must find the width of the window. It does this by calling *Applet.size,* which returns the size of the applet's window. It can't do this once in the *init* member because the user might resize the window.

Next it calculates the length of the string in the current font. This it does by calling *FontMetric.stringWidth,* passing it the *(x,y)* string. From this it calculates the proper place to draw the string. This calculation is shown graphically in Figure 13-2 for the string *(100,100).*

CrossHair Window

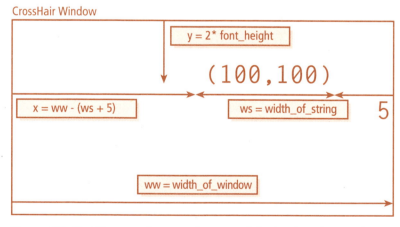

Figure 13-2. *The x and y coordinates of the* (x,y) *string in the CrossHair window.*

Execute the applet and notice that the string now appears in the upper right corner. It stays in the upper right even when the window is resized.

Mouse Clicks: The ConnectTheDots Applet

In this applet, we'll use the *mouseDown* event to create interesting
Spirograph-like patterns by drawing a line between each clicked location
and every other clicked location in the window.

Running the AppletWizard

Create a new ConnectTheDots project using the AppletWizard. Use the
same settings as in the CrossHair applet except also select the Mouse
Down/Up Interaction option. Pick your favorite size for the applet window.
Your applet summary should appear as follows:

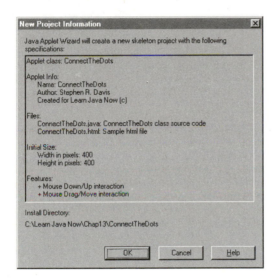

If your summary looks like this, click OK to build the applet boilerplate.

The ConnectTheDots applet

Modify the ConnectTheDots.java file you created with the AppletWizard
as indicated here:

```
//*******************************************************************
// ConnectTheDots.java:    Applet
//
//*******************************************************************
import java.applet.*;
import java.awt.*;

public class ConnectTheDots extends Applet
```

(continued)

```
{
    // user defined data
    // the following is a recording of all
    // previous clicked locations
    static final int m_nMAXLOCS = 100;
    Dimension m_dimLocs[];
    int m_nNumMouseClicks;

    // the current cursor location
    Dimension m_dimCursorLoc;


    public ConnectTheDots()
    {
        // initialize the object data members
        m_dimLocs = new Dimension[m_nMAXLOCS];
        m_nNumMouseClicks = 0;
        m_dimCursorLoc = new Dimension(0, 0);
    }

    public String getAppletInfo()
    {
        return "Name: ConnectTheDots\r\n" +
               "Author: Stephen R. Davis\r\n" +
               "Created for Learn Java Now (c)";
    }


    public void init()
    {
        resize(400, 400);
    }

    public void paint(Graphics g)
    {
        // put a cross where the cursor is located
        int nX = m_dimCursorLoc.width;
        int nY = m_dimCursorLoc.height;
        g.drawLine(nX - 2,      nY, nX + 2,      nY);
        g.drawLine(    nX, nY - 2,      nX, nY + 2);

        // now draw a line from each clicked location
        // to every other clicked location
        for (int i = 0; i < m_nNumMouseClicks - 1; i++)
        {
            for (int j = i + 1; j < m_nNumMouseClicks; j++)
            {
                g.drawLine(m_dimLocs[i].width,
                           m_dimLocs[i].height,
```

```
                                    m_dimLocs[j].width,
                                    m_dimLocs[j].height);
              }
          }
      }

      public boolean mouseDown(Event evt, int x, int y)
      {
          // record the click location (if there's enough room)
          if (m_nNumMouseClicks < m_nMAXLOCS)
          {
              m_dimLocs[m_nNumMouseClicks] = new Dimension(x, y);
              m_nNumMouseClicks++;

              // now force the window to repaint
              repaint();
          }
          return true;
      }

      public boolean mouseUp(Event evt, int x, int y)
      {
          // ignore the mouseUp event
          return true;
      }

      public boolean mouseDrag(Event evt, int x, int y)
      {
          // ignore the mouseDrag event
          return true;
      }

      public boolean mouseMove(Event evt, int x, int y)
      {
          // record the mouse location and repaint it
          m_dimCursorLoc = new Dimension(x, y);
          repaint();
          return true;
      }
  }
```

This applet is similar to the CrossHair applet in that it records the location of the mouse in the *mouseMove* event handler. (This applet ignores the *mouseDrag* event.)

In addition to recording the current mouse location, however, the applet also records the location of the mouse every time a *mouseDown* is called.

It records these mouse locations in the array *m_dimLocs* using the following statement:

```
m_dimLocs[m_nNumMouseClicks] = new Dimension(x, y);
m_nNumMouseClicks++;
```

The *Dimension* class is normally used to hold the size of a window, but it can also be used to store any x and y pair. Notice how the program creates a new *Dimension* object to store into the array. Remember that the statement *m_dimLocs = new Dimension[m_nMAXLOCS]* back in the constructor allocated room not for 100 *Dimension* objects but for 100 references to *Dimension* objects.

The *m_nNumMouseClicks* member keeps track of how many positions in the array are in use. Each new mouse location is stored at the position stored in *m_nNumMouse; m_nNumMouseClicks* is then incremented. The test against *m_nMAXLOCS* is to make sure that the bounds of the array are not exceeded. Each time a new mouse location is added to the list, a call to *repaint* causes the window to be updated.

The *paint* method starts out by painting a crosshair at the current mouse location, much like the CrossHair applet does. It then loops through the mouse click locations recorded in the *m_dimLocs* array. The outer loop starts at 0 and loops through the next to last recorded location (*m_nNumMouseClicks - 1*). The inner loop starts at the outer loop plus one and continues to the last recorded location (*m_nNumMouseClicks*). The *drawLine* method draws a line from the outer location to the inner location.

For example, assume that four clicked locations are recorded. On the first pass, *i* is 0. The inner loop then draws a line from location 0 to location 1, 0 to 2, and 0 to 3. The next pass through the outer loop draws a line from 1 to 2 and 1 to 3. On the third and final pass, *i* is 2 and the inner loop draws from location 2 to 3 and stops.

Figure 13-3 shows a typical execution run from this applet demonstrating just one of the interesting patterns you can create.

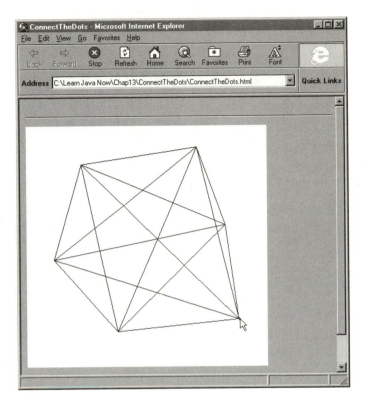

Figure 13-3. *The results of executing the ConnectTheDots applet.*

 OTE You might notice that as the Spirograph-like pattern gets more and more complicated, it starts to flicker a bit as you move the mouse or add a node. The effect is barely noticeable on most machines; however, this is just a hint of bigger problems to come when we start performing applet animation. We'll discuss how to cure the flickers in Chapter 15.

Mouse Double-Clicks

At times it is convenient to distinguish between a single click and a double-click. Both come through the *mouseDown* method; however, the *click-Count* field of the *Event* object passed to the *mouseDown* method is set to indicate the number of times in a row the mouse has been clicked. If the click count is 1, this is a single click; if 2, it's a double-click, and so forth.

 OTE Don't forget that the first click of a double-click is reported with the *clickCount* set to 1. The second click is then reported at the same location with the *clickCount* set to 2.

The updated ConnectTheDots applet

The ConnectTheDots applet has two minor problems. The first problem
is that there is no way to clear the screen. Let's use the double-click as a
clear-the-screen indication. While we're at it, we can fix the second problem: The applet is limited to storing *m_nMAXLOCS* number of mouse
clicks. While this number can be made arbitrarily large, we want the array
to grow as necessary to accommodate however many mouse clicks the
user might enter.

```java
//***************************************************************
// ConnectTheDots.java:     Applet
//
//***************************************************************
import java.applet.*;
import java.awt.*;
import java.util.Vector;

public class ConnectTheDots extends Applet
{
    // the following is a recording of all
    // previous clicked locations
    Vector m_vLocs;

    // the current cursor location
    Dimension m_dimCursorLoc;


    public ConnectTheDots()
    {
        m_vLocs = new Vector();
        m_dimCursorLoc = new Dimension(0, 0);
    }

    public String getAppletInfo()
    {
        return "Name: ConnectTheDots\r\n" +
               "Author: Stephen R. Davis\r\n" +
               "Created for Learn Java Now (c)";
    }


    public void init()
    {
        resize(400, 400);
    }

    public void paint(Graphics g)
```

```
    {
        // put an x where the cursor is located
        int nX = m_dimCursorLoc.width;
        int nY = m_dimCursorLoc.height;
        g.drawLine(nX - 2,      nY, nX + 2,      nY);
        g.drawLine(    nX, nY - 2,      nX, nY + 2);

        // now draw a line from each click location
        // to every other click location
        Dimension dimFrom;
        Dimension dimTo;
        int nSize = m_vLocs.size();
        for (int i = 0; i < nSize - 1; i++)
        {
            dimFrom = (Dimension)m_vLocs.elementAt(i);
            for (int j = i + 1; j < nSize; j++)
            {
                dimTo = (Dimension)m_vLocs.elementAt(j);
                g.drawLine(dimFrom.width, dimFrom.height,
                           dimTo.width,   dimTo.height   );
            }
        }
    }

    public boolean mouseDown(Event evt, int x, int y)
    {
        // in the event of a double-click...
        if (evt.clickCount > 1)
        {
            // ...remove all elements from the vector...
            m_vLocs.removeAllElements();
        }
        else
        {
            // ...otherwise, add an element
            m_vLocs.addElement(new Dimension(x, y));
        }
        repaint();
        return true;
    }


    public boolean mouseMove(Event evt, int x, int y)
    {
        // record the mouse location and repaint it
        m_dimCursorLoc = new Dimension(x, y);
        repaint();
        return true;
    }
}
```

In this version, the fixed array *m_dimLocs* has been replaced by an object named *m_vLocs,* which is of class *Vector*. *Vector* is like a dynamically re-sizable array. This array can grow as necessary to accommodate the number of objects you want to hold (up to the bounds of available memory, of course). *m_vLocs* is initialized in the *ConnectTheDots* class constructor. The constructor creates an empty *Vector* object.

The *mouseDown* method records a mouse click location by creating a *Dimension* object, just as it did before. This time, however, it adds the *Dimension* object to *m_vLocs* using the *Vector.addElement* method.

The loop within *paint* sports only two differences from the fixed array model. First, it is no longer necessary to keep a count of the number of elements in the array. *Vector* does that for us. *paint* asks *m_vLocs* how many elements it has by calling *size*. Second, *paint* uses the method *element-At* to fetch a reference to the object at that index. However, the object returned from *elementAt* must be cast to a *Dimension* before it can be used.

 OTE   Remember that *Vector* does not know what kind of object it is storing; but also remember that this cast is type safe. Thus, if *Vector* contains something other than *Dimension* objects, the cast throws a *BadCastException*.

The test for screen clear is in *mouseDown*. If *mouseDown* sees a double-click, it clears the list of recorded mouse locations by calling *Vector*'s *removeAllElements* method. Calling *repaint* removes all lines from the window.

Keyboard Events: The ScreenType Applet

The keystroke event signals that a key has been pressed or released. These events are normally processed by the *keyDown* and *keyUp* methods. The Unicode character of the key pressed or released is passed to the function; special codes are assigned to unprintable keys like the function keys and the arrow keys.

The ScreenType applet demonstrates the fielding of the key events. It is nothing more than a very simple notepad. The user clicks the mouse where she wants to type and then begins typing. The applet has little or no intelligence—it does not interpret backspace or carriage returns and it cannot save the notes to disk.

Running the AppletWizard

You create the boilerplate for the ScreenType applet using the Applet-Wizard. The only mouse event option to select is Mouse Down/Up inter-action. (The AppletWizard does not offer a menu option to automatically create *keyUp* and *keyDown* methods. We have to add these ourselves.)

The summary for the ScreenType applet should appear as follows:

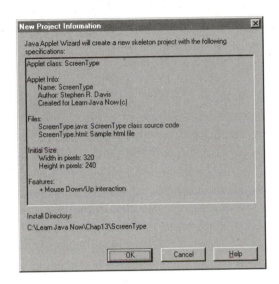

The ScreenType Applet

The additions to the ScreenType boilerplate are indicated in bold:

```
//*****************************************************************
// ScreenType.java:      Applet
//
//*****************************************************************
import java.applet.*;
import java.awt.*;
import java.util.Vector;

public class ScreenType extends Applet
{
    // key the keystrokes in a vector
    private Vector m_vKeys;

    // the current character location
    private Dimension m_dimLoc;
```

(continued)

```java
    // the font metrics for this applet's window
    private FontMetrics m_fm;

    public ScreenType()
    {
        // create a vector with enough room for 100 key
        // objects. Let it grow by 100 at a time. This will
        // be faster than the default.
        m_vKeys = new Vector(100, 100);

        // get a dimension object somewhere in the window
        m_dimLoc = new Dimension(10, 10);
    }

    public String getAppletInfo()
    {
        return "Name: ScreenType\r\n" +
               "Author: Stephen R. Davis\r\n" +
               "Created for Learn Java Now (c)";
    }

    public void init()
    {
        // set initial screen size
        resize(320, 240);

        // get font metrics here to save time
        m_fm = getFontMetrics(getFont());
    }

    public void paint(Graphics g)
    {
        // loop through the saved Key objects
        int nSize = m_vKeys.size();
        for (int i = 0; i < nSize; i++)
        {
            // get the key
            Key key = (Key)m_vKeys.elementAt(i);

            // from the key get the keystroke and the location
            Dimension dimLoc = key.GetLoc();
            char[] cKey = key.GetKey();

            // output the key and location
            g.drawChars(cKey, 0, 1, dimLoc.width, dimLoc.height);
        }
    }

    public boolean mouseDown(Event evt, int x, int y)
```

```
        {
            // on double-clicks...
            if (evt.clickCount > 1)
            {
                // ...clear everything out;...
                m_vKeys.removeAllElements();
                repaint();
            }
            else
            {
                // ...otherwise, just update the location
                m_dimLoc.width = x;
                m_dimLoc.height = y;
            }
            return true;
        }

        public boolean keyDown(Event evt,
                               int nKey)
        {
            // add key at the current location
            m_vKeys.addElement(new Key(nKey, m_dimLoc));

            // now update the location for the next character
            // by moving it over the width of this character
            // (remember that different characters are different
            // widths)
            m_dimLoc.width += m_fm.charWidth(nKey);

            // okay to repaint now
            repaint();
            return true;
        }
}
```

ScreenType takes essentially the same approach for keystrokes as the ConnectTheDots applet does for mouse clicks. Each keystroke is recorded in the *Vector* data member *m_vKeys*. In addition, ScreenType saves the character write location in *m_dimLoc* and the font metrics in *m_fm*. (The character write location is the location within the window where the next character will go.)

The *ScreenType* class constructor demonstrates a different constructor of the *Vector* class. This constructor tells *Vector* how much space to allocate initially and how much more space to allocate each time the available space runs out. (The ConnectTheDots applet simply left it up to the

Vector class to decide on its own. The *Vector* class will still work with these default values, but performance might not be optimal. If we have an idea of how many objects we might be putting in the *Vector,* we should pass that knowledge along.)

Jumping ahead to the event methods: *mouseDown* works basically the same as it did in the ConnectTheDots applet. *mouseDown* updates the write location each time the user performs a single click. One difference, however, is that this version of *mouseDown* does not allocate a new *Dimension* object every time the write location changes. Since the *width* and *height* members of *Dimension* are public, it simply updates their value. This is more efficient than allocating a new one each time.

The *keyDown* method uses the *Key* class to store the keystroke along with the current write location. The *Key* class appears at the bottom of this section. Once the keystroke has been recorded, *keyDown* updates the write location for the next character by moving *m_dimLoc* to the right one character width. This raises a question, however. How far should *keyDown* move the write location?

As you've seen already, *FontMetrics* defines a *getHeight* that returns the height of the current font. It might be logical to assume that there is a similar *getWidth* function to return the width of a character in the current font, but there isn't. The problem is that most fonts are proportional. This means that each character is allocated only the amount of space from left to right that it needs to display. The result is more pleasing to the eye than the older nonproportional or monospaced fonts. (This text is in a proportional font, while the code listings in this book are monospaced.)

Fortunately, there is a *FontMetrics.charWidth(int)* method that returns the width of a particular character in the specified font.

> **NOTE** Of course, if there were no *charWidth* method in the *FontMetrics* class, I could use *stringWidth(String)* and pass an entire string. (This is the function I used in the CrossHair applet.) This method returns the width of an entire string in the current font.

Once the character has been saved and the write location has moved over, it is time to repaint the window to make the new character visible.

The *paint* method is straightforward. The function loops through the *Key* objects saved in *m_vKeys*. It draws each one using the *Graphics.drawChars* method at the location stored in the *Key* object.

The *Key* helper class used to store keystrokes and their location appears as follows:

```
class Key
{
    private char[] m_cKey;
    private Dimension m_dimLoc;

    public Key(int nKey, Dimension dimLoc)
    {
        // store the character in an array of 1;
        // this is more convenient because drawChars
        // back up in paint wants an array
        m_cKey = new char[1];
        m_cKey[0] = (char)nKey;

        // use the same type constructor to make our own
        // copy of the Dimension object with the location
        m_dimLoc = new Dimension(dimLoc);
    }

    Dimension GetLoc()
    {
        return m_dimLoc;
    }

    char[] GetKey()
    {
        return m_cKey;
    }
}
```

This class contains the normal access methods *GetLoc* and *GetKey*. One interesting point is that the character is saved not as a single key but as an array of keys of the length one. This is only because the *drawChars* function back in *paint* wants an array of characters. Saving the character in an array, therefore, makes the class easier for ScreenType to use.

A second point is more fundamental. The constructor for the *Key* class makes its own copy of the *Dimension* object provided. This is shown graphically in Figure 13-4. It does this by calling one of the constructors for the *Dimension* class as follows:

```
m_dimLoc = new Dimension(dimLoc);
```

Once the constructor finishes, *m_dimLoc* does not reference *dimLoc* but rather a new *Dimension* object that contains the same information that *dimLoc* contains. In this way, the new *Key* object is not affected if the calling program later changes the width or height stored in its copy of the *Dimension* object passed to *Key*.

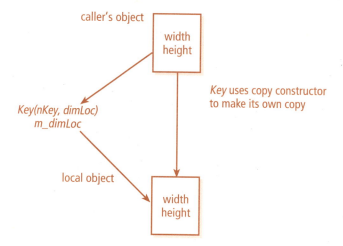

Figure 13-4. *The results of making our own copy of* dimLoc.

> **NOTE** In ScreenType, the *Key* class must make a copy of the *Dimension* object because the *Dimension* object in the calling method is changing all the time. However, any time you don't know or can't assume the calling function doesn't change the object, it is safer to make your own copy of passed objects. That way, you don't care whether the calling function changes the original object or not.

> **NOTE** The *Key* class can appear in the same .java file as ScreenType because *Key* is not declared public. If it were public, it would have to be in its own .java file. If you want to move *Key* to its own .java file anyway, don't forget to add the new Key.java file to the project.

A Faster ScreenType Applet

All of the applets we've seen so far use the *repaint* method with no arguments to force the entire window to be repainted whenever anything changes. In most cases, this is overkill. In particular, the ScreenType applet redraws the entire window even when the only thing that has happened is the addition of a single character. It would be much faster to redraw only the part of the screen that has changed.

Java supports this using the *repaint(int, int, int, int)* method. This function accepts the upper left and lower right corners of the box to be repainted. This box is known as the **invalid rectangle**. Anything within the invalid rectangle is assumed to be invalid and needs to be repainted. Only changes that fall within the invalid rectangle are repainted. The *repaint* method with no arguments builds an invalid rectangle that includes the entire window.

The following version of *keyDown* calls the more conservative *repaint(int, int, int, int)* method to invalidate only the box containing the newly typed character:

```
public boolean keyDown(Event evt,
                       int nKey)
{
    // add key at the current location
    m_vKeys.addElement(new Key(nKey, m_dimLoc));

    // perform a minimal repaint (just the box containing
    // the character)
    int nL, nR, nT, nB;
    nL = m_dimLoc.width;
    nR = nL + m_fm.charWidth(nKey);
    nB = m_dimLoc.height;
    nT = nB - m_fm.getHeight();

    repaint(nL, nT, nR, nB);

    // now update the location for the next character
    // by moving it over the width of this character
    // (remember that different characters are different
    // widths)
    m_dimLoc.width += m_fm.charWidth(nKey);

    return true;
}
```

The function starts with *nL*, which is the left side of the invalid rectangle. This is set to the x value of the current write location. From this the function calculates *nR*, the right side, by adding the width of the current character. *nB*, the bottom of the invalid rectangle, is the y value of the current write location. *nT*, the top, is therefore *nB* minus the height of the current font.

 N **OTE** Remember that y increases down the screen. Thus, *nB* is numerically larger than *nT*.

This is shown graphically in Figure 13-5.

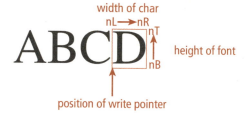

Figure 13-5. *The box surrounding the character shows only the area we really need repainted.*

Notice that the *paint* method still goes through the motions of attempting to repaint all of the characters stored. However, the *Graphics* object passed to *paint* ignores attempts to draw to areas outside the invalid rectangle.

Why doesn't *paint* limit itself to redrawing only the most recent character instead of messing around with this invalid rectangle stuff? Remember that *paint* is called for a lot of different reasons that have nothing to do with typing characters. For example, *paint* is called when the applet's window has been hidden and is redisplayed. In this case, the entire window is invalid and needs to be refreshed. Thus, *paint* must be prepared to restore the entire window.

Maintaining an invalid rectangle in the *Graphics* object is the best compromise between performance (avoiding repainting areas that don't need to be repainted) and code complexity (forcing *repaint* to keep track of why it has been called and exactly what it should repaint).

Conclusion

In this chapter, you've learned how to process the most common event types. In addition, you've learned a few tricks along the way, such as how to use the *Vector* class and how to build an invalid rectangle to repaint only those portions of the screen that need repainting.

In the next chapter, you'll find out how to use Java's multithreading mechanism to create, control, and terminate multiple threads of control.

Multithreading

Many of the Web pages that you see these days feature a so-called Panning Marquee. This is a marquee-type window in which text slowly pans from left to right like the Times Square marquee in Manhattan. In fact, the Panning Marquee is probably the single most popular Java applet in use today. Not to be outdone, let's build a Panning Marquee of our own.

The StaticMarquee Applet

You have to learn to crawl before you can walk, so let's start by creating a marquee that doesn't scroll. Once we have this StaticMarquee applet working, we can add panning capability relatively easily.

Creating the Boilerplate

First we'll create the boilerplate for the StaticMarquee applet using the AppletWizard. This time we won't need any of the special event handlers or multithreading. However, we will use the parameters feature. When you get to the Step 4 dialog box, fill in the parameters as shown in Figure 14-1 on the next page.

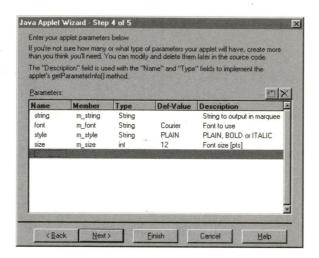

Figure 14-1. *The completed Step 4 dialog box for the StaticMarquee applet.*

The parameter window is a bit tricky to fill in until you get used to it. I use the following steps:

■ Name—Click in the first blank row in the Name column and fill in the name of the parameter. Don't worry about the rest of the columns at this point. Repeat this procedure for each parameter you want to enter.

■ Type—The AppletWizard sets each parameter to the default type *String*. For any parameters for which this is incorrect, go back and double-click on the *String* type label. A little arrow will appear on the right of the field. Click on this arrow and a drop-down menu will appear showing the intrinsic types. Select the type you want for this parameter from the list.

■ Default value—Update the default value in a similar way. When entering a string, don't include the quotes.

■ Description—Repeat the process for the description. The description is optional (but a good idea); it isn't used for anything except documentation.

When you finish, the applet summary should appear as shown on the facing page. (The box is scrolled down to show the important information.)

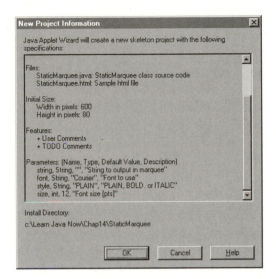

If yours looks like this, click OK to create the applet framework.

Filling In the Blanks

The amount of code we have to enter to complete this applet is quite small compared to the amount of code that is generated for us. The added code that makes this applet unique is shown below in bold type:

```
import java.applet.*;
import java.awt.*;

public class StaticMarquee extends Applet
{
    String m_string = "";
    String m_font = "Courier";
    String m_style = "PLAIN";
    int m_size = 12;

    // parameter names. to change the name of a parameter,
    // you need only make a single change. simply modify
    // the value of the parameter string below.
    //-----------------------------------------------------------
    final String PARAM_string = "string";
    final String PARAM_font = "font";
    final String PARAM_style = "style";
    final String PARAM_size = "size";
```

(continued)

231

```
public StaticMarquee()
{
}

public String getAppletInfo()
{
    return "Name: StaticMarquee\r\n" +
            "Author: Stephen R. Davis\r\n" +
            "Created for Learn Java Now (c)";
}

public String[][] getParameterInfo()
{
    String[][] info =
    {
        { PARAM_string, "String",
                            "String to output in marquee" },
        { PARAM_font, "String", "Font to use" },
        { PARAM_style, "String", "PLAIN, BOLD or ITALIC" },
        { PARAM_size, "int", "Font size [pts]" },
    };
    return info;
}

public void init()
{
    String param;

    param = getParameter(PARAM_string);
    if (param != null)
        m_string = param;

    param = getParameter(PARAM_font);
    if (param != null)
        m_font = param;

    param = getParameter(PARAM_style);
    if (param != null)
        m_style = param;

    param = getParameter(PARAM_size);
    if (param != null)
        m_size = Integer.parseInt(param);

    // resize(600, 80);

    // create the font here based on the parameters entered
    int nStyle = Font.PLAIN;
    if (m_style.equalsIgnoreCase("BOLD"))
```

```
        {
            nStyle = Font.BOLD;
        }
        if (m_style.equalsIgnoreCase("ITALIC"))
        {
            nStyle = Font.ITALIC;
        }

        Font font = new Font(m_font, nStyle, m_size);

        // now make this the font for this applet's window
        setFont(font);
    }

    public void paint(Graphics g)
    {
        // nVertOffset is calculated to center the string
        // vertically in the window
        int nVertOffset = size().height;
        nVertOffset = (nVertOffset - m_size) / 2;
        g.drawString(m_string, 5, nVertOffset + m_size);
    }
}
```

The StaticMarquee applet uses the PARAM feature of the HTML language to determine both what to output and the details of the font to use in outputting it. (If you don't remember PARAM, look back at Table 11-1, which describes some of the HTML commands.) If you look into the example HTML file that the AppletWizard created, you'll see several examples of the PARAM command:

```
<applet
    code=StaticMarquee.class
    width=600
    height=80 >
    <param name=string value="">
    <param name=font value="Courier">
    <param name=style value="PLAIN">
    <param name=size value=12>
</applet>
```

Suppose I edit the default StaticMarquee.html file to the following:

```
<applet
    code=StaticMarquee.class
    width=600
    height=80 >
```

(continued)

233

```
        <param name=string value="This is a test string">
        <param name=font value="Algerian">
        <param name=style value="PLAIN">
        <param name=size value=12>
</applet>
```

To see how this works, let's consider the font selection. The AppletWizard-generated code reads this parameter using the *getParameter* method, as follows:

```
param = getParameter(PARAM_font);
if (param != null)
    m_string = param;
```

PARAM_font is a string with the value *font*. The *getParameter* function searches the parameter list of the applet HTML command for a PARAM command whose name has the value *font*. If it finds one, *getParameter* returns a string with the contents of the corresponding *value* field. In our case, that would be the string *Algerian*. If *getParameter* doesn't find a parameter with that name, it returns null, in which case the program stays with the default string *Courier*. Thus, if the user doesn't specify otherwise, she gets a Courier font; however, the program provides a straightforward method for selecting a font without having to edit the actual Java code.

 OTE Using a default font, font size, and font style seems okay, but it might make more sense to throw an exception and exit if there is no string defined in the HTML file.

Notice that in the case of the *int m_size,* the AppletWizard code converts the string returned by *getParameter* using the *Integer.parseInt* method.

I then create a *Font* object based on the font name, style, and size specified by the parameters. (The style was calculated by comparing the style provided against "PLAIN", "BOLD", and "ITALIC".) The *Font* object is then passed to *setFont(Font)* to become the default font for this applet window.

 OTE You can use any font that your computer knows about. Basically, this means any font that shows up in the list of fonts in your word processor.

The marquee string is displayed in the *paint* method. *paint* displays the string five units from the left side of the window and centered roughly vertically. The line is centered vertically by subtracting the height of the font from the height of the window and dividing the result by 2. The result should be the amount of "pad" above the line of text drawn in the applet.

 OTE I commented out the *size* command in *init* so that it won't override the height and width set in the HTML file. This way, all aspects of the static marquee can be controlled from the HTML file.

Figure 14-2 shows the typical output from StaticMarquee after editing the HTML file to display the text *Learn Java Now.*

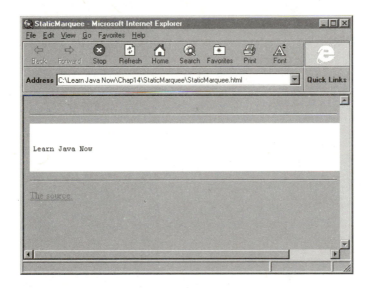

Figure 14-2. *The output from the StaticMarquee applet. This marquee doesn't scroll.*

A Panning Marquee

Now that you've seen the StaticMarquee applet at work, let's go back and do it again, but this time we'll add panning capability. To do that we have to make use of Java's multithreading capability.

Multithreading? What's That?

The key to making the marquee scroll is to repeatedly repaint the display string inside the marquee window with the x offset set progressively further to the left (that is, progressively smaller in value). Java automatically clips any part of the string that extends outside the window, either to the left or the right.

You might be tempted to try something like the following:

```java
void paint(Graphics g)
{
    while (true)
    {
        sleep(10);      // wait a little while between moves
        g.drawString(m_string, nXOffset, nYOffset);
        nXOffset--;     // move offset to the left
    }
}
```

This appears to solve the problem. The first time the browser calls *paint* to repaint the marquee window, the function enters an infinite loop. The call to *sleep* pauses some amount of time (in this case, 10 milliseconds). The function then draws the string at the current x offset. Decrementing the x offset causes the string to move over one unit to the left the next time it's displayed.

Unfortunately, this doesn't work. The problem is that when the browser calls *paint* to repaint the window, *paint* never returns. The marquee might or might not pan, but the user won't notice because he'll be so mad that the browser hung up. The problem is that as long as control is tied up in the *paint* method, the browser can't service any of the other events that might be occurring. What we have to do is to move the infinite loop with the *sleep* to another thread that can execute in parallel with the browser.

Java supports multithreading through the *Thread* class. To create a thread, the program creates an object of class *Thread*. The *Thread* object is used to store the state of the system when the thread doesn't have control. The argument to the *Thread* constructor is an object of a class that implements the *Runnable* interface. There's only one member in the *Runnable* interface, the method *run*.

The new thread doesn't actually start executing until the parent thread calls *Thread.start*. At this point, the parent thread returns from the call to *start* while the new thread begins executing the *run* method of your *Runnable* class.

Calling *Thread.stop* stops the thread from executing. Returning from the *run* method causes an automatic call to *stop.*

In practice this appears as follows:

```
class MyRunnableClass implements Runnable
{
    // this is a reference to the thread object that
    // will describe the thread that we are executing
    Thread m_thread;

    // control passes here as soon as the thread starts.
    // if this method returns, the thread stops automatically
    public void run()
    {
        // do whatever you like, including sitting in an
        // infinite loop
    }

    // this function starts executing MyRunnableClass.run as
    // a separate thread of execution
    void startNewThread()
    {
        // create a new thread of control; tie this thread
        // to our MyRunnableClass object
        m_thread = new Thread(this);

        // now start the thread executing; this will cause
        // the run function to be called under a new
        // thread. the function that called this function
        // will continue to execute in parallel.
        m_thread.start();
    }
}
```

NOTE This is not the only way to use the *Thread* class to create a new thread of execution, but this is the way the AppletWizard uses it. This approach is also the most flexible.

> ## Multithreading vs. Multiprocessing
>
> You've seen multiprocessing already—undoubtedly you've learned how to play Solitaire during long downloads from the Internet or long print jobs. Multiprocessing allows the operating system to execute more than one program at a time. (Of course, they don't really execute at the same time. Each program executes until it is blocked, at which time control of the CPU is passed to the next process.)
>
> Under Microsoft Windows 95 and Microsoft Windows NT, each process has its own memory space to prevent one process from interfering with the others. Multithreading is similar to multiprocessing except that the different threads execute in the same memory space. This means that when one thread crashes it can crash the other threads in the same process. On the other hand, there is less overhead in keeping track of a thread than there is in keeping track of a process.

Creating the Boilerplate

You create the boilerplate for the Marquee applet using the AppletWizard. In the Step 3 dialog box, select Yes for "Would you like your applet to be multi-threaded?" Select No for "Would you like support for animation?" In Step 4 set up the same parameters as you used in the StaticMarquee program except add the parameter *fps,* which is an *int* with the default value 10 and the description *Frame rate.* The applet summary window should appear as shown on the facing page. (Again, the box is scrolled down.)

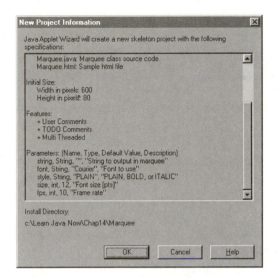

Making the Marquee Scroll

The code for the panning marquee appears as follows. Again, the code in bold represents additions to the code generated by the AppletWizard.

```java
import java.applet.*;
import java.awt.*;

public class Marquee extends Applet implements Runnable
{
    Thread m_Marquee = null;

    String m_string = "";
    String m_font = "Courier";
    String m_style = "PLAIN";
    int m_size = 12;
    int m_fps = 10;

    // parameter names. to change a name of a parameter,
    // you need only make a single change. simply modify
    // the value of the parameter string below.
    //-------------------------------------------------------
    final String PARAM_string = "string";
    final String PARAM_font = "font";
    final String PARAM_style = "style";
    final String PARAM_size = "size";
    final String PARAM_fps = "fps";
```

(continued)

```
// the following data members are used to keep track of the
// minimum and maximum x offset of the text. this is what
// makes the applet scroll.
private int m_nOffset;
private int m_nMax;
private int m_nMin;

public String getAppletInfo()
{
    return "Name: Marquee\r\n" +
            "Author: Stephen R. Davis\r\n" +
            "Created for Learn Java Now (c)";
}

public String[][] getParameterInfo()
{
    String[][] info =
    {
        { PARAM_string, "String", "String to output" },
        { PARAM_font, "String", "Font to use" },
        { PARAM_style, "String", "PLAIN, BOLD or ITALIC" },
        { PARAM_size, "int", "Font size [pts]" },
        { PARAM_fps, "int", "Frame rate" },
    };
    return info;
}

public void init()
{
    String param;

    param = getParameter(PARAM_string);
    if (param != null)
        m_string = param;

    param = getParameter(PARAM_font);
    if (param != null)
        m_font = param;

    param = getParameter(PARAM_style);
    if (param != null)
        m_style = param;

    param = getParameter(PARAM_size);
    if (param != null)
        m_size = Integer.parseInt(param);

    param = getParameter(PARAM_fps);
    if (param != null)
```

```
            m_fps = Integer.parseInt(param);

    // resize(600, 80);

    // create the font here based on the parameters entered
    int nStyle = Font.PLAIN;
    if (m_style.equalsIgnoreCase("BOLD"))
    {
        nStyle = Font.BOLD;
    }
    if (m_style.equalsIgnoreCase("ITALIC"))
    {
        nStyle = Font.ITALIC;
    }

    Font font = new Font(m_font, nStyle, m_size);

    // now make this the font for this applet's window
    setFont(font);

    // now calculate the size of the string in the current
    // font. use this information to set the minimum and
    // maximum x offset.
    // calculate the left boundary by measuring the
    // size of the message in the current font.
    FontMetrics fm = getFontMetrics(font);
    m_nMin = -fm.stringWidth(m_string);

    // the right margin is the width of the window
    m_nMax = size().width;

    // now start the string at the far right of the window
    m_nOffset  = m_nMax;
}

public void destroy()
{
    // TODO: Place applet cleanup code here
}

public void paint(Graphics g)
{
    int nVertOffset = size().height;
    nVertOffset = (nVertOffset - m_size) / 2;
    g.drawString(m_string, m_nOffset, nVertOffset + m_size);

    // now decrement the offset so that the next
    // time the string will appear one pixel to the left
```

(continued)

241

```
        // (once the entire string has scrolled off to the left,
        // restart it at the far right)
        m_nOffset--;
        if (m_nOffset < m_nMin)
        {
            m_nOffset = m_nMax;
        }
    }

    public void start()
    {
        if (m_Marquee == null)
        {
            m_Marquee = new Thread(this);
            m_Marquee.start();
        }
    }

    public void stop()
    {
        if (m_Marquee != null)
        {
            m_Marquee.stop();
            m_Marquee = null;
        }
    }

    public void run()
    {
        while (true)
        {
            // calculate the sleep time based on the frames
            // per second. sleep time is in units of
            // milliseconds.
            int nSleepValue = 1000 / m_fps;
            try
            {
                // repaint the window every nSleepValue
                // milliseconds
                repaint();

                // Thread.sleep(50); // we don't want the default
                Thread.sleep(nSleepValue);
            }
            catch (InterruptedException e)
            {
                // TODO: Place Exception handling code here in
                // case an InterruptedException is thrown by
```

```
                    // Thread.sleep(), meaning that another thread
                    // has interrupted this one
                    stop();
                }
            }
        }
    }
```

The beginning of the Marquee applet's *init* method is identical to the StaticMarquee *init* method except for the addition of the *fps* parameter. The *fps* parameter is the pan rate in frames per second. The final section of *init* calculates the width of the window and the length of the string in the specified font. The latter is used to decide when it is time to restart the display at the far right of the window.

Skipping ahead, you see that the *start* method is invoked when the window is displayed. This function creates a thread with the *Marquee* class. Notice that the *Marquee* class still extends *Applet,* but in addition it now implements *Runnable.* *Marquee.start* then calls the *Thread.start* method. When the new thread starts, it calls *Marquee.run* in its own execution thread. This method sits in a loop, alternately sleeping for the proper length of time commensurate with the requested frame rate and then invoking *repaint* to force the browser to repaint the marquee's window.

The *paint* method starts out the same as that of the StaticMarquee applet. Once the string is displayed, however, this version of *paint* decrements *m_nOffset,* the x offset of the string, so that the next time the string is displayed it moves to the left one unit (pixel). Once *m_nOffset* is less than *m_nMin,* meaning that the entire string has scrolled off the left of the window, *m_nOffset* is reset to *m_nMax,* which is the far right of the window.

The result of executing this program appears identical to the Static-Marquee output on the printed page, but a static view doesn't do it justice. Try executing the program for yourself with different settings for *string, font, size,* and *fps.*

Notice that as you increase the frame rate the panning speed of the marquee gradually speeds up. After a certain point, however, the program starts spending all of its time panning. Increasing the frame rate beyond that point has no effect on the panning speed.

Multiple Marquees

The panning Marquee applet gives me an opportunity to demonstrate graphically two points to which I alluded earlier:

- An applet is associated with an APPLET command within an HTML page and should be viewed in the context of that page.

- A single HTML page can have multiple applets.

The following HTML page invokes the *Marquee* class twice, each with a different string, a different font, and a different frame rate.

```
<html>
<head>
<title>Marquee</title>
</head>
<body>
<hr>
<h2> This is one marquee: </h2>
<applet
    code=Marquee.class
    width=600
    height=80 >
    <param name=string value="Learn Java Now with Visual J++">
    <param name=font value="Courier">
    <param name=style value="PLAIN">
    <param name=size value=18>
    <param name=fps value=10>
</applet>
<hr>
<h2> This is a second marquee: </h2>
<applet
    code=Marquee.class
    width=600
    height=60 >
    <param name=string
            value="The AppletWizard makes Java programming easy">
    <param name=font value="Arial">
    <param name=style value="ITALIC">
    <param name=size value=16>
    <param name=fps value=30>
</applet>
<hr>
<a href="Marquee.java">The source.</a>
</body>
</html>
```

The results of executing this HTML page under Netscape Navigator 2.0 are shown in Figure 14-3. The upper marquee displays the text *Learn Java Now with Visual J++* in an 18-point Courier font and pans across at 10 frames per second. The lower marquee simultaneously displays the text *The AppletWizard makes Java programming easy* in a 16-point italic Arial font that pans at 30 frames per second.

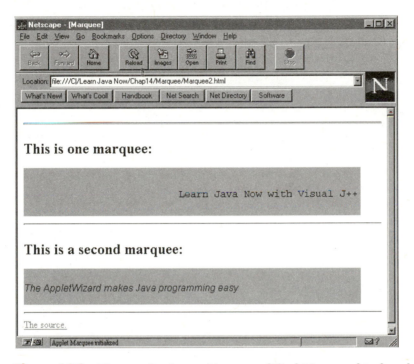

Figure 14-3. *The result of executing a modified Marquee.html under Netscape Navigator 2.0 showing two marquees panning at different rates.*

Resource Locking

One of the most complicated areas of multithreaded programming is resource collisions. A **collision** occurs when two threads attempt to update the same memory location simultaneously. Resource collisions can arise in extremely subtle ways. In addition, since such collisions sometimes rely on very small timing windows, the program might execute for hours before the problem arises.

For a graphic example of a collision, consider our old *BankAccount* class:

```
class BankAccount
{
    private double dBalance;
    public void Withdrawal(double dAmount)
    {
        // let's make this function as simple as possible
        dBalance = dBalance - dAmount;
    }
}
```

The *Withdrawal* method seems simple enough, but believe it or not, it isn't correct. If two different threads have access to the same bank account, the following scenario is certainly possible (although unlikely):

1. Thread 1 reads the current *dBalance* into a register of the CPU.

2. Thread 1 subtracts *dAmount* from the register.

3. Thread 1 loses control of the CPU to thread 2.

4. Thread 2 reads the current *dBalance* (the original balance, since thread 1 hasn't gotten around to updating it yet), performs the subtraction of its *dAmount,* and stores the result back into *dBalance.*

5. Thread 1 regains control.

6. Thread 1 stores the register back into *dBalance,* thereby losing any record of the withdrawal performed by thread 2. (See what I mean about subtle?)

This type of resource contention is a collision. To avoid collisions, Java uses the **synchronize** keyword to mark a method so that only one thread can be in that method at a time. If thread 2 starts to enter the method and thread 1 is already in the method, thread 2 is blocked until thread 1 vacates the method.

 OTE The synchronization of threads is implemented using locks. The lock is not on the method but on the object. Thus, thread 2 cannot enter any synchronized method with that object if thread 1 is paused in any synchronized method with the same object, whether it's the same method or another synchronized method.

Since *Deposit* also updates *dBalance,* it must also be flagged. Thus, the following solves the problem:

```
class BankAccount
{
    private double dBalance;
    public synchronized void Withdrawal(double dAmount)
    {
        // let's make this function as simple as possible
        dBalance = dBalance - dAmount;
    }
    public synchronized void Deposit(double dAmount)
    {
        dBalance = dBalance + dAmount;
    }
}
```

It is also possible to get the lock on an object from within a section of code, as follows:

```
class MyClass
{
    public void someFunc(BankAccount ba)
    {
        // I don't want anyone messing with the BankAccount
        // ba until I'm done with it
        synchronized (ba)
        {
            // ...whatever I want to do BUT don't call
            // a function that tries to get the lock
            // again!...
        }
    }
}
```

While it is common to see methods declared synchronized, it is not common to see methods allocate a lock on an object.

Conclusion

The addition of multitasking allows us to write applets that really move. However, applet animation brings with it a few problems, one of which is screen flicker. In the next chapter, we'll use more advanced animation techniques to reduce screen flicker to a minimum.

Chapter 15

Animation Techniques

You might have noticed that if you set the pan rate in the Marquee applet in Chapter 14 too high, the display begins to flicker slightly. Unfortunately, this flickering increases with the complexity of the image being painted. The flickering effect in the Marquee applet isn't too objectionable because the output from this applet is fairly simple. Applets with more complicated output flicker more noticeably. Since pictures are much more complex than just a line of text, almost any animation involving images generates enough flickering to drive you batty.

In this chapter, you'll learn how to cure the flickers. We'll start with an applet that has a bad case of the flickers. We'll then explore two different ways to reduce the flicker problem. In the next chapter we'll apply these techniques to a program that animates images.

The Flickering Stock Applet

The following applet creates a chart for a simulated stock. It's the kind of chart you might find in the business section of the newspaper. Since I don't have access to real data, this applet simulates the data by creating random up and down movements.

Creating the Boilerplate

Create the Stock applet boilerplate using the AppletWizard. Use a fairly large window size. (I chose 600x240 pixels.) We'll need multithreading, but we won't need sample images in the Step 3 dialog box. We won't need any of the special mouse event handlers. In Step 4, create an *int* parameter *fps* with a default value of 10.

The applet summary should appear as shown in Figure 15-1.

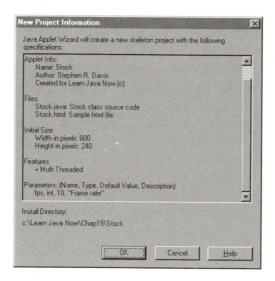

Figure 15-1. *The summary window for the Stock applet.*

If yours looks like this, click OK to generate the applet boilerplate.

Filling In the Blanks

The completed Stock applet appears as follows. (The lines shown in bold were added to the code generated by the AppletWizard.)

```
// Stock1 - this applet displays a scrolling graph of
//          data similar to that produced by plotting
//          stock price against time. this version
//          flickers badly when the frame rate is too
//          high.
```

```
import java.applet.*;
import java.awt.*;
import java.util.Random;

public class Stock extends Applet implements Runnable
{
    Thread      m_Stock = null;

    int m_fps = 10;
    final String PARAM_fps = "fps";

    // use the random object to create stock movements
    private Random  m_r = new Random();

    // m_dValue[] - contains the closing price of the stock
    //              for day that is visible. [0] is today
    //              day, [1] yesterday, etc.
    private double[] m_dValue;
    private int m_nSize;  // length of value array
    private int m_nMax;   // maximum value in value array

    public String getAppletInfo()
    {
        return "Name: Stock\r\n" +
               "Author: Stephen R. Davis\r\n" +
               "Created for Learn Java Now (c)";
    }

    public String[][] getParameterInfo()
    {
        String[][] info =
        {
            { PARAM_fps, "int", "Frame rate" },
        };
        return info;
    }

    public void init()
    {
        String param;
```

(continued)

```
            param = getParameter(PARAM_fps);
            if (param != null)
                m_fps = Integer.parseInt(param);

            // resize(600, 240);

            // initialize the m_dValue array to the current
            // width of the window
            Dimension dim = size();
            int m_nSize = XToIndex(dim.width);
            m_dValue = new double[m_nSize];
            m_nMax = 100;
        }

        public void paint(Graphics g)
        {
            // paint the data
            PaintData(g);

            // paint the frame
            PaintFrame(g);
        }

        private void PaintFrame(Graphics g)
        {
            // get the dimensions of the window
            Dimension d = size();
            int nWidth  = d.width;
            int nHeight = d.height;

            // put up axis along the left and bottom
            g.drawString(Integer.toString(m_nMax), 5, 10);
            g.drawString("0", 5, d.height - 10);
            g.drawLine(0, nHeight - 1, nWidth, nHeight - 1);
            g.drawLine(0, nHeight - 1, 0, 0);
            int nMark = 50;
            while (nMark < m_nMax)
            {
                int nL = 3;
                if ((nMark % 100) == 0)
                {
                    nL = 6;
                }
```

```
                int nH = ValueToY(nHeight, nMark);
                g.drawLine(0, nH, nL, nH);
                nMark += 50;
        }
}

synchronized private void PaintData(Graphics g)
{
        // get the dimensions of the window
        Dimension d = size();
        int nWidth = d.width;
        int nHeight = d.height;

        // check to see if the array needs resizing
        ResizeArray(d.width);

        // repaint the data
        for (int i = 0; i < m_nSize; i++)
        {
                int x = IndexToX(nWidth, i);
                int y = ValueToY(nHeight, m_dValue[i]);
                g.drawLine(x - 1, y, x + 1, y);
                g.drawLine(x, y - 1, x, y + 1);
        }
}

public void start()
{
        if (m_Stock == null)
        {
                m_Stock = new Thread(this);
                m_Stock.start();
        }
}

public void stop()
{
        if (m_Stock != null)
        {
                m_Stock.stop();
                m_Stock = null;
        }
}

public void run()
```

(continued)

```
    {
        // calculate the proper time to delay
        int nSleepTime = 1000 / m_fps;

        // start with the first value stored.
        // if it's zero then this must be
        // the first time into the applet -
        // start with an initial value of 50.
        double dValue = m_dValue[0];
        if (dValue == 0.0)
        {
            dValue = 50.0;
        }

        while (true)
        {
            try
            {
                // create a new stock value
                // this is the part that's random
                // (here I assume that movement of plus
                // or minus two points a day or so is
                // reasonable - the 0.2 offset gives it
                // a slight upward drift)
                dValue += 2 * m_r.nextGaussian() + 0.2;
                AddValue(dValue);

                // now repaint the window
                repaint();

                // repaint at the fps speed
                Thread.sleep(nSleepTime);
            }
            catch (InterruptedException e)
            {
                stop();
            }
        }
    }

    // ResizeArray - resize the array of stock prices
    //               (if necessary)
    private void ResizeArray(int nWidth)
    {
        // if the window is the same size...
        int nNumPts = XToIndex(nWidth);
        if (nNumPts == m_nSize)
```

```
    {
        // ...then ignore it
        return;
    }

    // otherwise, we need to resize the array:
    // allocate room
    double[] dNewArray = new double[nNumPts];

    // now copy the points from the old, smaller
    // array to the new, larger array
    int nNumToCopy = Math.min(nNumPts, m_nSize);
    for (int i = 0; i < nNumToCopy; i++)
    {
        dNewArray[i] = m_dValue[i];
    }

    // finally, make the new array our own
    m_dValue = dNewArray;
    m_nSize = nNumPts;
}

// AddValue - add a value to the array
synchronized private void AddValue(double dValue)
{
    // move everything over one to make
    // room for the new data item
    for (int i = m_nSize - 1; i > 0; i--)
    {
        m_dValue[i] = m_dValue[i - 1];
    }

    // add the new data item as the
    // the first entry
    m_dValue[0] = dValue;

    // make sure to keep track of the max
    while (dValue >= m_nMax)
    {
        m_nMax += 50;
    }
}

// XToIndex - convert the display window dimension
//            to the corresponding array index
private static final int m_PIXELS_PER_POINT = 3;
static private int XToIndex(int nWidth)
```

(continued)

```
        {
            return nWidth / m_PIXELS_PER_POINT;
        }
        // IndexToX - convert the array index to the window
        //            x offset
        static private int IndexToX(int nWidth, int nIndex)
        {
            return (nWidth - 1) - (m_PIXELS_PER_POINT * nIndex);
        }
        // ValueToY - convert the stock value to the y
        //            offset in the window to plot the point
        private int ValueToY(int nHeight, double dValue)
        {
            return nHeight - ((int)dValue * nHeight) / m_nMax;
        }
}
```

While this applet might seem a bit lengthy, it isn't too bad if we take it one method at a time. First, I added four data structures. *m_dValue* is an array that contains the stock closing prices for each day—[1] is today, [2] is yesterday, [3] is the day before, and so forth. This is the data we want to plot. *m_nSize* is simply the number of elements in *m_dValue*. *m_nMax* is the maximum value in the array rounded up to the nearest multiple of 50. (This is used to decide what scale to use in plotting the data.) The *Random* object *m_r* will be used to generate the random day-to-day fluctuations in the stock's closing price.

In the initialization method *init*, *m_dValue* is initialized to hold enough elements to fill the window. Each data point takes up three units across in the applet window. The *XToIndex* method that appears at the bottom of the class converts a window x offset to the corresponding array size.

The AppletWizard-generated *start* method invokes *run* with a new thread. *run* calculates the proper amount of time to sleep to match the selected frame rate. It then takes the first location from *m_dValue* as the starting value for the stock. Upon returning to the applet from another browser window, this is correct; however, when entering the applet for the first time, this first location contains a 0. In that case, *run* uses an initial stock value of 50. It then sits in a tight loop—updating the stock's value, adding the new value to the array, repainting the window, and then going to sleep.

To update the stock value, *run* calls the function *Random.nextGaussian,* which returns a pseudorandom number taken from a Gaussian distribution centered about 0 with a standard deviation of 1. Multiplying this number by 2 gives the stock a little more volatility. Adding 0.2 gives the stock a slightly upward bias. (I'm an optimistic investor.)

The calculated stock price is added to the list by calling *AddValue.* This method starts by moving every element in the array over by one to make room for the new value. The last value is lost. The new value is then placed at offset 0—the first element in the array. Finally, a check is made to make sure that *m_nMax* is greater than or equal to the current stock value. This ensures that all of the data fits within the chart.

The *paint* method repaints the window by first painting the data using the *PaintData* method and then painting the frame using the *PaintFrame* method.

PaintData repaints the data by looping through the array of stored values and plotting each one. The x and y offsets are calculated using the *IndexToX* and *ValueToY* methods, which are defined at the end of the class. The program draws small crosses around the data point by drawing a line from one unit to the left of the point to one unit to the right and then again from one unit below to one unit above.

The *PaintFrame* method paints the x and y axes. It places the range at the bottom and top of the y axis and tick marks every 50 units (with the 100 unit tick marks slightly larger) to make reading the chart easier.

The *ResizeArray* method is called from within *PaintData* to resize the *m_dValue* array in the event that the window changes size. *ResizeArray* first checks to see if the array size should change. If not, it returns without doing anything. If the window changes size, however, the *ResizeArray* method allocates a new array of the proper size. It then copies the data out of *m_dValue* into the new array. Finally, it stores the location of this new array into *m_dValue,* making this our value array.

The output from this program is different every time you execute it because the pseudorandom number generator uses the system clock for its seed value; however, Figure 15-2 on the next page shows the result of a typical run.

What you don't see from this figure is how badly the image flickers. For slow frame speeds (such as two or three frames per second), the flicker isn't too bad. As soon as the frame speed gets over 5 to 10 frames per second, however, the flicker is so bad that the applet is completely unusable.

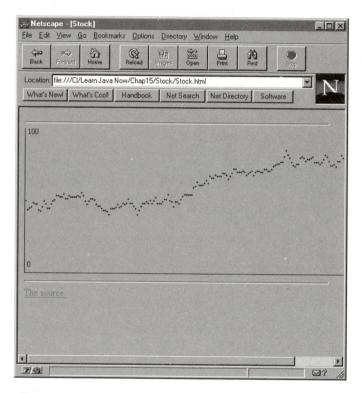

Figure 15-2. *A typical display from the Stock applet.*

What Causes Flicker?

If you look carefully at the Stock applet, the source of its flicker problem becomes clear. When the browser repaints the window as a result of someone calling *repaint,* it actually calls *Applet.update,* not *Applet.paint.* The default version of *Applet.update* clears the applet window (by repainting it with the background color) and then calls *Applet.paint* to recreate the display. As you know, *Applet.paint* puts the new data into the window and returns.

For slow frame rates, there is a considerable pause after *update* and *paint* finish and before *run* calls *repaint* to start the whole process over again. During this time the eye has a chance to take in the window's contents.

For higher frame rates, however, *run* calls *repaint* before the *update/paint* pair can finish servicing the last request. As soon as *update/paint* finishes updating the display, it's time to do it again. In effect, the process looks like the following:

```
loop forever
{
    clear the screen (update())
    paint object 1   (paint())
    paint object 2   (   "   )
    ....
    paint object N   (   "   )
}
```

update clears the screen and then calls *paint* to paint each of the objects. When *update* returns to the browser, the browser immediately calls *update* again to service the pending *repaint* request.

This means that whatever *paint* puts on the display last spends almost no time being displayed. Just as soon as *paint* puts it up, the next call to *update* clears it again. You can verify this by examining the Stock applet. The x and y axes, which are painted last, are barely visible at higher frame rates they flicker so badly. On the other hand, the data at the far right of the applet window, which is painted first, appears stable at all frame rates. This is because, being painted first, it stays visible on the display while the rest of the data is being painted.

Knowing this, we can reduce the effect without actually changing the amount of flicker by repainting the following types of data first:

■ Anything we know the user will be concentrating on a lot. That way, he won't notice the flicker as much.

■ Anything that draws relatively quickly. That way, the majority of the window is painted most of the time.

Simply reversing the order that things are displayed within *paint* helps the apparent flicker a lot. The following version paints the axes before it paints the data:

```
public void paint(Graphics g)
{
    // paint the frame
    PaintFrame(g);

    // paint the data
    PaintData(g);
}
```

The axes paint relatively quickly compared to the mound of data that needs to be displayed. This allows the user to concentrate on the new data and the more recent trends. The resulting effect is more pleasing even though we haven't actually done anything to reduce the flicker.

Synchronizing Tricky Stock Options

You might have noticed that *PaintData* reads data from the *m_dValue* array at the same time that *AddValue* is adding new elements to it. This is because *PaintData* is called from a different thread than *AddValue*. Thus, it's entirely possible that *AddValue* might add a new entry just as *PaintData* is in the middle of displaying the list. In this particular case, this interaction doesn't cause much grief, but in general we don't like two methods accessing the same data structures simultaneously. (The next version of Stock is not nearly so forgiving.)

Such interaction problems are alleviated by declaring *PaintData* and *AddValue* to be **synchronized**. This means that the two methods are mutually exclusive. *run* can't call *AddValue* to add a new value to the *m_dValue* array if *PaintData* is using it. *run* is blocked until *PaintData* is finished. Similarly, the browser must wait for *AddValue* to complete before *PaintData* can repaint the values in the *m_dValue* array.

Decreasing Flicker by Avoiding Screen Clear

If the applet doesn't clear the screen before repainting the window, the old data stays on the display while the new data is being painted. This reduces flicker considerably.

We can do this by providing our own version of *update,* which doesn't clear the screen. However, since the screen isn't being cleared, *update* must remove the old data point before it puts up the next. It can't just loop through removing data points and then start over repainting them—the result would flicker just as badly as before. Instead, it must remove and repaint as it makes its way through the data. That way, even though the window is in constant flux, only a small part of the window is being changed at a time.

Even though this *update* doesn't call *paint,* the *paint* method is still necessary. The browser calls *paint* directly to restore the applet window if it has suffered damage. However, *paint* can call *update* to repaint the data.

This flickerless version of Stock appears as follows. Changes are in bold.

```
// Stock2 - this applet is an "improved" version of the
//          Stock1 applet. this version avoids applet
//          flicker by carefully removing each symbol
//          before putting up the new position. however,
//          this version is slow and difficult to write.
import java.applet.*;
import java.awt.*;
import java.util.Random;

public class Stock extends Applet implements Runnable
{
    Thread      m_Stock = null;

    int m_fps = 10;
    final String PARAM_fps = "fps";

    // use the random object to create stock movements
    private Random  m_r = new Random();

    // m_dValue[] - contains the closing price of the stock
    //              for day that is visible. [0] is today
    //              day, [1] yesterday, etc.
    private double[] m_dValue;
    private int m_nSize;  // length of value array
    private int m_nMax;   // maximum value in value array

    // m_nOffset - number of values to move the display
    //             during a pan
    private int m_nOffset = 0;
```

(continued)

```java
        // m_bRepaintAll - setting this flag to true forces
        //                 update to perform a full repaint
        //                 of the applet's window
        private boolean m_bRepaintAll = true;

        // m_nWinWidth - the width of the window
        private Dimension m_dimWin = new Dimension(0, 0);

        public String getAppletInfo()
        {
            return "Name: Stock\r\n" +
                    "Author: Stephen R. Davis\r\n" +
                    "Created for Learn Java Now (c)";
        }

        public String[][] getParameterInfo()
        {
            String[][] info =
            {
                { PARAM_fps, "int", "Frame rate" },
            };
            return info;
        }

        public void init()
        {
            String param;

            param = getParameter(PARAM_fps);
            if (param != null)
                m_fps = Integer.parseInt(param);

            // resize(600, 240);

            // initialize the value array to the current
            // width of the window
            Dimension dim = size();
            int m_nSize = XToIndex(dim.width);
            m_dValue = new double[m_nSize];
            m_nMax = 100;
        }
```

```java
public void paint(Graphics g)
{
    // before we repaint, make sure the whole
    // screen is cleared
    Dimension dim = size();
    g.clearRect(0, 0, dim.width, dim.height);

    // paint the frame
    PaintFrame(g);

    // paint the data
    PaintData(g);

    // no need to repaint the world again
    m_bRepaintAll = false;
}

public void update(Graphics g)
{
    // make sure that the window registers exactly
    Dimension dim = size();
    if (dim.width != m_dimWin.width ||
        dim.height!= m_dimWin.height)
    {
        // window has changed size - repaint everything
        m_bRepaintAll = true;
        m_dimWin = new Dimension(dim.width, dim.height);
    }

    // if we need to repaint everything...
    if (m_bRepaintAll)
    {
        // ...then repaint the world...
        paint(g);
    }
    else
    {
        // ...otherwise, just repaint the data
        PaintData(g);
    }
}
```

(continued)

```
private void PaintFrame(Graphics g)
{
    // get the dimensions of the window
    Dimension d = size();
    int nWidth  = d.width;
    int nHeight = d.height;

    // check to see if the array needs resizing
    ResizeArray(nWidth);

    // put up axis along the left and bottom
    g.drawString(Integer.toString(m_nMax), 5, 10);
    g.drawString("0", 5, d.height - 10);
    g.drawLine(0, nHeight - 1, nWidth, nHeight - 1);
    g.drawLine(0, nHeight - 1, 0, 0);
    int nMark = 50;
    while (nMark < m_nMax)
    {
        int nL = 3;
        if ((nMark % 100) == 0)
        {
            nL = 6;
        }
        int nH = ValueToY(nHeight, nMark);
        g.drawLine(0, nH, nL, nH);
        nMark += 50;
    }
}

synchronized private void PaintData(Graphics g)
{
    // get the dimensions of the window
    Dimension d = size();
    int nWidth = d.width;
    int nHeight = d.height;

    // if m_nOffset is zero, there's nothing to do
    if (m_nOffset == 0)
    {
        return;
    }

    // repaint the data
    Color bg = getBackground();
    Color fg = getForeground();
    int nMax = m_nSize - m_nOffset - 1;
    for (int i = 0; i < nMax; i++)
```

```
        {
            int x = IndexToX(nWidth, i);

            // remove the old mark in this column
            int y;
            y = ValueToY(nHeight, m_dValue[i + m_nOffset]);
            g.setColor(bg);
            g.drawLine(x - 1, y, x + 1, y);
            g.drawLine(x, y - 1, x, y + 1);

            // now draw the new mark in this column
            y = ValueToY(nHeight, m_dValue[i]);
            g.setColor(fg);
            g.drawLine(x - 1, y, x + 1, y);
            g.drawLine(x, y - 1, x, y + 1);
        }

        // now that we've repainted, note that by setting
        // the offset back to zero
        m_nOffset = 0;
    }

    public void start()
    {
        if (m_Stock == null)
        {
            m_Stock = new Thread(this);
            m_Stock.start();
        }
    }

    public void stop()
    {
        if (m_Stock != null)
        {
            m_Stock.stop();
            m_Stock = null;
        }
    }

    public void run()
    {
        // calculate the proper time to delay
        int nSleepTime = 1000 / m_fps;

        // start with the first value stored
        // off. if it's zero then this must be
```

(continued)

```
            // the first time into the applet -
            // start with an initial value of 50.
            double dValue = m_dValue[0];
            if (dValue == 0.0)
            {
                dValue = 50.0;
            }

            while (true)
            {
                try
                {
                    // create a new stock value
                    // this is the part that's random
                    // (here I assume that movement of plus
                    // or minus two points a day or so is
                    // reasonable - the 0.2 offset gives it
                    // a slight upward drift)
                    dValue += 2 * m_r.nextGaussian() + 0.2;
                    AddValue(dValue);

                    // now repaint the window
                    repaint();

                    // repaint at the fps speed
                    Thread.sleep(nSleepTime);
                }
                catch (InterruptedException e)
                {
                    stop();
                }
            }
        }

    // ResizeArray - resize the array of stock prices
    //                (if necessary)
    private void ResizeArray(int nWidth)
    {
        // if the window is the same size...
        int nNumPts = XToIndex(nWidth);
        if (nNumPts == m_nSize)
        {
            // ...then ignore it
            return;
        }

        // otherwise, we need to resize the array:
        // allocate room
        double[] dNewArray = new double[nNumPts];
```

```
        // now copy the points from the old, smaller
        // array to the new, larger array
        int nNumToCopy = Math.min(nNumPts, m_nSize);
        for (int i = 0; i < nNumToCopy; i++)
        {
            dNewArray[i] = m_dValue[i];
        }

        // finally, make the new array our own
        m_dValue = dNewArray;
        m_nSize = nNumPts;
    }

// AddValue - add a value to the array
synchronized private void AddValue(double dValue)
{
    // indicate to update how far we've moved the
    // data points over since the last time it repainted
    m_nOffset++;

    // move everything over one to make
    // room for the new data item
    for (int i = m_nSize - 1; i > 0; i--)
    {
        m_dValue[i] = m_dValue[i - 1];
    }

    // add the new data item as the
    // the first entry
    m_dValue[0] = dValue;

    // make sure to keep track of the max
    while (dValue >= m_nMax)
    {
        m_nMax += 50;
        m_bRepaintAll = true;
    }
}

// XToIndex - convert the display window dimension
//            to the corresponding array index
private static final int m_PIXELS_PER_POINT = 3;
static private int XToIndex(int nWidth)
{
    return nWidth / m_PIXELS_PER_POINT;
}
```

(continued)

```
    // IndexToX - convert the array index to the window
    //             x offset
    static private int IndexToX(int nWidth, int nIndex)
    {
        return (nWidth - 1) - (m_PIXELS_PER_POINT * nIndex);
    }
    // ValueToY - convert the stock value to the y
    //             offset in the window to plot the point
    private int ValueToY(int nHeight, double dValue)
    {
        return nHeight - ((int)dValue * nHeight) / m_nMax;
    }
}
```

This version of *update* does not clear the screen. Instead, under normal circumstances, it simply calls *PaintData* to repaint the data points. This version of *PaintData* is considerably more complicated than its predecessor, however. Not only must it paint the new data, it must paint over the previous data in the same column by drawing at the same location in the background color. *PaintData* switches back to the foreground color to paint the new data. *m_nOffset* records how many data points have been added to the *m_dValue* array since the last time the array was painted.

Under certain circumstances, *update* needs to repaint the entire display. For example, when *m_nMax* changes or when the window changes size it is too difficult to keep track of where the old data points are on the display. Setting the flag *m_bRepaintAll* to *true* tells *update* to call *paint* as it normally does to clear the window and repaint it from scratch. Normally, however, *m_bRepaintAll* is *false,* signaling to *update* that it's safe to update only the data by calling *PaintData*.

There must still be a *paint* method, since this method is called when the window has been damaged and needs to be completely repainted (for example, when a portion of the window is deiconified). This version of *paint* is very similar to its predecessor except for the addition of *Graphics.clearRect,* which was added to ensure that the window is cleared since *update* is no longer performing that function.

How Are We Doing?

The updated Stock applet has a much improved appearance compared with the original. It displays no flicker even at the highest refresh rates.

However, it does suffer from several problems common to this approach to flickerless applets.

First, it repaints even more slowly than the original Stock applet. This is because *PaintData* must remove the old data by painting over it one line at a time in addition to painting the new data. Since painting to the screen is a painfully slow operation, this makes the applet almost twice as slow as its flickering twin.

Second, this version of Stock displays a curious "inchworm" effect. As the update makes its way from right to left, the display appears to creep along like a caterpillar, expanding as the data on the left is moved and contracting as the data on the right catches up. While it's not as objectionable as the original flicker, it is distracting.

Finally, this updated Stock applet is more complicated than the original. Thought must be given to the different paths through the code, including the possible interactions. If any symbol gets inadvertently left on the display, it remains there until the user forces a full refresh.

This approach to flicker reduction works, but it's an imperfect solution at best.

Avoiding Flicker Through Double Buffering

Let's go back. Isn't there some other approach we can take to reduce flicker? The fundamental problem with the original Stock applet is that the user can see each step the applet takes as it updates the display. The updated Stock applet minimizes the effect by only updating a little bit of the window at a time.

What if we could let Stock update some off-screen *Graphics* object instead of directly updating the screen? While Stock is updating this object, the user will see an unchanging, rock-solid applet window. Once the off-screen *Graphics* object is updated and ready for view, the applet can then perform a block copy of the off-screen object to the applet window.

This approach is called **double buffering**. The double buffer refers to the fact that the off-screen image is a second image buffer. (The first is the image that the user sees in the applet window.)

The Double Buffer Stock Solution

The following is the double-buffered version of Stock. Again, the changes compared to the original flickering Stock applet are in bold.

 N OTE   Since this applet is more similar to Stock1 than to Stock2, I have used bold for changes from Stock1 and not from Stock2.

```
// Stock3 - this version of the Stock applet uses
//          double buffering to avoid the flickers.
//          it is much faster than Stock2 and just
//          as easy to write as Stock1.
import java.applet.*;
import java.awt.*;
import java.util.Random;

public class Stock extends Applet implements Runnable
{
    Thread     m_Stock = null;

    int m_fps = 10;
    final String PARAM_fps = "fps";

    // use the random object to create stock movements
    private Random  m_r = new Random();

    // m_dValue[] - contains the closing price of the stock
    //              for day which is visible. [0] is today
    //              day, [1] yesterday, etc.
    private double[] m_dValue;
    private int m_nSize;  // length of value array
    private int m_nMax;   // maximum value in value array

    // double buffering image
    private Image m_image;// off-screen image
    private Graphics m_g; // associated graphics object
    Dimension m_dimImage; // size of off-screen image

    public String getAppletInfo()
    {
```

```
        return "Name: Stock\r\n" +
               "Author: Stephen R. Davis\r\n" +
               "Created for Learn Java Now (c)";
    }

    public String[][] getParameterInfo()
    {
        String[][] info =
        {
            { PARAM_fps, "int", "Frame rate" },
        };
        return info;
    }

    public void init()
    {
        String param;

        param = getParameter(PARAM_fps);
        if (param != null)
            m_fps = Integer.parseInt(param);

        // resize(600, 240);

        // initialize the value array to the current
        // width of the window
        Dimension dim = size();
        int m_nSize = XToIndex(dim.width);
        m_dValue = new double[m_nSize];
        m_nMax = 100;
    }

    public void paint(Graphics g)
    {
        // repaint existing image
        if (m_image != null)
        {
            g.drawImage(m_image, 0, 0, null);
        }
    }

    public void update(Graphics g)
```

(continued)

```
    {
        // make sure that the image is the same size as
        // the applet's window
        ResizeImage();

        // clear the off-screen image (not the on-screen one)
        Color colFG = getForeground();
        Color colBG = getBackground();
        m_g.setColor(colBG);
        m_g.fillRect(0, 0, m_dimImage.width, m_dimImage.height);
        m_g.setColor(colFG);

        // paint the frame
        PaintFrame(m_g);

        // then repaint the data
        PaintData(m_g);

        // now repaint the image
        paint(g);
    }

    private void PaintFrame(Graphics g)
    {
        // get the dimensions of the window
        Dimension d = size();
        int nWidth  = d.width;
        int nHeight = d.height;

        // put up axis along the left and bottom
        g.drawString(Integer.toString(m_nMax), 5, 10);
        g.drawString("0", 5, d.height - 10);
        g.drawLine(0, nHeight - 1, nWidth, nHeight - 1);
        g.drawLine(0, nHeight - 1, 0, 0);
        int nMark = 50;
        while (nMark < m_nMax)
        {
            int nL = 3;
            if ((nMark % 100) == 0)
            {
                nL = 6;
            }
            int nH = ValueToY(nHeight, nMark);
            g.drawLine(0, nH, nL, nH);
            nMark += 50;
        }
    }
```

```
synchronized private void PaintData(Graphics g)
{
    // get the dimensions of the window
    Dimension d = size();
    int nWidth = d.width;
    int nHeight = d.height;

    // check to see if the array needs resizing
    ResizeArray(d.width);

    // repaint the data
    for (int i = 0; i < m_nSize; i++)
    {
        int x = IndexToX(nWidth, i);
        int y = ValueToY(nHeight, m_dValue[i]);
        g.drawLine(x - 1, y, x + 1, y);
        g.drawLine(x, y - 1, x, y + 1);
    }
}

public void start()
{
    if (m_Stock == null)
    {
        m_Stock = new Thread(this);
        m_Stock.start();
    }
}

public void stop()
{
    if (m_Stock != null)
    {
        m_Stock.stop();
        m_Stock = null;
    }
}

public void run()
{
    // calculate the proper time to delay
    int nSleepTime = 1000 / m_fps;

    // start with the first value stored
    // off. if it's zero then this must be
    // the first time into the applet - start
    // with an initial value of 50.
```

(continued)

```
        double dValue = m_dValue[0];
        if (dValue == 0.0)
        {
            dValue = 50.0;
        }

        while (true)
        {
            try
            {
                // create a new stock value
                // this is the part that's random
                // (here I assume that movement of plus
                // or minus two points a day or so is
                // reasonable - the 0.2 offset gives it
                // a slight upward drift)
                dValue += 2 * m_r.nextGaussian() + 0.2;
                AddValue(dValue);

                // now repaint the window
                repaint();

                // repaint at the fps speed
                Thread.sleep(nSleepTime);
            }
            catch (InterruptedException e)
            {
                stop();
            }
        }
    }

    // ResizeImage - resize the off-screen image (if necessary)
    private void ResizeImage()
    {
        // get the size of the applet's window
        Dimension dim = size();
        int nWidth = dim.width;
        int nHeight= dim.height;

        // compare that to the size of our image;
        // if it hasn't changed...
        if (m_dimImage != null &&
            m_dimImage.width == nWidth &&
            m_dimImage.height== nHeight)
        {
            // ...don't do anything
            return;
        }
```

```
        // create a graphics image to paint to
        m_dimImage = new Dimension(nWidth, nHeight);
        m_image = createImage(nWidth, nHeight);
        m_g = m_image.getGraphics();
}

// ResizeArray - resize the array of stock prices
//                (if necessary)
private void ResizeArray(int nWidth)
{
        // if the window is the same size...
        int nNumPts = XToIndex(nWidth);
        if (nNumPts == m_nSize)
        {
            // ...then ignore it
            return;
        }

        // otherwise, we need to resize the array:
        // allocate room
        double[] dNewArray = new double[nNumPts];

        // now copy the points from the old, smaller
        // array to the new, larger array
        int nNumToCopy = Math.min(nNumPts, m_nSize);
        for (int i = 0; i < nNumToCopy; i++)
        {
            dNewArray[i] = m_dValue[i];
        }

        // finally, make the new array our own
        m_dValue = dNewArray;
        m_nSize = nNumPts;
}

// AddValue - add a value to the array
synchronized private void AddValue(double dValue)
{
        // move everything over one to make
        // room for the new data item
        for (int i = m_nSize - 1; i > 0; i--)
        {
            m_dValue[i] = m_dValue[i - 1];
        }

        // add the new data item as the
        // the first entry
```

(continued)

```
            m_dValue[0] = dValue;

            // make sure to keep track of the max
            while (dValue >= m_nMax)
            {
                m_nMax += 50;
            }
        }

        // XToIndex - convert the display window dimension
        //            to the corresponding array index
        private static final int m_PIXELS_PER_POINT = 3;
        static private int XToIndex(int nWidth)
        {
            return nWidth / m_PIXELS_PER_POINT;
        }
        // IndexToX - convert the array index to the window
        //            x offset
        static private int IndexToX(int nWidth, int nIndex)
        {
            return (nWidth - 1) - (m_PIXELS_PER_POINT * nIndex);
        }
        // ValueToY - convert the stock value to the y
        //            offset in the window to plot the point
        private int ValueToY(int nHeight, double dValue)
        {
            return nHeight - ((int)dValue * nHeight) / m_nMax;
        }
    }
}
```

There are a few new data members at the top of the class. *m_image* is a private, off-screen image. This is created in the *ResizeImage* method whenever the applet window is resized. *ResizeImage* ensures that the off-screen image is the same size as the applet window.

ResizeImage also initializes the *Graphics* object *m_g*, which is simply the *Graphics* object that writes to *m_image*. *m_dimImage* contains the dimensions of the off-screen image.

The double-buffered Stock applet still needs to override the *update* method to avoid clearing the applet window. This version of *update* first checks to make sure that the off-screen image is the same size as the visible image by calling *ResizeImage*.

ResizeImage compares the size of the off-screen image to that of the on-screen version. If they are the same size, *ResizeImage* returns immediately.

If they are not the same size, *ResizeImage* allocates a new off-screen image of the appropriate size.

 OTE *ResizeImage* displays a typical use of the && operator. The first time that *ResizeImage* is called, *m_dimImage* is null. Since the first test in the *if* statement fails, the second and third tests, which involve *m_dimImage,* are short circuited. (See the discussion of short circuit evaluation in Chapter 2.)

Once *update* assures itself that the off-screen image is the proper size, it clears this image. To do so, it paints over the entire image with the applet's background color using the *fillRect* method.

 OTE Notice that *update* acts on the off-screen *Graphics* object *m_g* and not on the visible *Graphics* object *g.*

After clearing the off-screen image, *update* paints the axes followed by the data into the off-screen image using the *PaintFrame* and *PaintData* methods. These methods are identical to the originals in the original Stock applet.

Finally, *update* calls *paint* to transfer the off-screen image onto the display.

paint does nothing more than transfer the off-screen image onto the visible applet window image using the method *drawImage*. The first argument to *drawImage* is the off-screen image to transfer. The second and third are the offset. An offset of 0 keeps the two images aligned. The last argument is called the *ImageObserver* and is optional. We will see how to use an *ImageObserver* in the next chapter.

The Advantages of Double Buffering

The double-buffered Stock applet has all the advantages we are looking for:

- It demonstrates no flickering at all, no matter what the frame rate is set to.

- It is as simple as the original Stock applet.

- Since it rebuilds the screen from scratch every frame, it doesn't suffer from screen droppings caused by the applet forgetting to remove some small pieces of image from an earlier frame.

- It's nearly as fast as the flickering version.

About the only disadvantage of the double-buffered applet compared to its flickering cousin is the extra memory it consumes for the off-screen images. A high-resolution, multicolored image can consume more than a megabyte of RAM. Nevertheless, this seems a small price to pay to preserve the user's sanity.

Conclusion

In this chapter, we started with a nice applet that suffered from a socially unacceptable flicker problem. After analyzing the origins of the problem, we first solved the flicker using a conservative redraw policy. We then solved the problem using a double-buffering scheme. Finally, we saw why the double-buffering solution is preferable for most applets.

In the next chapter, we'll use this double-buffering animation technique to load and replay real video animation.

Animating Images

Animation means replaying images to the display so quickly that the user perceives continuous motion. In the types of animations we have performed so far, these images have been created by the computer in real time. Occasionally, however, we want to replay a sequence of previously stored picture-like images.

Ideally, we want to read these images from the disk while displaying them. Remember, however, that Java is meant to execute remotely over a modem connection. There is no way that images can be transmitted to the applet in anything approaching real time. Some other approach is needed to solve this problem.

 N **OTE**   Java applets do not have access to the client computer's disk.

The Animation Applet

In the previous chapter, you saw how to use double buffering to avoid screen flicker. Double buffering allows the application to keep a second copy of the screen image in an off-screen buffer. The application meticulously updates that image just as it would the on-screen image. Once the off-screen image is ready to be presented, it is transferred to the screen in a relatively quick and painless block transfer operation.

What if we could keep multiple images, one for each frame of the video to be replayed? During initialization, we would load each .gif file containing the proper image for a frame into a separate off-screen buffer. To play the video, we would sequentially copy each off-screen buffer to the screen. This is the way Java creates full-motion video.

 OTE You might think that this unnecessarily limits the number of frames of animation that the applet can replay. In reality, the number of frames is already severely limited by the user's patience. No one will tolerate an applet that takes 30 minutes to download all of the video images it needs to execute.

 OTE Java uses the .gif file format to store images to disk.

Creating the Boilerplate

The AppletWizard is capable of generating a fully functional animation applet. This applet replays a series of images that display a rotating globe. I will demonstrate here how to modify that applet to replay any series of .gif files you have.

Use the AppletWizard to create a new applet called Animation.

In Step 3 of the wizard, be sure to answer Yes to both "Would you like your applet to be multi-threaded?" and "Would you like support for animation?"

In Step 4, create three parameters. First create an *int* parameter *fps* with a default value of 10. This will be used to control the replay frame rate. Then create a *String* parameter *imageFile*. This will contain the prefix of the .gif files that are replayed in the animation. These files are numbered using two digits starting with 01 and they carry the suffix *.gif.* Since I am using image files named LJN01.gif through LJN22.gif for my version of the applet, I have defaulted to the prefix *LJN*. The final field, *numImages,* is an *int* field that specifies the number of images. This is defaulted to 22 to match the number of LJN files.

The applet summary should appear as follows:

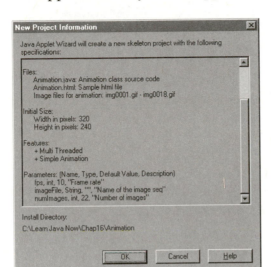

If your applet summary looks like this, click OK to instruct the Applet-Wizard to create your application framework.

Filling In the Blanks

Below is the Animation applet with additions and changes to the Applet-Wizard-generated code marked in bold. I deleted do-nothing methods for the sake of brevity.

```
//***********************************************************************
// Animation.java: this version of Animation uses the MediaTracker
//                 to monitor the progress of loading the images
//***********************************************************************
import java.applet.*;
import java.awt.*;

public class Animation extends Applet implements Runnable
{
    // THREAD SUPPORT:
    //          m_Animation    is the Thread object for the applet
    //--------------------------------
    Thread    m_Animation = null;

    // ANIMATION SUPPORT:
    //--------------------------------
    private Graphics m_Graphics;         // used for graphics context
```

(continued)

```
private Image     m_Images[];        // array of image objects
private int       m_nCurrImage;      // index of current image
private int       m_nImgWidth  = 0;  // width and...
private int       m_nImgHeight = 0;  // ...height of images
private boolean   m_fAllLoaded = false; // TRUE->images loaded


// m_numImages replaces the following supplied by the AppletWizard
// private final int NUM_IMAGES = 18;

// PARAMETER SUPPORT:
// Members for applet parameters
// <type>         <MemberVar>     = <Default Value>
//-------------------------------
private int      m_fps = 10;
private String   m_imageFile = "LJN";
private int      m_numImages = 22;

private int      m_nSleepTime;   // sleep time based on m_fps

// Parameter names.  To change a name of a parameter, you need
// only make a single change.  Simply modify the value of the
// parameter string below.
//-------------------------------
private final String PARAM_fps = "fps";
private final String PARAM_imageFile = "imageFile";
private final String PARAM_numImages = "numImages";

// APPLET INFO SUPPORT:
//   The getAppletInfo() method returns a string describing the
// applet's author, copyright date, or miscellaneous information.
//-------------------------------
public String getAppletInfo()
{
    return "Name: Animation\r\n" +
           "Author: Stephen R. Davis\r\n" +
           "Created for Learn Java Now (c)";
}

// PARAMETER SUPPORT
//   The getParameterInfo() method returns an array of strings
// describing the parameters understood by this applet.
//
// Animation Parameter Information:
//   { "Name", "Type", "Description" },
//-------------------------------
public String[][] getParameterInfo()
{
    String[][] info =
    {
```

```
            { PARAM_fps, "int", "Frame Rate" },
            { PARAM_imageFile, "String", "Name of the image seq" },
            { PARAM_numImages, "int", "Number of images" },
        };
        return info;
}

// The init() method is called by the AWT when an applet is first
// loaded or reloaded.
//---------------------------------
public void init()
{
    // PARAMETER SUPPORT
    //   The following code retrieves the value of each
    // parameter specified with the <PARAM> tag and stores it in
    // a member variable.
    //---------------------------------
    String param;

    param = getParameter(PARAM_fps);
    if (param != null)
        m_fps = Integer.parseInt(param);

    param = getParameter(PARAM_imageFile);
    if (param != null)
        m_imageFile = param;

    param = getParameter(PARAM_numImages);
    if (param != null)
        m_numImages = Integer.parseInt(param);

    // If you use a ResourceWizard-generated "control creator"
    // class to arrange controls in your applet, you may want to
    // call its CreateControls() method from within this method.
    // Remove the following call to resize() before adding the
    // call to CreateControls(); CreateControls() does its own
    // resizing.
    //---------------------------------
    resize(320, 240);

    // Calculate the sleep time based on fps
    if (m_fps != 0)
    {
        m_nSleepTime = 1000 / m_fps;
    }
}
```

(continued)

```
// ANIMATION SUPPORT:
//   Draws the next image, if all images are currently loaded
//---------------------------------
private void displayImage(Graphics g)
{
    if (!m_fAllLoaded)
        return;

    // Draw Image in center of applet
    //----------------------------------
    g.drawImage(m_Images[m_nCurrImage],
                (size().width - m_nImgWidth)   / 2,
                (size().height - m_nImgHeight) / 2, null);

    // display the frame number (this is optional)
    g.setColor(Color.white);
    g.drawString("Image #" + m_nCurrImage, 10,40);
}

// Animation Paint Handler
//----------------------------------
public void paint(Graphics g)
{
    // ANIMATION SUPPORT:
    //   The following code displays a status message until all
    // the images are loaded. Then it calls displayImage to
    // display the current image.
    //----------------------------------
    if (m_fAllLoaded)
    {
        Rectangle r = g.getClipRect();

        g.clearRect(r.x, r.y, r.width, r.height);
        displayImage(g);
    }
    else
        g.drawString("Loading images...", 10, 20);
}

// The start() method is called when the page containing the
// applet first appears on the screen.
//----------------------------------
public void start()
{
    if (m_Animation == null)
    {
        m_Animation = new Thread(this);
        m_Animation.start();
    }
```

```
}

// The stop() method is called when the page containing the
// applet is no longer on the screen.
//--------------------------------
public void stop()
{
    if (m_Animation != null)
    {
        m_Animation.stop();
        m_Animation = null;
    }
}


// THREAD SUPPORT
//    The run() method is called when the applet's thread is
// started.
//--------------------------------
public void run()
{
    m_nCurrImage = 0;

    // If re-entering the page, then the images have already been
    // loaded.
    // m_fAllLoaded == TRUE.
    //--------------------------------
    if (!m_fAllLoaded)
    {
        repaint();
        m_Graphics = getGraphics();
        m_Images   = new Image[m_numImages];

        // Load in all the images
        //--------------------------------
        MediaTracker tracker = new MediaTracker(this);
        String strImage;

        // For each image in the animation, this method first
        // constructs a string containing the path to the image
        // file; then it begins loading the image into the
        // m_Images array. Note that the call to getImage will
        // return before the image is completely loaded.
        //--------------------------------
        for (int i = 1; i <= m_numImages; i++)
        {
            // Build path to next image
            //--------------------------------
```

(continued)

285

```
                    // the AppletWizard code uses a hard-coded filename;
                    // replace with a parameter from the HTML file
                    strImage = // "images/img00"
                            m_imageFile          // initialized in init()
                            + ((i < 10) ? "0" : "")
                            + i
                            + ".gif";
                    m_Images[i-1] = getImage(getDocumentBase(),strImage);
                    tracker.addImage(m_Images[i-1], 0);
                }

                // Wait until all images are fully loaded
                //--------------------------------
                try
                {
                    tracker.waitForAll();
                    m_fAllLoaded = !tracker.isErrorAny();
                }
                catch (InterruptedException e)
                {
                }

                if (!m_fAllLoaded)
                {
                    stop();
                    m_Graphics.drawString("Error loading images!",
                                          10, 40);
                    return;
                }

                // Assume all images are same width and height.
                //--------------------------------
                m_nImgWidth  = m_Images[0].getWidth(this);
                m_nImgHeight = m_Images[0].getHeight(this);
            }
        repaint();

        while (true)
        {
            try
            {
                // Draw next image in animation
                //--------------------------------
                displayImage(m_Graphics);
                m_nCurrImage++;
                if (m_nCurrImage == m_numImages)
                    m_nCurrImage = 0;
```

```
                    // replace with a value based on the fps parameter:
                    Thread.sleep(m_nSleepTime);
                }
                catch (InterruptedException e)
                {
                }
            }
        }
    }
```

Note that I made the following slight modifications to the Animation applet created by the AppletWizard.

- The animation applet generated by the AppletWizard hard-codes both the name of the image file and the number of frames in the file. I added a little flexibility by allowing the user to indicate the image filename in the HTML file.

- I changed *NUM_IMAGES* to *m_numImages* globally. This was necessary to indicate that the number of image frames is now in the HTML file.

- I allowed the frame rate to be read from the HTML file as well.

I highlighted in bold the changes necessary to implement these improvements.

This applet must go through a number of steps before you get to see animated video. Let's take each one in turn.

As always, the *init* method is invoked when the applet is first loaded and begins executing. *init* reads any parameters from the HTML file. The parameters that this applet supports are the standard *fps*, which specifies the frames-per-second replay rate; *imageFile*, which is used to specify the name of the image file, and *numImages*, which is used to specify the number of .gif files. Finally, *init* calculates the time to sleep based on the frame rate.

The next function to execute is *start*. This function creates a new thread and starts it. This new thread begins executing with the *Animation.run* method.

What Is *getDocumentBase?*

The first argument to *getImage* is a URL. Why is this so? Remember that a Java applet is meant to be executed over the Web. That means that the HTML page might be at a different location than the applet to which it refers. The *getDocumentBase* method returns the URL of the HTML page that invoked the Java applet. This applet assumes that the image files are at the same location as the HTML page. By comparison, the *getCodeBase* method returns the URL address of the applet itself.

What Is a *MediaTracker* Object?

Notice how the Animation program attaches each frame to a *Media-Tracker* object. What's this object for? A *MediaTracker* object provides a way to monitor the status of media objects such as image and sound files. The *getImage* method does not actually load the image file. It merely establishes an association between the image object and the image file. The image isn't loaded until specifically requested or until the *Image* object is used. Even then, the loading process normally goes on in the background. This allows the applet (and the browser that is executing it) to continue doing useful work during the relatively long file uploads.

A *MediaTracker* object can monitor the loading of such image files. The *MediaTracker* object keeps track of whether the images are loading, whether the load is complete, and, if the load is complete, whether an error of some sort has occurred.

Once the images are attached to the *MediaTracker* object, this program forces all images to be loaded by calling the *MediaTracker.waitForAll* method. *waitForAll* does not return until all images signal that they have been loaded (or until the load has failed).

When *MediaTracker.waitForAll* returns, the program checks to make sure that they loaded successfully by calling *MediaTracker.isErrorAny*.

run begins by checking whether the images have already been loaded. (They would have been loaded if the user had gone on to another page and then returned.) If the images have not been loaded previously, *run* calls the *repaint* method. Since the images have yet to be loaded, *paint* displays a "Loading images…" message. Meanwhile, *run* allocates an array of *Image* objects, one for each frame to be replayed. Finally, run creates a *MediaTracker* object that it will use to monitor the image frames as they are loaded.

The program then enters a loop in which it takes the file prefix (let's say *LJN,* which is the default) and concatenates the frame number in a string called *strImage.* Thus, the first time through the loop *strImage* is equal to LJN01.gif, the second time LFN02.gif, and so on. The call to *getImage* creates an *Image* object associated with this .gif file and sets *m_Images[i-1]* to refer to it. Finally, the program adds this image to the *MediaTracker* object.

Finally, *run* enters a final loop during which it displays each frame in turn by calling the *displayImage* method in a loop, incrementing the frame number as it goes. As a lark, the last two lines in *displayImage* display the frame number along with the image.

How's It Look?

The image files LJN01.gif through LJN22.gif display a sequence of the word *Java* morphing into the word *VJ++* and back. A selection of frames from the sequence is shown in Figures 16-1 through 16-13. Frames 12, 13, and 14 are identical, which gives the user the impression that the animation has stopped for an instant. From there, the animation morphs *VJ++* back into *Java* to repeat the process.

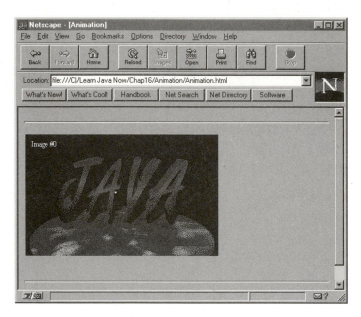

Figure 16-1. *Frame 0 of the morphing sequence showing the word* Java.

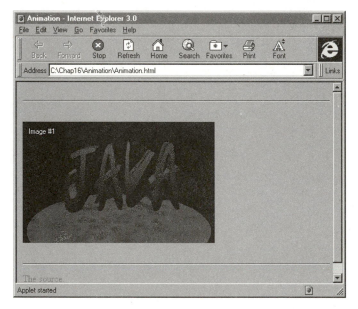

Figure 16-2. *Frame 1 of the animation sequence.*

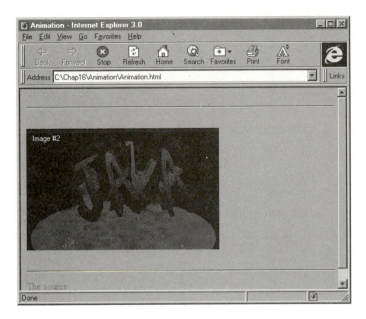

Figure 16-3. *Frame 2 of the animation sequence.*

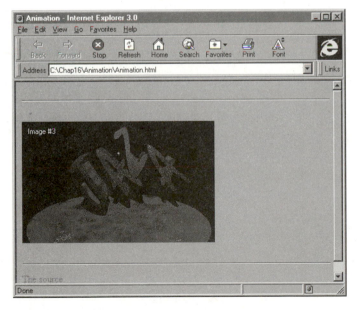

Figure 16-4. *Frame 3 of the animation sequence.*

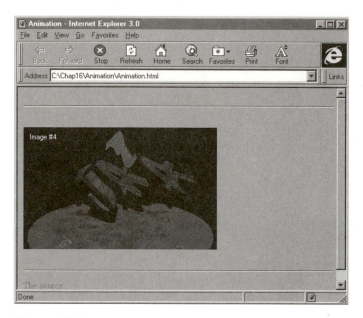

Figure 16-5. *Frame 4 of the animation sequence.*

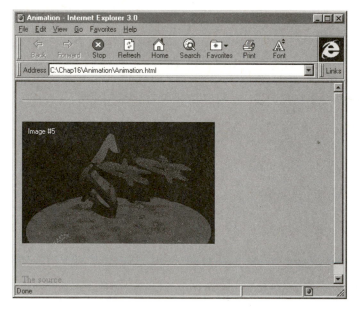

Figure 16-6. *Frame 5 of the animation sequence.*

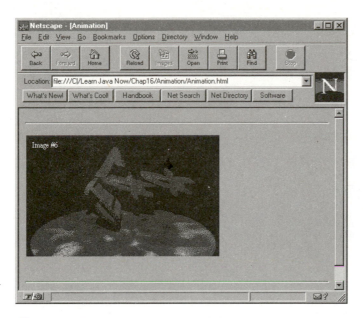

Figure 16-7. *Frame 6 is roughly halfway between* Java *and* VJ++. *Neither word is clearly visible.*

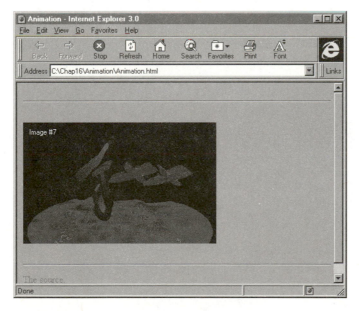

Figure 16-8. *Frame 7 of the animation sequence.*

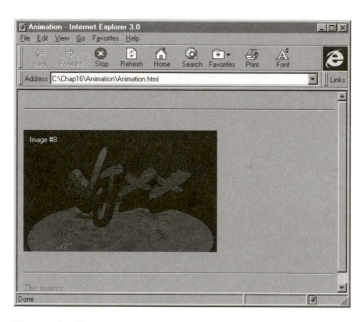

Figure 16-9. *Frame 8 of the animation sequence.*

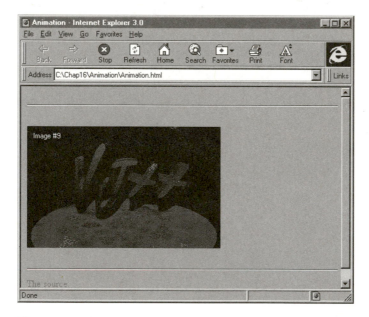

Figure 16-10. *Frame 9 of the animation sequence.*

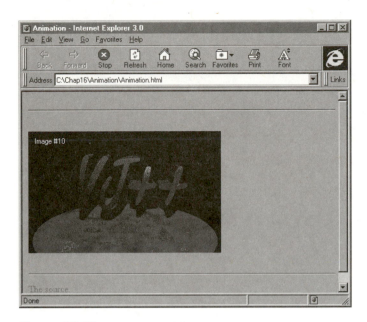

Figure 16-11. *Frame 10 of the animation sequence.*

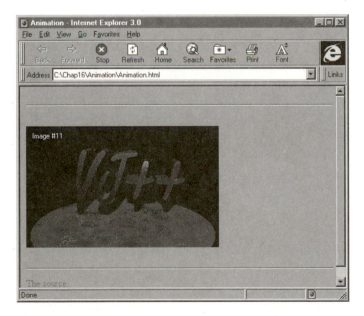

Figure 16-12. *Frame 11 of the animation sequence.*

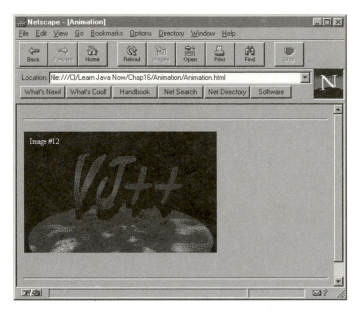

Figure 16-13. *By Frame 12 the morph is complete.*

Adding Audio

The *AudioClip* class is provided to add sound capability to your applet. In much the same way that a .gif image file is associated with an *Image* object, an .au audio file is associated with an *AudioClip* object.

The *AudioClip* class provides three methods: *play* plays the *AudioClip* once, *loop* plays the *AudioClip* in a loop, and *stop* stops the *AudioClip* from playing.

What Is an .au File?

Unfortunately for PC users, Java does not understand .wav files. However, this is only a minor nuisance, since several utilities are available for converting .wav files into .au format.

To add a little sound capability, I converted the Microsoft Windows 95 logon music to .au format and associated it with the replay by making the following additions to the *run* method.

```
public void run()
{
    // ...same as before...

    repaint();

    // get the audio clip that goes with the animation above
    String sSoundClip = new String(m_imageFile + ".au");
    AudioClip ac = getAudioClip(getCodeBase(), sSoundClip);

    // now play it in a loop
    ac.loop();

    while (true)
    {

        //...same here as well
    }
}
```

run constructs the name of the .au file to load by appending the *.au* suffix to the prefix *(LJN)* provided for the image files. Thus, the default filename is LJN.au. It then loads this audio file by calling the *getAudioClip* method, which returns an *AudioClip* object. Finally, *run* starts replaying this audio clip in a loop by calling the *AudioClip.loop* method before replaying the video images.

When the user exits the applet, *run* calls the *AudioClip.stop* method to turn the sound off.

 OTE The Java specification says that the *MediaTracker* class will eventually support audio loading; however, at this time, it supports only image files.

Conclusion

In this chapter, you've seen how to add replay of stored video images to your applets using the *MediaTracker* class. In addition, you've learned how to add audio replay to your applets to accompany image replay.

The Abstract Window Toolkit

Since way back in Chapter 8, we've been importing the java.awt package. At that time I explained that *awt* stood for Abstract Window Toolkit, but I didn't explain what that meant. Let's correct that omission.

The Abstract Window Toolkit (AWT) is Java's mapping package. The AWT creates the windows that you see displayed. In fact, the *Applet* class is a member of the AWT. There are a lot of other members of that package that we haven't looked into at all. Let's take a closer look at some of those classes now.

Using the Abstract Window Toolkit

The super class of most of the classes that make up the AWT package is *Component*. This is shown in Figure 17-1 on the next page. Our old favorite, *Applet*, extends *Component* through the classes *Container* and *Panel*.

 OTE Many of the *Applet* methods used in earlier applets, such as *getBackground*, *getForeground*, and *size*, are inherited from *Component*. This means that these same methods are available to the other AWT methods as well.

Broadly speaking, the AWT breaks down into two sets of classes: the simple components and the container components. The simple components are the classes along the right side of Figure 17-1. These classes, such as *Button, Label,* and *Scrollbar,* mirror their like-named equivalents in other windowing packages such as the C++-based Microsoft Foundation Classes.

The *Container* component, which appears on the left side of Figure 17-1, serves as a generic holder of other components. For example, a container can contain multiple buttons, labels, text fields, and the like. The subclasses of *Container* add specific behavior. For example, a *Dialog* is a modal, fixed-size window that the application can pop up.

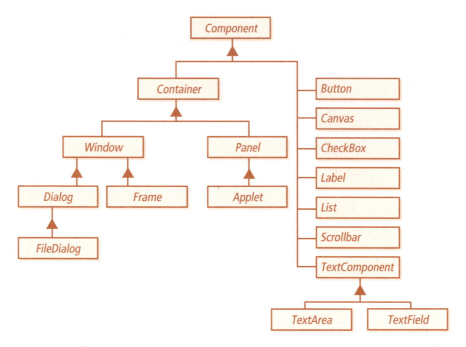

Figure 17-1. *The subclasses of the* Component *class, the super class of most of the classes that make up the Abstract Window Toolkit.*

Using Simple Components

Since *Applet* is a subclass of *Container,* it can contain AWT components. Let's make our initial foray into the AWT by attaching a few simple components to an applet.

This applet displays a label, a text box, and a button. The user can enter text into the text box. Selecting the button transfers whatever text is in the text box to the label.

Creating the Boilerplate

Use the AppletWizard to create the applet boilerplate. I call this applet *SimpleComponent*. Make the normal selections in Steps 1 and 2. This time select "No, thank you" to the question, "Would you like your applet to be multi-threaded?" in Step 3. There are no parameters in Step 4.

When you finish, the applet summary should appear as follows:

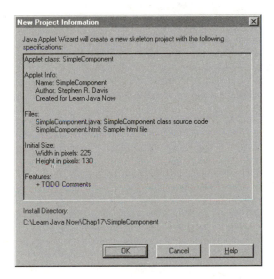

If your summary matches this one, click OK to create the applet boilerplate.

Filling In the Blanks

Make the additions marked in bold to the applet boilerplate created by the AppletWizard:

```
// SimpleComponent - demonstrates how to attach simple
//                   Abstract Window Toolkit components
//                   to an applet
import java.applet.*;
import java.awt.*;
```

(continued)

```java
public class SimpleComponent extends Applet
{
    // Label - a label is a string of text that can be
    //         modified by the program but not by
    //         the user
    private Label  m_label = new Label("Type in the text field");

    // TextField - a text field represents a one-line,
    //             optionally editable area of text
    private TextField m_textField = new TextField(10);

    // Button - a button is a simple object that you can
    //          select using the mouse or by tabbing to it
    //          and pressing Enter
    private Button m_button = new Button("Read Text Field");

    public String getAppletInfo()
    {
        return "Name: SimpleComponent\r\n" +
               "Author: Stephen R. Davis\r\n" +
               "Created for Learn Java Now (c)";
    }

    public void init()
    {
        resize(320, 240);

        // TODO: Place Addition Initialization code here
        // Attach the label, text field, and button to the
        // applet
        add(m_label);
        add(m_textField);
        add(m_button);
    }

    public void paint(Graphics g)
    {
    }

    public boolean action(Event event, Object obj)
    {
```

```
    // if this action sprung from a button...
    Object oTarget = event.target;
    if (oTarget instanceof Button)
    {
        // ...and if the button label is the same
        // as "our button"
        Button buttonTarget = (Button)oTarget;
        String sButtonString = buttonTarget.getLabel();
        if (sButtonString.compareTo("Read Text Field") == 0)
        {
            String s = m_textField.getText();
            m_label.setText(s);
            return true;
        }
    }
    return false;
    }
}
```

Figure 17-2 shows a possible result from executing the SimpleComponent applet.

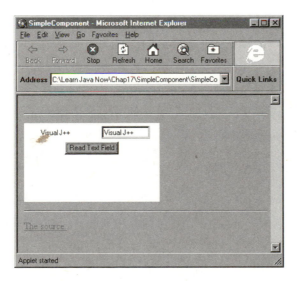

Figure 17-2. *A possible result of executing the SimpleComponent applet.*

Three simple components are constructed when the SimpleComponent applet is constructed:

- A label with the initial text *Type in the text field*
- A text field
- A button with the label *Read Text Field*

Both the label and the button are autosized to match their text. The empty text field is set to a width of 10 characters by the constructor.

The applet's *init* function attaches these components to the applet using the *Component.add* method. Once a component is attached to a container, the container takes care of most of the mundane chores associated with maintaining the component. For example, *SimpleApplet.paint* doesn't have to do anything. The container already calls the *paint* method for each of the components attached to it. Simple components know how to paint themselves without additional help from the application program.

You do have to provide a method if you want to receive events from the components, however. We could override the *handleEvent* method to handle events directed at the applet such as mouse clicks, mouse movements, and so forth. The event we are looking for is called the action event.

An **action event** is the event created by activating a simple component. The action event for a button is generated by clicking the button. The action event for a text field is generated by pressing Enter with the cursor in the text field. There is no action event for a label.

It is not necessary to override the *handleEvent* method to snag action events. In the case of mouse events, the default *handleEvent* method calls special mouse methods such as *mouseDown* and *mouseMoves,* which can be overridden to intercept the specific event. In the case of action events, the default *handleEvent* method invokes a method called *action*. The *action* method can be overridden to take whatever action you desire.

To provide an action event handler for a component, you can inherit from the component and override the *action* method. In this example program we could have created a new class, say *OurButton*, which extends *Button*.

The *OurButton.action* method would receive the action event generated by clicking *OurButton*. However, creating a separate class for each component in the applet can get pretty laborious.

Fortunately, it's not necessary. The default *action* method for each component simply invokes the *action* method of its parent. The **parent** of a component is the container to which the component is attached. In this case the parent of the button is the SimpleComponent applet. Thus, by overriding the single *action* method in the applet, we can intercept in one place action events for all components attached to the applet.

If we do that, however, the problem becomes "How do we know which component generated the action?" In this case, we have two sources of action events: the text field and the button. We want to take action only when the user clicks the button.

The *Event* object passed to *action* contains two arguments that are particularly useful in deciding what action to take. *target* is a reference to the object (in this case, *Component*) that initiated the action. Thus, when the user selects our button object, *target* is a reference to that button. In addition to that, *Event.arg* describes the new state of the target object. *arg* can be a string containing text. In the case of a scroll bar, it is the position to scroll to. (*arg* is passed to *action* as the second argument.)

We are now in position to understand the *action* method above. *action* starts out by asking whether the *Event.target* is a type of *Button* object. If it is not, it cannot possibly be the Read Text Field button we are looking for. It performs this test as follows:

```
Object oTarget = event.target;
if (oTarget instanceof Button)
{
    // ...whatever
}
```

The *instanceof* operator is *true* if the object on the left is of the same type (or a subtype) of the class on the right.

If *oTarget* is a button, we still don't know whether it's our button.

OTE Actually, we do know that *oTarget* is our button; there's only one but-ton in this applet. However, I wrote this applet to be as general as possible. If your applet has only one button, you can remove this test.

To determine whether this is our button, *action* reads the button label and compares it to the expected value. It does this by first casting the generic *oTarget Object* into a button. We know this cast is safe since we wouldn't be here if *instanceof* hadn't already said that *oTarget* is a button. The method then reads the button label and compares it to Read Text Field. If *compareTo* returns a 0, indicating that the two strings are the same, we know that the user selected our button.

Once the applet determines that yes, indeed, this is our button, it transfers the contents of the text field *m_textField* to the label *m_label*. Returning a *true* informs the super class that we have handled the action in this case. The applet returns *false* in all other cases to indicate that it really hasn't handled the action event.

More Complicated *action* Methods

There is another way that *action* can determine whether *event.target* refers to our button. The following version of *action* is simpler, if not as generic:

```
public boolean action(Event event, Object obj)
{
    // if this is our action button...
    if (event.target == m_button)
    {
        // ...transfer text from text field to label
        String s = m_textField.getText();
        m_label.setText(s);
        return true;
    }
    return false;
}
```

This version of *action* simply looks to see if *event.target* refers to the same object as *m_button*. This approach is simple and just as valid, but it relies on the fact that *action* has access to a reference to the de-sired object, which might not always be the case.

More complicated applets will want to take different actions for different components. This is handled using multiple tests:

```
public boolean action(Event event, Object obj)
{
    Object objTarget = event.target;
    if (objTarget instanceof Button)
    {
        // ...handle buttons here...
    }
    if (objTarget instanceof TextField)
    {
        // ...handle Enter within text fields here...
    }
    // ...etc...

    // get here for objects we don't handle
    return false;
}
```

Using this approach, a single *action* method can handle actions originating from any one of several AWT components.

Layout Policies

Figure 17-2 on page 303 shows a possible result of executing the Simple-Component applet. Figure 17-3 and Figure 17-4 on the next page show other, less desirable results that depend on the size of the applet window.

The problem is that when SimpleComponent attaches the components to the applet container, it doesn't tell the container where to put them. In fact, there is no direct way of telling the container where to display the components attached to it. Instead, every container is assigned what is called a layout policy.

The **layout policy** determines how the components that are attached to a container are displayed. The default layout policy for the *Applet* class is *FlowLayout*. Under *FlowLayout,* components are positioned from left to right across the window in the order in which they are attached. When there is no more room on the right, the next component is placed at the beginning of the next line. You can see how *FlowLayout* works by comparing Figures 17-2 through 17-4.

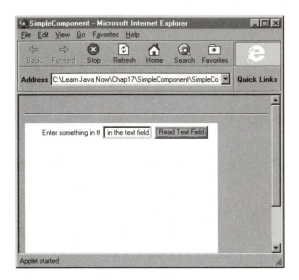

Figure 17-3. *Another possible result of executing the SimpleComponent applet.*

Figure 17-4. *Yet a third possible result of executing the SimpleComponent applet.*

The layout policy is enforced by the *LayoutManager* interface. You can change the layout policy by assigning the container a new class that implements the *LayoutManager* interface via the *Container.setLayout* method. Several such classes are provided.

The most common layout manager class besides *FlowLayout* is *Border-Layout*. This layout manager allows the application to position components relative to the window borders, which are labeled North, South, West, and East. One other "border" is the center of the window, which is called Center. These directions are also known as **gravity**. Thus, we might say that a component has West gravity, meaning that as the window changes size, the component moves with the left border. A window that uses *BorderLayout* tends to keep its shape when it is resized.

For example, consider the following version of the *SimpleComponent* applet:

```java
// SimpleComponent - demonstrates how to attach simple
//                   Abstract Window Toolkit components
//                   to an applet using a Border Layout
import java.applet.*;
import java.awt.*;

public class SimpleComponent extends Applet
{
    // Label - a label is a string of text that can be
    //         modified by the program but not by
    //         the user
    private Label  m_label = new Label("Type in the text field");

    // TextField - a text field represents a one-line,
    //             optionally editable area of text
    private TextField m_textField = new TextField(10);

    // Button - a button is a simple object that you can
    //          select using the mouse or by tabbing to it
    //          and pressing Enter
    private Button m_button = new Button("Read Text Field");

    public String getAppletInfo()
    {
        return "Name: SimpleComponent\r\n" +
               "Author: Stephen R. Davis\r\n" +
               "Created for Learn Java Now (c)";
    }
```

(continued)

```
public void init()
{
    resize(320, 240);

    // TODO: Place Addition Initialization code here
    // Use a BorderLayout manager
    setLayout(new BorderLayout());

    // Attach the label, text field, and button to the
    // applet
    add("North", m_label);
    add("Center", m_textField);
    add("South", m_button);
}

public void paint(Graphics g)
{
}

public boolean action(Event event, Object obj)
{
    // if this action sprung from a button...
    Object oTarget = event.target;
    if (oTarget instanceof Button)
    {
        // ...and if the button label is the same
        // as "our button"
        Button buttonTarget = (Button)oTarget;
        String sButtonString = buttonTarget.getLabel();
        if (sButtonString.compareTo("Read Text Field") == 0)
        {
            String s = m_textField.getText();
            m_label.setText(s);
            return true;
        }
    }
    return false;
}
```

Creating a *BorderLayout* object and making it the *LayoutManager* for the applet changes the layout policy. This allows the *add* method to specify the gravity as the first argument. The results of these minor changes has a big change on the appearance of the applet, as shown in Figure 17-5.

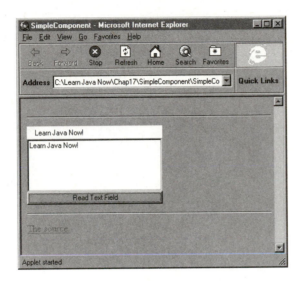

Figure 17-5. *The SimpleComponent applet with a* BorderLayout *object.*

The order in which objects are allocated space under the *BorderLayout* policy is very important:

- North and South objects are allocated as much vertical space as they need. Horizontal space is divided among them.

- West and East objects are then allocated as much space as they need horizontally within any remaining vertical space.

- Center objects are allocated the remainder.

BorderLayout is particularly well suited for windows, which are resizable, because it tends to position components in terms of the window edges and it allocates space in a fair and predictable fashion.

Other layout managers are possible. For example, *GridLayout* implements a regularly spaced grid much like a spreadsheet. *GridBagLayout* implements a grid of irregularly sized objects.

Compound Containers

It is possible to achieve sophisticated results using *BorderLayout* by creating components within components. For example, a subclass of *Container* (such as a *Panel*) can be attached as a single component to an existing container. Of course, the child container has its own layout policy, which might or might not be the same as that of the parent.

For example, the following version of SimpleComponent combines the label and text into a single panel and places it on the left, leaving the button on the right:

```
// SimpleComponent - demonstrates how to attach simple
//                    Abstract Window Toolkit components
//                    to an applet using a Border Layout
import java.applet.*;
import java.awt.*;

public class SimpleComponent extends Applet
{
    // Label - a label is a string of text that can be
    //         modified by the program but not by
    //         the user
    Label m_label = new Label("Enter something in the TextField");

    // TextField - a text field represents a one-line,
    //             optionally editable area of text
    TextField m_textField = new TextField(10);

    // Button - a button is a simple object that you can
    //          select using the mouse or by tabbing to it
    //          and pressing Enter
    Button m_button = new Button("Read Text Field");

    public String getAppletInfo()
    {
        return "Name: SimpleComponent\r\n" +
                "Author: Stephen R. Davis\r\n" +
                "Created for Learn Java Now (c)";
    }

    public void init()
    {
        resize(320, 240);

        // TODO: Place Addition Initialization code here
```

```
        // Use a BorderLayout manager
        setLayout(new BorderLayout());

        // create a panel with the label and text together
        // (put the label above the text field - using Center
        // for the text field gives it any remaining room
        // after the label takes its cut)
        Panel panelText = new Panel();
        panelText.setLayout(new BorderLayout());
        panelText.add("North", m_label);
        panelText.add("Center", m_textField);

        // now add the panel to the applet on the left and
        // the button on the right
        add("Center", panelText);
        add("East", m_button);
    }

public void paint(Graphics g)
{
}

public boolean action(Event event, Object obj)
{
    // if this action sprung from a button...
    Object oTarget = event.target;
    if (oTarget instanceof Button)
    {
        // ...and if the button label is the same
        // as "our button"
        Button buttonTarget = (Button)oTarget;
        String sButtonString = buttonTarget.getLabel();
        if (sButtonString.compareTo("Read Text Field") == 0)

        {
            String s = m_textField.getText();
            m_label.setText(s);
            return true;
        }
    }
    return false;
    }
}
```

This applet creates a *Panel* container with a *BorderLayout* policy into which it places the label and the text field. Giving the label North gravity places the label along the top edge of the panel. Giving the text field Center gravity assigns it any remaining space in the panel. (If I assign it South gravity, the text field scrunches down at the bottom of the panel, which looks funny when the applet window is expanded.)

Once the panel is completed, it is attached to the left of the button in the applet window. (Again, Center gravity is used instead of West gravity. This assigns the panel any remaining room after the button has taken what it needs to accommodate its label.) The results of executing this applet are shown in Figure 17-6.

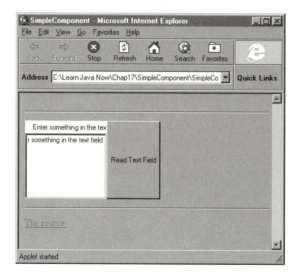

Figure 17-6. *The SimpleComponent applet with the label and the text field in their own* Panel *container.*

The *Frame* Class

As you saw in Figure 17-1 on page 300, there are other container classes besides *Applet*. One of the more popular is *Frame*. *Frame* implements a top-level, framed window separate from the applet's window. It can be moved around the screen. It is generally resizable. It has a title bar across the top, and it might have a menu bar across the top underneath the title bar. Since *Frame* is resizable, its default layout is *BorderLayout*.

OTE From within a browser such as Microsoft Internet Explorer or Netscape Navigator, the applet window is neither resizable nor movable. This makes it appear as part of the HTML page that contains it. By comparison, the fact that a frame is movable and resizable makes it appear to be a separate window above and slightly separate from the HTML page that spawned it.

The following simple applet demonstrates how to create a frame and attach a menu to it.

Creating the Boilerplate

Use the AppletWizard to create the same applet boilerplate, and use the same options that you used for the SimpleComponent applet. Call this applet FrameComponent. When you finish, the applet summary should appear as follows:

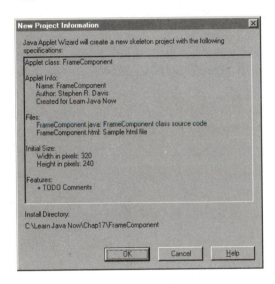

When your summary appears like the one above, click OK to create the applet boilerplate.

Filling In the Blanks

The following listing shows additions to the AppletWizard-generated boilerplate marked in bold:

```java
// FrameComponent - demonstrates how to create a frame with
//                   a simple menu and how to read menu selections
import java.applet.*;
import java.awt.*;
import TestFrame;

public class FrameComponent extends Applet
{
    // m_frame - this is the frame we create
    private Frame m_frame;

    // m_object - the action object passed from the
    //            Frame menu
    private Object m_object;

    public String getAppletInfo()
    {
        return "Name: FrameComponent\r\n" +
               "Author: Stephen R. Davis\r\n" +
               "Created for Learn Java Now (c)";
    }


    public void init()
    {
        resize(320, 240);

        // TODO: Place Addition Initialization code here
        // create a frame of type TestFrame
        m_frame = new TestFrame(this);

        // size the frame
        Dimension d = size();
        m_frame.resize(d);

        // now make it visible (frames are created hidden)
        m_frame.show();
    }

    // paint - if there is an action object, output it
    //         to the applet window
    public void paint(Graphics g)
    {
        if (m_object != null)
```

```
        {
            g.drawString(m_object.toString(), 10, 20);
        }
    }

// action - record the action object for
//          display (this method is not normally invoked -
//          it's only called here because the TestFrame
//          class passes the event along

public boolean action(Event event, Object obj)
{
    m_object = obj;
    repaint();
    return true;
}
}
```

This applet generates an object of class *TestFrame,* which is a subclass of *Frame.* (I will define this class in a minute.) It then sizes the *TestFrame* object and shows it. Calling the *show* method to make the *Frame* visible is necessary since frames (and most other container objects) are created invisible. This allows the applet to attach components and resize the window appropriately before making the window visible. If the window were always visible, the user would see these things occur and the effect would be rather messy.

 OTE   The applet does not try to add the *Frame* object to the applet window. This is because the *Frame* class is a top-level window.

The *TestFrame* class is defined as follows:

```
// TestFrame - implement our own frame
import java.applet.*;
import java.awt.*;
class TestFrame extends Frame
{
    // m_appletParent - this is the applet that
    //                  created the frame
    private Applet  m_appletParent;

    // m_MenuBar - goes along the top of the frame
    private MenuBar m_MenuBar;
```

(continued)

```
    // m_objSelected - this is the menu item selected
    private Object m_objSelected;


    TestFrame(Applet appletParent)
    {
        super("Test Frame");

        // save the parent applet
        m_appletParent = appletParent;

        // now create the menu bar
        m_MenuBar = new MenuBar();

        // add the File menu with its items
        Menu menuFile = new Menu("File");
        menuFile.add(new MenuItem("Open"));
        menuFile.add(new MenuItem("Close"));
        m_MenuBar.add(menuFile);

        // now the Edit menu with its items
        Menu menuEdit = new Menu("Edit");
        menuEdit.add(new MenuItem("Copy"));
        menuEdit.add(new MenuItem("Cut"));
        menuEdit.add(new MenuItem("Paste"));
        m_MenuBar.add(menuEdit);

        setMenuBar(m_MenuBar);
    }

    // action - called if any of the menu items are selected
    public boolean action(Event event, Object o)
    {
        // save the string of the MenuItem selected
        m_objSelected = o;

        // and cause the string to be painted
        repaint();

        // it is also possible to signal the parent
        if (m_appletParent != null)
        {
            m_appletParent.action(event, o);
        }
        return true;
    }

    public void paint(Graphics g)
```

```
    {
        String s;
        if (m_objSelected == null)
        {
            s = "No menu item selected";
        }
        else
        {
            s = "You selected " + m_objSelected.toString();
        }

        Dimension dimWin = size();
        Insets insFrame = insets();
        int nWinWidth  =
                dimWin.width  - (insFrame.left + insFrame.right);
        int nWinHeight =
                dimWin.height - (insFrame.top  + insFrame.bottom);

        FontMetrics fm = getFontMetrics(getFont());
        int nStringHeight = fm.getHeight();
        int nStringWidth  = fm.stringWidth(s);

        int nLeftOffset = (nWinWidth  - nStringWidth) / 2;
        int nTopOffset  = (nWinHeight + nStringHeight)/ 2;

        g.drawString(s, nLeftOffset, nTopOffset);
        g.drawRect(0, 0, nWinWidth - 1, nWinHeight - 1);
    }
}
```

The constructor for the *TestFrame* class starts by passing the title of the frame, *Test Frame,* to the *Frame(String)* constructor. This creates the basic frame and initializes the title bar. It then records the parent object before creating a menu bar.

To create a menu bar, *TestFrame* first creates an object of class *MenuBar*. To the menu bar, *TestFrame* adds two menus: File and Edit. A *Menu* object represents a drop-down menu. Passing a *true* as an optional second argument to the *Menu* constructor makes the menu tearable. Tearable menus can be removed from the menu bar and placed anywhere within the frame. *TestFrame* then adds the individual *MenuItem* objects to the menus. It is the menu items that the user actually selects. Selecting a menu item generates a call to the *action* method of the associated *MenuItem* object. This action object is passed up to the menu and ultimately to the frame.

N OTE   The object passed to *Frame.action* is not the menu item, but a string representing the label of the *MenuItem*.

Once the *MenuBar* object is completed, it is added to the frame using the *setMenuBar* method. Notice that a frame can have zero or one menu bar. Calling *setMenuBar* to add a second menu bar replaces the old one.

The *TestFrame.action* method simply records the action object and invokes *repaint* to cause the object to be displayed. In a normal applet, this method would check to see which menu item was selected and then take appropriate action.

 N OTE   In addition, the *TestFrame.action* method also invokes the *Frame-Component.action* method of its parent. This is to show you how to pass the menu selection back in the applet should you prefer to do so. The default *Frame.action* does not invoke the *Applet.action* method, since the test frame is not a child component of the applet.

The *TestFrame.paint* method displays the string *You selected xxx,* where *xxx* is the menu item you selected, or it displays *No menu item selected* if you have yet to select a menu item. This would be easy, except that *TestFrame.paint* displays this string centered within the frame window.

You've seen how to display text centered in an applet's window. What makes the frame so much more complicated is that it devotes considerable window real estate to the title bar, the menu bar, and the scroll bar (if attached). The *size* method includes these window dressings in the size information it returns. Unfortunately, the offset passed to the draw methods is measured from the upper left corner of the writable area and does not include the size of the border. Thus, it is up to the application to subtract the size of the window dressings when calculating the size of the writable window.

To account for the size of any window dressings, *TestFrame* calls the *Container.insets* method, which returns an object of class *Insets*. This object contains four values that represent the size of the left, right, top, and bottom borders, including all window dressings.

The following calculation removes the effect of the border:

```
Dimension dimWin = size();
Insets insFrame = insets();
int nWinWidth  = dimWin.width  - (insFrame.left + insFrame.right);
int nWinHeight = dimWin.height - (insFrame.top  + insFrame.bottom);
```

For example, *dimWin.height* is the height of the entire frame, including title bar, menu, and horizontal scroll bar. *nWinHeight* represents the height of the writable window only.

The result of executing *TestFrame* from within the Visual J++ IDE is shown in Figure 17-7. Notice how the message in the *Frame* window is centered and displays the last menu option selected. Notice also that the menu option has been communicated back to the applet window.

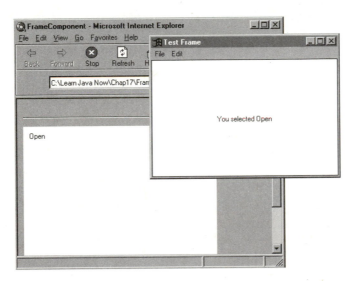

Figure 17-7. *The frame and applet windows from the TestFrame applet.*

Building a Container Automatically: The ResourceWizard

Visual J++ provides a utility to relieve much of the tedium of creating complicated windows by hand. The programmer can draw the window using the Resource Editor, a convenient drawing tool. The Resource-Wizard then converts these resource objects into Java classes.

OTE The ResourceWizard does not support all types of resources. Visual J++ 1.0 supports only menus and dialog boxes—even then, it supports dialog boxes only incompletely. However, as the ResourceWizard evolves, it will undoubtedly handle more and more resource features.

Creating a ResourceWizard Menu

To create a menu using the ResourceWizard, you first need to create the .rct resource template file. Begin by choosing New from the File menu. Select Resource Template in the New dialog box and then click OK. Now insert a resource into the file by choosing Resource from the Insert menu. In the Insert Resource dialog box, select Menu and then click OK. At this point, the Resource Editor opens a window like that shown in Figure 17-8.

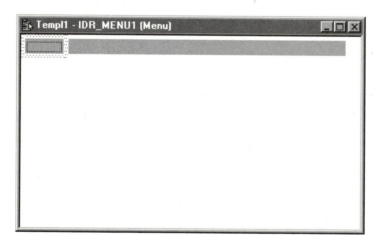

Figure 17-8. *The initial menu window in the Resource Editor.*

Double-click on the black rectangle at the upper left of this window to open the Menu Item Properties dialog box, and then click the push pin button in the upper left corner of the dialog box. (The dialog box remains on screen, even while the focus moves elsewhere, when this button is "pushed.") Type *File* in the Caption text box and notice that a blank menu item appears on the new File menu. Click on the blank menu item and type *Open* in the Caption text box. Repeat the process to create a Close menu item. To move to the next menu, click on the menu bar just to the right of *File*. Repeat the process to create an Edit menu with Copy, Cut, and Paste menu items.

Once you finish entering all menu items, close the menu by clicking the Close button. Since this is the only menu we want to create, close the resource file as well. Since the resource file has changed, the program responds by prompting, "Do you want to save the resource file?" Click Yes. You will then see a file selection dialog box. Save the file in the same directory as your project, using whatever name you prefer (but retain the .rct extension). In my case, I chose the name *RWMenu.rct*.

You must now convert the .rct resource template file into a .java source file. Choose Java Resource Wizard from the Tools menu. Now enter the name of the resource file and click Next. From here you can change the name of the menu class you want to create from that created by the Resource Editor. I chose the name *RWMenu*. Now click Finish.

The ResourceWizard should respond that RWMenu.java was successfully created. The RWMenu.java file created by the ResourceWizard for the menu above appears as follows:

```
//------------------------------------------------------------
// RWMenu.java:
//          Implementation for menu creation class RWMenu
//
//------------------------------------------------------------
import java.awt.*;

public class RWMenu
{
    Frame    m_Frame        = null;
    boolean m_fInitialized = false;

    // MenuBar definitions
    //--------------------------------------------------------
    MenuBar mb;

    // Menu and Menu item definitions
    //--------------------------------------------------------
    Menu m1;    // File
    MenuItem ID_FILE_OPEN;      // Open
    MenuItem ID_FILE_CLOSE;     // Close
    Menu m4;    // Edit
    MenuItem ID_EDIT_COPY;      // Copy
    MenuItem ID_EDIT_CUT;       // Cut
    MenuItem ID_EDIT_PASTE;     // Paste
```

(continued)

```
// Constructor
//----------------------------------------------------------------
public RWMenu (Frame frame)
{
    m_Frame = frame;
}

// Initialization.
//----------------------------------------------------------------
public boolean CreateMenu()
{
    // Can only init controls once
    //--------------------------------------------------------
    if (m_fInitialized || m_Frame == null)
        return false;

    // Create menubar and attach to the frame
    //--------------------------------------------------------
    mb = new MenuBar();
    m_Frame.setMenuBar(mb);

    // Create menu and menu items and assign to menubar
    //--------------------------------------------------------
    m1 = new Menu("File");
    mb.add(m1);
        ID_FILE_OPEN = new MenuItem("Open");
        m1.add(ID_FILE_OPEN);
        ID_FILE_CLOSE = new MenuItem("Close");
        m1.add(ID_FILE_CLOSE);
    m4 = new Menu("Edit");
    mb.add(m4);
        ID_EDIT_COPY = new MenuItem("Copy");
        m4.add(ID_EDIT_COPY);
        ID_EDIT_CUT = new MenuItem("Cut");
        m4.add(ID_EDIT_CUT);
        ID_EDIT_PASTE = new MenuItem("Paste");
        m4.add(ID_EDIT_PASTE);

    m_fInitialized = true;
    return true;
    }
}
```

The *RWMenu* class bears a striking resemblance to the menu we created by hand earlier. You should have little trouble understanding it.

Note that the ResourceWizard does not add the file to the project. As an example, let's create a do-nothing applet that opens the menu and takes its input.

Create a project file and applet boilerplate using the AppletWizard, as usual. Select the same options as in the TestFrame applet above. I named this applet *AutoFrame*. Now add the RWMenu.java file to the project by choosing Files Into Project from the Insert menu. This opens a file selection dialog box. Select RWMenu.java and then click Add.

Make the additions to the *AutoFrame* class indicated in bold:

```
// AutoFrame - exercise the RWMenu class
import java.applet.*;
import java.awt.*;
import RWMenu;

public class AutoFrame extends Applet
{

    public AutoFrame()
    {
    }

    public String getAppletInfo()
    {
        return "Name: AutoFrame\r\n" +
               "Author: Stephen R. Davis\r\n" +
               "Created for Learn Java Now (c)";
    }

    public void init()
    {
        resize(320, 240);

        // TODO: Place Addition Initialization code here
        // create a framed window
        Frame frame = new Frame("ResourceWizard created menu");
        frame.resize(400, 200);

        // now create a RWMenu on this frame
        RWMenu menu = new RWMenu(frame);

        // finally create the members of the RWMenu
        menu.CreateMenu();
```

(continued)

```
        // now show the frame with the menu attached
        frame.show();
    }

    public void paint(Graphics g)
    {
    }

    // TODO: Place additional applet Code here

}
```

The *init* method creates and sizes a *Frame* object. This is the frame window that will contain the *RWMenu*. It then creates an *RWMenu*, passing it the frame. The call to *RWMenu.CreateMenu* tells the *RWMenu* to create the constituent menu bar, menus, and menu items. Finally, the call to *Frame-.show* makes the frame visible.

The results of executing this applet are identical to those shown in Figure 17-7 on page 321 for the TestFrame applet.

 OTE   If this applet does not compile properly, make sure that the RW-Menu.java file has been added to the project. In addition, make sure that the RWMenu.class is in the Classfiles path. (To edit this path, choose Options from the Tools menu. In the Options dialog box, click the Directories tab and select Class Files from the Show Directories For drop-down list box.)

Creating a ResourceWizard Dialog Box

The following DialogWindow applet uses the dialog box feature of the ResourceWizard to create a sample dialog box that queries the user for his or her name and marital status (the latter is optional, of course).

The applet exercises the *AutoDialog* class sufficiently to allow you to see how to get user input into and out of the dialog box. Create the Dialog-Window applet using the AppletWizard, in the usual way. Make the same selections you made for *RWMenu*. The additions to the AppletWizard-generated boilerplate are marked in bold.

```
// DialogWindow - pop up the dialog box created by the
//                 ResourceWizard and wait for the user to enter
//                 OK. once he or she does, read the data out of
//                 the dialog box, close the dialog box, and
//                 display the data in the applet window
import java.applet.*;
import java.awt.*;
import AutoDialog;

public class DialogWindow extends Applet
{
    // the extra frame attached to the applet
    private OurFrame m_frame = null;

    public DialogWindow()
    {
    }

    public String getAppletInfo()
    {
        return "Name: DialogWindow\r\n" +
               "Author: Stephen R. Davis\r\n" +
               "Created for Learn Java Now (c)";
    }

    public void init()
    {
        resize(320, 240);

        // TODO: Place Addition Initialization code here
        // Create one of our dialog box frames
        m_frame = new OurFrame(this);
    }

    public void paint(Graphics g)
    {
        DialogData data = m_frame.getData();
        if (data != null)
        {
            g.drawString(data.toString(), 10, 20);
        }
    }
}
```

(continued)

```
class OurFrame extends Frame
{
    // child dialog box
    private AutoDialog m_autodialog = null;

    // parent applet
    private Applet m_parent = null;

    // data contained in dialog box
    private DialogData m_data = null;

    public OurFrame(Applet parent)
    {
        super("Auto Dialog");

        m_parent = parent;

        // be sure to set a font (the size is unimportant
        // because it will be changed by the AutoDialog class)
        setFont(new Font("Arial", Font.PLAIN, 12));

        // now create the AutoDialog and let it add the
        // components to our frame
        m_autodialog = new AutoDialog(this);
        m_autodialog.CreateControls();

        show();
    }

    public boolean action(Event event, Object obj)
    {
      // if this is our button...
      Object target = event.target;
      if (target instanceof Button)
      {
          Button button = (Button)target;
          String buttonLabel = button.getLabel();
          if (buttonLabel.compareTo("OK") == 0)

          {
              // ...get the data from the dialog box...
              String sFirstName=m_autodialog.IDC_EDIT1.getText();
              String sLastName =m_autodialog.IDC_EDIT2.getText();
              boolean bMarried =m_autodialog.IDC_CHECK1.getState();
```

```
                // ...create a DialogData object...
                m_data = new DialogData(sFirstName,
                                        sLastName,
                                        bMarried);

                // ...and force the applet to output the data
                m_parent.repaint();
            }

            // hide the dialog box if either button is pressed
            hide();
            return true;
        }
        return false;
    }

    public DialogData getData()
    {
        return m_data;
    }
}

class DialogData
{
    private String m_sFirstName;
    private String m_sLastName;
    private boolean m_bMarried;

    public DialogData(String sFN, String sLN, boolean bM)
    {
        m_sFirstName = sFN;
        m_sLastName  = sLN;
        m_bMarried   = bM;
    }

    public String toString()
    {
        String s;
        s   = m_sFirstName + " " + m_sLastName + " ";
        s += m_bMarried ? "(married)" : "(single)";
        return s;
    }
}
```

The first addition to DialogWindow is a member of *OurFrame* class. An *OurFrame* object is created when the applet window is initialized in the *init* method.

The *OurFrame* class is a locally created subclass of *Frame*. I chose to store the dialog box in a frame to make it resizable and give it a label. I created the *OurFrame* subclass so that I could override the *action* method of *Frame*. This method processes the OK and Cancel buttons.

The *OurFrame* constructor creates the *AutoDialog* object and then calls the *CreateControls* method. Remember that *CreateControls* creates the components that you draw into your dialog box using the Resource Editor. *CreateControls* adds these components to the *OurFrame* object. Finally, *OurFrame* unhides the frame with the dialog box information by calling *show*.

As the user enters data into the dialog box components, the action events make their way up to *OurFrame.action*. These events do not reach the applet's *action* method because the components were added not to the applet's window but to the newly created frame. This *action* method ignores all events except button clicks. If the user clicks the OK button, *action* first reads the data from the *AutoDialog* object. It does this by accessing the data members of *AutoDialog* directly. (These are left friendly in the class definition so they are accessible to other classes in the same package.) The data read from the *AutoDialog* object is used to create a *DialogData* object. This object is nothing more than a user-created repository for the dialog box data.

 NOTE   Creating a *DialogData* class to contain the data that appears in the dialog box is a good programming practice. This tends to isolate the remainder of the program from details such as the names of the data members in the *AutoDialog* class.

Once the *DialogData* has been created to hold the user-entered data, *OurFrame* calls the *repaint* method to force the parent applet to repaint its window. Finally, *OurFrame* hides itself to make the dialog box disappear.

If the user clicks the Cancel button, *OurFrame* simply hides itself without taking any further action.

DialogWindow.paint first looks to see if *OurFrame* has any user data to report (i.e., whether there is a *DialogData* object yet). Remember that this is the case only after the user enters data in the dialog box and then clicks OK. If not, *paint* doesn't do anything. If there is a *DialogData* object, *paint* calls its *toString* method and displays the results.

To create the dialog box resource, choose Resource from the Insert menu as before, except this time double-click the Dialog option. Now double-click the IDD_DIALOG1 dialog box. A default dialog box containing just an OK and a Cancel button should appear. In addition, off to the right you should see a Controls toolbar containing the different types of controls that you can add to a dialog box.

OTE If the Controls toolbar does not appear, it has probably been turned off. Choose Toolbars from the View menu and make sure that Controls is selected. If not, select it and the toolbar should appear.

Using the dialog box tools, create a dialog box with text fields (these are named Edit Box controls on the toolbar) for first name and last name and a check box labeled *Married*. Use static text controls to label the text fields. To add a component to the dialog box, simply click on the component on the Controls toolbar and then click where you want the component to go. To move a component, click it and drag it. Grab the corner of a component to resize it. Double-click the component to change its properties. There are several tools along the bottom that allow you to quickly and easily align components in the window. Double-click the dialog box itself to change generic properties such as font size. (I set the font to 14-point Arial to make the dialog box more visible.)

My dialog box appears as shown on the following page.

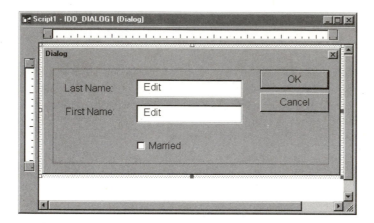

Figure 17-9. *A sample dialog box created using the Resource Editor.*

When you finish, close the dialog box and save the resource template file. I called my resource template file *AutoDialog*. Now execute the Resource-Wizard as before, specifying the name of the resource template file. This time I told the ResourceWizard to call my class *AutoDialog*. The Resource-Wizard created two Java files: AutoDialog.java and DialogLayout.java.

The *DialogLayout* class is created any time that your resource file contains a dialog box. This class is always the same. *DialogLayout* implements a simple layout policy that is more similar to that used by C++. Using the *DialogLayout* class reduces the amount of work that the *ResourceWizard* class must do.

The *AutoDialog* class appears as follows:

```
//------------------------------------------------------------
// AutoDialog.java:
//         Implementation for container control
//         initialization class AutoDialog
//
//------------------------------------------------------------
import java.awt.*;
import DialogLayout;

public class AutoDialog
{
    Container    m_Parent      = null;
    boolean      m_fInitialized = false;
    DialogLayout m_Layout;
```

```
// Control definitions
//-----------------------------------------------------------
Button          IDOK;
Button          IDCANCEL;
TextField       IDC_EDIT1;
TextField       IDC_EDIT2;
Label           IDC_STATIC1;
Label           IDC_STATIC2;
Checkbox        IDC_CHECK1;


// Constructor
//-----------------------------------------------------------
public AutoDialog (Container parent)
{
    m_Parent = parent;
}

// Initialization.
//-----------------------------------------------------------
public boolean CreateControls()
{
    // Can only init controls once
    //-------------------------------------------------------
    if (m_fInitialized || m_Parent == null)
        return false;

    // Parent must be a derivation of the Container class
    //-------------------------------------------------------
    if (!(m_Parent instanceof Container))
        return false;

    // since there is no way to know if a given font is
    // supported from platform to platform, we only change
    // the size of the font, and not type face name.  And, we
    // only change the font if the dialog resource specified
    // a font.
    //-------------------------------------------------------
    if (true)
    {
        Font OldFnt = m_Parent.getFont();
        Font NewFnt = new Font(OldFnt.getName(),
                               OldFnt.getStyle(),
                               16);

        m_Parent.setFont(NewFnt);
    }
```

(continued)

333

```
                    // All position and sizes are in Dialog Units, so, we use
                    // the DialogLayout manager.
                    //----------------------------------------------------------
                    m_Layout = new DialogLayout(m_Parent, 183, 74);
                    m_Parent.setLayout(m_Layout);
                    m_Parent.addNotify();

                    Dimension size  = m_Layout.getDialogSize();
                    Insets    insets = m_Parent.insets();

                    m_Parent.resize(insets.left + size.width  + insets.right,
                                    insets.top  + size.height + insets.bottom);

                    // Control creation
                    //----------------------------------------------------------
                    IDOK = new Button ("OK");
                    m_Parent.add(IDOK);
                    m_Layout.setShape(IDOK, 129, 7, 50, 14);

                    IDCANCEL = new Button ("Cancel");
                    m_Parent.add(IDCANCEL);
                    m_Layout.setShape(IDCANCEL, 129, 24, 50, 14);

                    IDC_EDIT1 = new TextField ("");
                    m_Parent.add(IDC_EDIT1);
                    m_Layout.setShape(IDC_EDIT1, 58, 13, 62, 14);

                    IDC_EDIT2 = new TextField ("");
                    m_Parent.add(IDC_EDIT2);
                    m_Layout.setShape(IDC_EDIT2, 58, 35, 62, 14);

                    IDC_STATIC1 = new Label ("First name:", Label.LEFT);
                    m_Parent.add(IDC_STATIC1);
                    m_Layout.setShape(IDC_STATIC1, 13, 13, 41, 8);

                    IDC_STATIC2 = new Label ("Last name:", Label.LEFT);
                    m_Parent.add(IDC_STATIC2);
                    m_Layout.setShape(IDC_STATIC2, 13, 37, 40, 8);

                    IDC_CHECK1 = new Checkbox ("Married");
                    m_Parent.add(IDC_CHECK1);
                    m_Layout.setShape(IDC_CHECK1, 59, 55, 39, 10);

                    m_fInitialized = true;
                    return true;
                }
            }
```

This code is not different in concept from that generated for *RWMenu*. The constructor does nothing more than save the parent. The *CreateControls* method creates a series of components and attaches them along with the *DialogLayout* policy to the parent.

Figure 17-10 shows the applet window after some sample information has been entered in the dialog box.

Figure 17-10. *The applet window resulting from entering my name and marital status and then clicking OK in the AutoDialog dialog box shown in Figure 17-9.*

 OTE Displaying the data from the dialog box in the applet's window is not particularly useful; however, it does demonstrate how to read data from the dialog box and use it in your applets as you see fit.

Conclusion

In this chapter, you've seen some of the classes that make up the Abstract Window Toolkit. You've learned how simple components can be added to containers in different ways to create intricate windows. You've learned how to receive the events created when these simple components such as buttons and menu items are selected. You've seen how to create and write to a framed window. Finally, you've learned how the ResourceWizard takes some of the drudgery out of creating complex containers.

I hope that this has been enough of an introduction to the Abstract Window Toolkit to pique your curiosity. You can spend hours of fun (and frustration) investigating the nooks and crannies of the Abstract Window Toolkit.

Installation and Other Basics

You'll need to install the enclosed Visual J++ CD-ROM before you can start having fun compiling and executing the Java programs contained in this book. In the following sections, I'll give you a few pointers about getting Visual J++ up and running.

 OTE Production schedules being what they are, these instructions were generated using a late beta version of Visual J++. While it's unlikely that much has changed, some of the details of the captured screens might vary slightly from what you see.

Installing Visual J++

To install Visual J++, start by loading the CD-ROM included with this book. This should bring up the Master Setup window automatically. If not, use the Microsoft Windows Explorer to execute the Setup program in the CD-ROM's root directory. The first window should look like that shown in Figure A-1 on the next page.

In the Master Setup window, select Install Visual J++ 1.0. In the next window, the Welcome window, click the Next button. This takes you to the Software License window. If you accept the conditions of the software license, click Yes to continue the installation process.

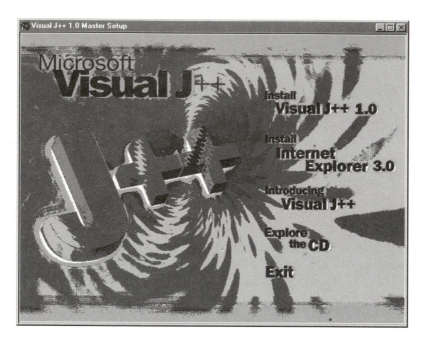

Figure A-1. *The Visual J++ 1.0 Master Setup window.*

The next window is the Registration window. Here you enter your name, the name of your organization, and your CD key. Your organization name is optional, but the CD key is not. This key is located on a yellow sticker contained within the CD crystal.

Click Next to go to the Installation Options window, which looks like the window shown in Figure A-2.

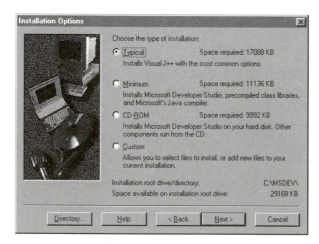

Figure A-2. *The Installation Options window.*

You can click the directory button in the lower left corner to change the directory into which Visual J++ will be installed. The default is C:\MSDEV.

The four option buttons allow you to select the type of installation. The CD-ROM option requires the least amount of hard disk space; however, you must have the CD-ROM loaded when you use Visual J++. (No listening to Lawrence Welk on CD while you're programming.) In addition, since the CD-ROM is considerably slower than a hard disk, selecting this option will result in slower execution.

The Typical installation copies most of what you need to the hard disk. While the F1-type context-sensitive Help files get copied, this option leaves the remaining Help files on the CD-ROM. This means that you must have the CD-ROM loaded to get detailed help. In addition, the Typical installation leaves the class library .java source files on the CD-ROM. These source files can be useful when you try to figure out why your perfectly reasonable program is being so cruelly misinterpreted by the standard library.

The Minimum option installs only the files that are absolutely necessary to run Visual J++ without requiring the CD-ROM.

The Custom installation option allows you to pick exactly which options you want. If hard disk space is not at a premium, select Custom and select Books Online in the next window to copy the online books to hard disk as well. The online books increase the hard disk footprint by a measly five megabytes. This will speed up displaying Help, plus nothing will get in the way of those cork-popping sounds.

 OTE When you select the Custom installation, the initial settings are the same as those of the Typical installation. Thus, by selecting the Custom option you can see exactly what the Typical option gives you.

After you select the installation options you want, click Next to begin the installation process. Once Visual J++ is installed, the setup program gives you the option of registering your copy with Microsoft via modem. If you do not select this option, be sure to fill out the yellow registration card and mail it in. Otherwise, you won't be informed of upgrades.

As part of the setup, Visual J++ installs the uninstall program, which you can use to remove Visual J++ from your system. To remove Visual J++, choose Add/Remove Programs in the Windows Control Panel. Microsoft Visual J++ will be listed as one of the installed programs. Select it and click OK to remove Visual J++.

 NOTE The uninstall program can be useful when upgrading versions. Normally it isn't needed for an upgrade, but if I'm having trouble installing the next version of a product, one of the first things I do is remove the old version before installing the new. This is something to keep in mind when Visual J++ 2.0 comes out.

Installing Internet Explorer

The companion CD-ROM also includes the Microsoft Internet Explorer browser. Visual J++ knows how to use external browsers such as Internet Explorer to execute the applets you build. In any case, you'll need a Java-aware browser to access Java applets on the Web. (If you already have Netscape Navigator or some other Java-aware browser installed on your system, this step is optional.)

Simply select Install Internet Explorer 3.0 in the Master Setup window. If you accept the terms of the license agreement, click OK and that's about all there is to it. (The Visual J++ Setup program automatically installs Internet Explorer 3.0.)

Internet Browsers and Peaceful Coexistence

Internet Explorer coexists peacefully with other Internet browsers in all ways except one. If you install Internet Explorer as the application of choice for HTML files, when you double-click an HTML file it brings up Internet Explorer automatically.

Unfortunately, Navigator also insists on being the registered application of choice. Thus, the first time you execute Navigator after you install Internet Explorer, Navigator will complain that it is no longer registered to handle HTML pages and will ask if you want to change that. Click Yes and Navigator will reregister itself to handle HTML.

This presents no problem except that the next time you execute Internet Explorer, it will complain in a similar fashion. Each time you change browsers, the current browser will complain about the presence of the other.

Both Navigator and Internet Explorer allow you to turn this warning message off, but I suggest that you not do that. The problem is that once you turn off the warning message, if you want to reregister Navigator or Internet Explorer as the main application for HTML files, you have to do it by hand. (In Internet Explorer, you can reenable the warning message in the Options dialog box. Choose Options from the View menu.)

Creating Your First Application

Once you install Visual J++, it's time to start creating applications and applets. Chapter 1 shows you the step-by-step procedure for creating a Java application. Chapter 11 shows you how to create a Java applet manually, and Chapter 12 takes you through the steps of creating a Java applet using the Visual J++ AppletWizard.

Creating a Project

To compile and execute a Java source file, you need a project file. The easiest way to create a project file is to let Visual J++ do it for you. Simply create a new file to be edited by choosing New from the File menu, and then in the New dialog box select Text File. Enter your program. Compile your project by choosing Compile from the Build menu. At this point, Visual J++ will warn that you need a project workspace to continue, and it will offer to build it for you. Click OK. If you haven't already saved the file, a window will open for you to save the file. If your file contains a public class, be sure that the filename you choose matches the name of the class. In addition, make sure that the file extension is *.java*.

You can also create a project manually. This process is described in Chapter 1 for simple Java applications and again in Chapter 11 for applets. The

AppletWizard creates an initial project file when it creates the boilerplate for your applet.

Executing Your Application

Once your Java application has been compiled successfully, choose Execute from the Build menu to execute it. You can also single-step the application by first placing the cursor where you want the application to stop and then choosing Debug/Run To Cursor from the Build menu or pressing F7. Once the application stops on the specified line, choose Debug/Step Into from the Build menu or press F8 to single-step through the application.

Executing Your Applet

When executing a Java applet, you have two options. You can use the internal viewer built into Visual J++, as you did above, or you can execute your applet using an external Java-aware browser such as Internet Explorer 3.0 or later (the version on the enclosed CD-ROM will work fine) or Netscape Navigator 2.0 or later.

Choose Settings from the Build menu to see the project settings. From here, click the Debug tab and then select General from the Category drop-down list box. Finally, click the Browser option button in the Debug Project Under window. Select Browser from the Category drop-down list box to select the particular browser to use for viewing your applets.

 OTE   If you are using Netscape Navigator as your Java browser, be sure that Java is enabled in the security window. Choose Security Preferences from the Options menu, click the General tab, and then deselect the Disable Java check box.

Using Visual J++ with the Sun JDK

Prior to the release of Visual J++, the main Java compiler for the 80x86 family of processors (and still the main compiler for UNIX-based systems) was Sun's Java Development Kit (JDK). You can have both the Visual J++ and JDK environments installed on the same computer if you take a few precautions.

The JDK consists primarily of three programs:

- javac, the Java compiler that produces .class object files from .java source files

- java, which is used to execute Java applications

- appletviewer, which is used to execute Java applets

All three of these programs are designed to be executed from an MS-DOS window within Windows 95 or Windows NT.

Both the java and appletviewer programs can execute .class files generated by Visual J++ as long as the CLASSPATH environment variable has been set to point to both the current directory and the JDK directory that contains the Java class library. Normally, CLASSPATH is initialized at bootup in the AUTOEXEC.BAT file. Unfortunately, that doesn't work in this case because it messes up Visual J++. To avoid this problem, initialize CLASSPATH in the SETUP.BAT file you execute when opening the MS-DOS window. Alternatively, you can create a .BAT file for each of the above commands that first initializes CLASSPATH and then executes the appropriate JDK command.

See the ReadMe.txt file for informaton on installing the *Learn Java Now* sample applications.

Selected Sun JDK Applets

When you're learning a new programming language, you can never have too many example programs. Therefore, in this Appendix I've included some of the more interesting applets from Sun's Java Development Kit (JDK). (I did/not write these applets; they are from Sun, which placed them in the public domain as a training aid.) These applets do not use the same naming and indention conventions that I've used in this book, and some of them are not commented as well as I might like; however, I've included descriptions of each applet to help you through the tricky parts. In addition, I've added comments to help you read the code. My comments are marked in bold.

 NOTE The Sun applets come with their own HTML files, each named *example1.html.* To execute these applets under the debugger, you need to build a project file containing the .java file. In addition, you must tell the debugger to use the existing HTML file rather than create one of its own. To do this, choose Settings from the Build menu. Select the Debug tab in the Project Settings dialog box, and under the General category select Browser in the Debug/Execute Project Under area. Next, select the Browser category and select Use Parameters From HTML Page, and then enter the name of the HTML file in the HTML Page edit box.

A complete set of the JDK applets is included on the companion CD-ROM. Each applet is in its own directory under \JDK Examples. To try one out, simply open the exam1.html file in the applet's directory. Some of my personal favorites didn't make it into this appendix because of their size; be sure to try out GraphLayout and MoleculeViewer.

CardTest

The CardTest applet is interesting in the way it demonstrates several different layout policies. This applet creates several components that it attaches to the panel. The user can select the layout manager used in attaching these components. By varying the layout manager, the user can see immediately how the different layout managers work.

Note that all of the Sun demo applets begin with a disclaimer. I have left the disclaimer on this applet but removed it from all subsequent applets to save space. (Of course, the applets on the CD-ROM retain the disclaimer.)

```
/*
 * @(#)CardTest.java    1.7 95/08/23 Arthur van Hoff
 *
 * Copyright (c) 1994-1995 Sun Microsystems, Inc. All Rights
 * Reserved.
 *
 * Permission to use, copy, modify, and distribute this software
 * and its documentation for NON-COMMERCIAL or COMMERCIAL
 * purposes and without fee is hereby granted.
 * Please refer to the file
 * http://java.sun.com/copy_trademarks.html for further important
 * copyright and trademark information and to
 * http://java.sun.com/licensing.html for further important
 * licensing information for the Java (tm) Technology.
 *
 * SUN MAKES NO REPRESENTATIONS OR WARRANTIES ABOUT THE
 * SUITABILITY OF THE SOFTWARE, EITHER EXPRESS OR IMPLIED,
 * INCLUDING BUT NOT LIMITED TO THE IMPLIED WARRANTIES OF
 * MERCHANTABILITY, FITNESS FOR A PARTICULAR PURPOSE, OR NON-
 * INFRINGEMENT. SUN SHALL NOT BE LIABLE FOR ANY DAMAGES SUFFERED
 * BY LICENSEE AS A RESULT OF USING, MODIFYING OR DISTRIBUTING
 * THIS SOFTWARE OR ITS DERIVATIVES.
 *
 * THIS SOFTWARE IS NOT DESIGNED OR INTENDED FOR USE OR RESALE AS
 * ON-LINE CONTROL EQUIPMENT IN HAZARDOUS ENVIRONMENTS REQUIRING
 * FAIL-SAFE PERFORMANCE, SUCH AS IN THE OPERATION OF NUCLEAR
 * FACILITIES, AIRCRAFT NAVIGATION OR COMMUNICATION SYSTEMS, AIR
 * TRAFFIC CONTROL, DIRECT LIFE SUPPORT MACHINES, OR WEAPONS
 * SYSTEMS, IN WHICH THE FAILURE OF THE SOFTWARE COULD LEAD
 * DIRECTLY TO DEATH, PERSONAL INJURY, OR SEVERE PHYSICAL OR
 * ENVIRONMENTAL DAMAGE ("HIGH RISK ACTIVITIES").  SUN
 * SPECIFICALLY DISCLAIMS ANY EXPRESS OR IMPLIED WARRANTY OF
```

```
 * FITNESS FOR HIGH RISK ACTIVITIES.
 */

import java.awt.*;
import java.applet.Applet;

// CardPanel - a CardPanel is a panel with the 5 buttons
//             labeled one through five and with a specified
//             layout manager.
class CardPanel extends Panel {
    Panel create(LayoutManager layout) {
    Panel p = new Panel();
    p.setLayout(layout);
    p.add("North",  new Button("one"));
    p.add("West",   new Button("two"));
    p.add("South",  new Button("three"));
    p.add("East",   new Button("four"));
    p.add("Center", new Button("five"));
    return p;
    }

    CardPanel() {
    setLayout(new CardLayout());
    add("one", create(new FlowLayout()));
    add("two", create(new BorderLayout()));
    add("three", create(new GridLayout(2, 2)));
    add("four", create(new BorderLayout(10, 10)));
    add("five", create(new FlowLayout(FlowLayout.LEFT, 10, 10)));
    add("six", create(new GridLayout(2, 2, 10, 10)));
    }

    public Dimension preferredSize() {
    return new Dimension(200, 100);
    }
}

public class CardTest extends Applet {
    CardPanel cards;

    public CardTest() {
    setLayout(new BorderLayout());
    add("Center", cards = new CardPanel());
    Panel p = new Panel();
    p.setLayout(new FlowLayout());
    add("South", p);
    p.add(new Button("first"));
    p.add(new Button("next"));
    p.add(new Button("previous"));
    p.add(new Button("last"));
```

(continued)

```
            Choice c = new Choice();
            c.addItem("one");
            c.addItem("two");
            c.addItem("three");
            c.addItem("four");
            c.addItem("five");
            p.add(c);
            }


            // the action is based on the label of the button;
            // this allows several buttons that share a common label,
            // ("one" for example), to have the same action
            public boolean action(Event evt, Object arg) {
            if (evt.target instanceof Choice) {
                ((CardLayout)cards.getLayout()).show(cards,(String)arg);
            } else {
                if ("first".equals(arg)) {
                ((CardLayout)cards.getLayout()).first(cards);
                } else if ("next".equals(arg)) {
                ((CardLayout)cards.getLayout()).next(cards);
                } else if ("previous".equals(arg)) {
                ((CardLayout)cards.getLayout()).previous(cards);
                } else if ("last".equals(arg)) {
                ((CardLayout)cards.getLayout()).last(cards);
                } else {
                ((CardLayout)cards.getLayout()).show(cards,(String)arg);
                }
            }
            return true;
            }


            // main is executed only when the applet is executed as
            // an application. main goes through the same steps a
            // browser would go through when displaying the applet's
            // window:
            // a) create a window in which to display the output
            // b) call the constructor for the applet class
            // c) call the applet init function
            // d) call the applet start function
            public static void main(String args[]) {
            Frame f = new Frame("CardTest");
            CardTest cardTest = new CardTest();
            cardTest.init();
            cardTest.start();

            f.add("Center", cardTest);
            f.resize(300, 300);
            f.show();
            }
        }
```

CardTest is designed to execute as either an application or an applet. The *main* function is provided to execute when CardTest is executed as an application. The *CardTest* class is invoked from the browser when CardTest is executed as an applet.

The *CardTest* constructor sets *BorderLayout* as the layout manager. It then creates five *CardPanel* objects and adds them to the center of the applet window. Along the bottom of the applet window it adds a panel containing the buttons *first, next, previous,* and *last* followed by a drop-down selection widget all in *FlowLayout*. The drop-down window offers the options *one* through *five*.

Each *CardPanel* is a panel window containing five buttons labelled *one* through *five*. Each of the *CardPanel* objects has a different layout manager. Since they are "stacked," only one is visible at a time. By selecting the buttons *one* through *five,* the user can make each of the five *CardPanel* objects visible in turn. Similarly, the user can select the *next* and *previous* buttons to cycle through the different *CardPanel* objects and display the different layout managers.

The first three card panels are shown in Figures B-1 through B-3.

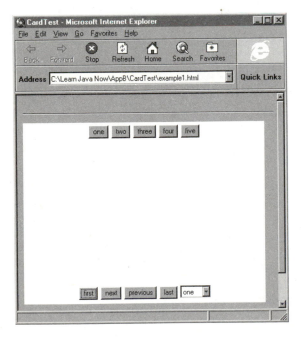

Figure B-1. *Card panel number 1 in the CardTest applet.*

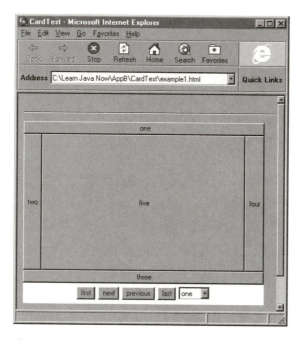

Figure B-2. *Card panel number 2.*

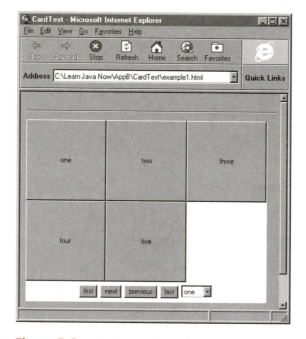

Figure B-3. *Card panel number 3.*

> **The Two Faces of Java**
> _____
>
> The fact that a Java program can be executed as either an application or an applet, depending on how it's written, is both a boon and a bane. It's sort of like having a language that can generate either MS-DOS—based applications or Microsoft Windows—based applications with equal ease. Interestingly enough, these two capabilities are not mutually exclusive. This is a good example of how the same class can be constructed to execute as both an application and an applet.
>
> When CardTest is executed as an applet, the *main* method is ignored and control passes straight to the members of the *CardTest* class, as described in Part 2 of this book. However, when CardTest is executed as an application, the Java Virtual Machine starts executing with *main*. This function simulates the steps that a browser would go through, at least to the level that the *CardTest* class cares about.
>
> First, *main* creates a window in which the CardTest "applet" will display. In this case, the window is of class *Frame*. Then it creates a *CardTest* object and invokes the *init* and *start* methods. These are the same steps that the browser would go through as part of displaying the applet. The *CardTest* class never knows that it isn't being invoked from a browser.

NervousText

The NervousText applet is an interesting alternative to marquee-style applets such as the Marquee applet demonstrated in Chapter 14. Nervous-Text displays a character string within a window, but rather than scroll it one way or the other it makes the characters dance about as if they are being shaken. It does this by repeatedly repainting the string with each character offset from its normal position by some random value. The amount of jiggling is adjusted so that the character string remains readable.

```
/*  Daniel Wyszynski
    Center for Applied Large-Scale Computing (CALC)
    04-12-95

    Test of text animation.

    kwalrath: Changed string; added thread suspension. 5-9-95
*/
import java.awt.Graphics;
import java.awt.Font;

public class NervousText extends java.applet.Applet
                                        implements Runnable {

    // this array holds the individual characters of the string s
    // (this allows each character to be displayed separately)
    char separated[];

    // the string to display
    String s = null;

    // the current thread (curious name though)
    Thread killme = null;

    // miscellaneous controls
    int i;
    int x_coord = 0, y_coord = 0;
    String num;
    int speed=35;
    int counter =0;

    // keep track of whether we're suspended or not
    // (clicking the mouse suspends the applet)
    boolean threadSuspended = false; //added by kwalrath

public void init() {
    // read the text to display from the HTML file;
    // default is "HotJava"
    s = getParameter("text");
    if (s == null) {
        s = "HotJava";
    }

    // now pull the string apart into its individual characters
    separated = new char [s.length()];
    s.getChars(0,s.length(),separated,0);
```

```
    // set up the window size and font
    resize(150,50);
    setFont(new Font("TimesRoman",Font.BOLD,36));
 }

// start - normal stuff here
public void start() {
    if(killme == null)
    {
        killme = new Thread(this);
        killme.start();
    }
 }

// stop - normal here too
public void stop() {
    killme = null;
 }

// run - all the work is in paint
public void run() {
    while (killme != null) {
    try {Thread.sleep(100);} catch (InterruptedException e){}
    repaint();
    }
    killme = null;
 }

// paint - repaint the string with each character adjusted
//         slightly by some random amount
public void paint(Graphics g) {
    // loop through the characters in the string
    for(i=0;i<s.length();i++)
    {

    // allocate 15 pixels horizontally for each character (this
    // is based on the size of the font selected in init) -
    // BUT jiggle each character by anywhere from 0 to 10 pixels
    // both horizontally and vertically
    x_coord = (int) (Math.random()*10+15*i);
    y_coord = (int) (Math.random()*10+36);

    // now draw the one character from the i'th position of the
    // "separated" array at the calculated coordinates
    g.drawChars(separated, i,1,x_coord,y_coord);
    }
 }
```

(continued)

```
// mouseDown - clicking the mouse stops the nervous animation
/* Added by kwalrath. */
public boolean mouseDown(java.awt.Event evt, int x, int y) {
        if (threadSuspended) {
            killme.resume();
        }
        else {
            killme.suspend();
        }
        threadSuspended = !threadSuspended;
    return true;
    }
}
```

NervousText.init starts by reading the "text" parameter from the HTML file. If the parameter is not present, the string "HotJava" is used. Since the applet must display each character separately, it immediately pulls the string apart into the *char* array *separated* using the *String.getChars* method. NervousText then sets the font type and size. Notice that NervousText hard-codes this information, but the information could just as well have been read from the HTML file, as we did in the Marquee applet.

The *start, stop,* and *run* methods are conventional and simple. All the work is performed in the *paint* method. *paint* loops through the characters stored in the *separated* array, displaying each character one at a time using the *Graphics.drawChars* method. The second argument to *drawChars* is the offset of where in *separated* to start, and the third is the number of characters to display.

The x coordinate of each character is calculated by multiplying the character offset, *i,* by 15 (the width of the 36-point Times Roman font selected). A random factor of from 0 to 9 is added to this offset to create the jiggling effect. A similar calculation is used to place the y coordinate.

The results of executing the NervousText applet are shown in Figure B-4.

Figure B-4. *Output from the NervousText applet appears to jiggle continuously.*

MouseTrack and MouseRun

The MouseTrack applet in the JumpingBox directory represents a simple but entertaining game. It draws a small box within a large playing field. This small box jumps about randomly. Every time you click the mouse button with the mouse pointer within the rectangle, the applet scores a hit. Your job is to "chase" the rectangle, scoring as many hits in a row as possible.

```
import java.awt.Graphics;
import java.lang.Math;

public class MouseTrack extends java.applet.Applet {

    // mx, my are the mouse x and y positions
    int mx, my;

    // onaroll counts the number of times in a row you hit
    int onaroll;

    // init - set the window size and let it go at that
    public void init() {
    onaroll = 0;
    resize(500, 500);
    }
```

(continued)

```
// paint - paint target rectangle
public void paint(Graphics g) {
// start by drawing a bounding rectangle around entire
// window
g.drawRect(0, 0, size().width - 1, size().height - 1);

// now calculate a random location for the target window
// and draw it there
mx = (int)(Math.random()*1000) %
                    (size().width - (size().width/10));
my = (int)(Math.random()*1000) %
                    (size().height - (size().height/10));
g.drawRect(mx, my,
        (size().width/10) - 1,
        (size().height/10) - 1);
}

/*
 * Mouse methods
 */
// mouseDown - determine if you got a hit
public boolean mouseDown(java.awt.Event evt, int x, int y) {
requestFocus();
if((mx < x && x < mx+size().width/10-1) &&
   (my < y && y < my+size().height/10-1)) {
    if(onaroll > 0) {
    switch(onaroll%4) {
    case 0:
        play(getCodeBase(),
                        "sounds/tiptoe.thru.the.tulips.au");
        break;
    case 1:
        play(getCodeBase(), "sounds/danger,danger...!.au");
        break;
    case 2:
        play(getCodeBase(), "sounds/adapt-or-die.au");
        break;
    case 3:
        play(getCodeBase(), "sounds/cannot.be.completed.au");
        break;
    }
    onaroll++;
    if(onaroll > 5)
        getAppletContext().showStatus(
                "You're on your way to THE HALL OF FAME:"
                + onaroll + "Hits!");
    else
        getAppletContext().showStatus(
                "YOU'RE ON A ROLL:" + onaroll + "Hits!");
```

```
        }
        else {
        getAppletContext().showStatus("HIT IT AGAIN! AGAIN!");
        play(getCodeBase(), "sounds/that.hurts.au");
        onaroll = 1;
        }
    }
    else {
        getAppletContext().showStatus(
            "You hit nothing at (" + x + ", " + y + "), exactly");
        play(getCodeBase(), "sounds/thin.bell.au");
        onaroll = 0;
    }
    repaint();
    return true;
    }

    // mouseMove - repaint the rectangle whenever the mouse
    //            moves, enters the window, or exits the window
    public boolean mouseMove(java.awt.Event evt, int x, int y) {
    if((x % 3 == 0) && (y % 3 == 0))
        repaint();
    return true;
    }

    public void mouseEnter() {
    repaint();
    }

    public void mouseExit() {
    onaroll = 0;
    repaint();
    }

    /**
     * Focus methods
     */
    public void keyDown(int key) {
    requestFocus();
    onaroll = 0;
    play(getCodeBase(), "sounds/ip.au");
    }
}
```

The core of this applet lies in the *paint* method, which draws the target rectangle at a random location within the playing field. *paint* is invoked under a variety of conditions, including whenever the mouse moves more than 3 pixels. The only other nontrivial method, *mouseDown,* calculates whether the user scores a hit.

 N OTE   Notice how MouseTrack uses the *showStatus* method to paint to the status bar.

The problem with MouseTrack is that the target rectangle jumps randomly rather than running away. After studying MouseTrack, I created the following MouseRun applet. In this variation, the rectangle runs away from the mouse pointer. When it gets far enough away, it stops running. When it gets to a wall, the target rectangle jumps back to the center of the applet window.

```java
// MouseRun - based on the Sun demo applet MouseTrack. MouseTrack
//           moves a rectangle randomly on the screen and
//           challenges the user to try to "hit it" with the
//           mouse. MouseRun causes the rectangle to run away
//           from the mouse (not just jump about randomly).
import java.awt.*;
import java.lang.Math;
import java.applet.Applet;

public class MouseRun extends Applet implements Runnable {

    // location of the mouse
    Point mouse = new Point(0, 0);

    // the target rectangle
    Rectangle rectangle = new Rectangle(20, 20);

    // the bounding rectangle contains the entire playing area
    Rectangle bounds = new Rectangle();

    // direction to run
    Point vector = new Point(1, 1);

    // save our thread
    Thread me = null;

    // counts the number of hits in a row
    int onaroll = 0;

    // init - size the window and the bounding rectangle
    public void init()
    {
```

```
        bounds.resize(size().width - 1, size().height - 1);
}

// start - start the thread to move the rectangle
public void start()
{
    if(me == null)
    {
        me = new Thread(this);
        me.start();
    }
}

// stop - stop the thread
public void stop()
{
    me = null;
}

// run - repeatedly repaint the screen to let the rectangle
//         move away
public void run() {
    while (me != null)
    {
        try
        {
            Thread.sleep(20);
        }
        catch (InterruptedException e)
        {
            me = null;
        }
        repaint();
    }
}

// paint - move and display the target rectangle
public void paint(Graphics g)
{
    // repaint the bounding rectangle
    g.drawRect(0, 0, bounds.width, bounds.height);

    // move the rectangle away from the mouse; as soon as
    // the rectangle is "far enough" away, stop moving it
    Point center = new Point(rectangle.x + rectangle.width/2,
                             rectangle.y + rectangle.height/2);
```

(continued)

```
            vector.x = -1;
            if (mouse.x < center.x)
            {
                vector.x = 1;
            }
            if ((center.x - mouse.x) * vector.x > 100)
            {
                vector.x = 0;
            }

            vector.y = -1;
            if (mouse.y < center.y)
            {
                vector.y = 1;
            }
            if ((center.y - mouse.y) * vector.y > 100)
            {
                vector.y = 0;
            }
            rectangle.translate(vector.x, vector.y);


            // make sure rectangle doesn't leave the window
            Rectangle intersect = rectangle.intersection(bounds);
            if (!intersect.equals(rectangle))
            {
                rectangle.move(bounds.width/2, bounds.height/2);
            }

            // now draw the target rectangle
            g.drawRect(rectangle.x,      rectangle.y,
                       rectangle.width, rectangle.height);
    }

    /*
     * Mouse methods
     */
    // mouseDown - count the number of hits/misses
    public boolean mouseDown(java.awt.Event evt, int nX, int nY)
    {
        // first position the mouse
        mouse.move(nX, nY);

        // now see if we hit it
        if(rectangle.inside(nX, nY))
        {
            switch (++onaroll)
            {
                case 1:
```

```
                            getAppletContext().showStatus(
                                           "HIT IT AGAIN! AGAIN!");
                        break;
                    case 2:
                    case 3:
                    case 4:
                        getAppletContext().showStatus(
                                           "YOU'RE ON A ROLL:"
                                           + onaroll
                                           + "Hits!");
                        break;
                    default:  // this handles 5 or more hits in a row
                        getAppletContext().showStatus(
                            "You're on your way to THE HALL OF FAME:"
                            + onaroll
                            + "Hits!");
                }
                play(getCodeBase(), "sounds/that.hurts.au");
            }
            else
            {
                // miss!
                getAppletContext().showStatus("You missed at ("
                                              + nX
                                              + ", "
                                              + nY
                                              + ")");
                play(getCodeBase(), "sounds/thin.bell.au");
                onaroll = 0;
            }
            return true;
        }

        // mouseMove - record the mouse location
        public boolean mouseMove(java.awt.Event evt, int nX, int nY)
        {
            mouse.move(nX, nY);
            return true;
        }
    }
```

This version of the applet uses a separate thread to continuously repaint the window. This allows the target rectangle to continuously move away from the cursor.

paint starts by drawing the bounding rectangle just like before. It then calculates the center of the target rectangle. By comparing this center point with the position of the cursor, it decides which direction to run. Once the rectangle is 100 pixels or more away from the mouse in a given dimension, it stops moving away in that dimension. *paint* calls *translate* to update the location of the rectangle.

paint makes sure that the target rectangle is completely within the bounding rectangle by calculating the intersection between the two. If the result is not equal to the target rectangle, *paint* knows that some part of the target rectangle is outside of the bounding rectangle. If it is, *paint* moves the target rectangle back to the center of the window.

The *mouseDown* method is a simplified version of its MouseTrack predecessor, calculating the number of hits in a row and displaying the results in the status window.

DitherTest

The DitherTest applet is much larger than the first three applets, but it's still not too complicated. This applet demonstrates Java's ability to generate an extremely large palette of colors, either directly or via dithering.

Dithering is a technique by which the software generates a color that the screen is not otherwise capable of generating, by alternating pixels of two other colors in close proximity. When the eye views the result, it perceives the desired color somewhere between the alternating colors. Java supports dithering through a class known as *MemoryImageSource*.

MemoryImageSource allows you to paint to a palette one pixel at a time by providing a matrix of integers, each representing the intensity and the red, green, and blue hues of that pixel. The color of a particular pixel is encoded as follows:

```
pixel[height*y + w] = (nIntensity << 24) +
                      (nRed       << 16) +
                      (nGreen     << 8)  +
                      (nBlue);
```

Thus, each primary color as well as the intensity is represented by 8 bits in the 32-bit pixel value.

Once the value of each pixel is calculated, it is passed to the constructor for *MemoryImageSource,* which returns an image ready for display. The following example taken from the Sun documentation shows an applet snippet that creates a 100-by-100 palette that fades from black to blue along the x axis and from black to red along the y axis:

```
// allocate a 100x100 palette of pixels
int w = 100;
int h = 100;
int pix[] = new int[w * h];

// now set the color of each
int index = 0;
for (int y = 0; y < h; y++) {

    // calculate the red value as a percentage of where the
    // pixel is from top to bottom
    int red = (y * 255) / (h - 1);
    for (int x = 0; x < w; x++) {

        // calculate the blue value as a percentage of where the
        // pixel is from left to right
        int blue = (x * 255) / (w - 1);

        // now combine the red and blue values into the current
        // pixel (notice that the intensity is set to full on
        // (255) and that the green is set to off (it's stored at
        // bit offset 8 through 15))
        pix[index++] = (255 << 24) | (red << 16) | blue;
    }
}

// now create an image using the palette we just created
Image img = createImage(new MemoryImageSource(w, h, pix, 0, w));
```

The DitherTest applet creates a color palette that gradually fades from one color to another along both the x axis and the y axis. The user selects the color and range to sweep horizontally by using a select widget above the image and vertically from a selection widget below the image. Clicking the New Image button causes the applet to calculate a new palette image based on the user's selections.

The DitherTest applet appears here. As before, I've added comments in bold to the original applet to help explain certain points. In addition, I've removed the disclaimer that appears at the beginning of each Sun demo applet.

```java
import java.applet.Applet;
import java.awt.*;
import java.awt.image.ColorModel;
import java.awt.image.MemoryImageSource;
import java.lang.InterruptedException;

// DitherTest - this is the applet itself
public class DitherTest extends Applet implements Runnable {

    // these represent color "methods" referred to throughout
    // the program (NOOP means don't change color)
    final static int NOOP = 0;
    final static int RED = 1;
    final static int GREEN = 2;
    final static int BLUE = 3;
    final static int ALPHA = 4;
    final static int SATURATION = 5;

    Thread kicker;

    // controls for the x and y dimensions (this tells
    // the application which color to vary and the range)
    DitherControls XControls;
    DitherControls YControls;

    // the window in which the color image is displayed
    // (a canvas is a component like a window, except it is
    // not a subclass of Container and cannot hold other
    // components)
    DitherCanvas canvas;

    // init - read the HTML page for the initial color and
    //        ranges and then create the controls and canvas
    public void init() {
    String xspec, yspec;
    int xvals[] = new int[2]; // holds the min and max x vals
    int yvals[] = new int[2]; // holds the min and max y vals

    // the following reads the initial x and y ranges and
    // colors from the HTML page (the default x color is red and
    // the default y color is blue)
    try {
        xspec = getParameter("xaxis");
    } catch (Exception e) {
        xspec = null;
    }
    try {
        yspec = getParameter("yaxis");
    } catch (Exception e) {
```

```
        yspec = null;
    }
if (xspec == null) xspec = "red";
if (yspec == null) yspec = "blue";
int xmethod = colormethod(xspec, xvals);
int ymethod = colormethod(yspec, yvals);

// put buttons across the top and bottom; add a New Image
// (render) button to the bottom controls
setLayout(new BorderLayout());
XControls = new DitherControls(this, xvals[0], xvals[1],
                    xmethod, false);
YControls = new DitherControls(this, yvals[0], yvals[1],
                    ymethod, true);
YControls.addRenderButton();
add("North", XControls);
add("South", YControls);

// now put the canvas in the middle
add("Center", canvas = new DitherCanvas());
}

// start - build the palette in a background thread to
//         avoid locking up the browser for long periods
public synchronized void start() {
if (canvas.getImage() == null) {
    kicker = new Thread(this);
    kicker.start();
}
}

public synchronized void stop() {
try {
    if (kicker != null) {
    kicker.stop();
    }
} catch (Exception e) {
}
kicker = null;
}

public void restart() {
stop();
canvas.setImage(null);
start();
}
```

(continued)

```
// main - same sort of thing as before - make it so the
//         applet can execute as an application
public static void main(String args[]) {
Frame f = new Frame("ArcTest");
DitherTest     ditherTest = new DitherTest();

ditherTest.init();

f.add("Center", ditherTest);
f.pack();
f.show();

ditherTest.start();
}

// colormethod - parse the string s into color and ranges
int colormethod(String s, int vals[]) {
int method = NOOP;

if (s == null)
    s = "";

String lower = s.toLowerCase();
int len = 0;
if (lower.startsWith("red")) {
    method = RED;
    lower = lower.substring(3);
} else if (lower.startsWith("green")) {
    method = GREEN;
    lower = lower.substring(5);
} else if (lower.startsWith("blue")) {
    method = BLUE;
    lower = lower.substring(4);
} else if (lower.startsWith("alpha")) {
    method = ALPHA;
    lower = lower.substring(4);
} else if (lower.startsWith("saturation")) {
    method = SATURATION;
    lower = lower.substring(10);
}

if (method == NOOP) {
    vals[0] = 0;
    vals[1] = 0;
    return method;
}

int begval = 0;
int endval = 255;
```

```
try {
    int dash = lower.indexOf('-');
    if (dash < 0) {
    begval = endval = Integer.parseInt(lower);
    } else {
    begval = Integer.parseInt(lower.substring(0, dash));
    endval = Integer.parseInt(lower.substring(dash+1));
    }
} catch (Exception e) {
}

if (begval < 0) begval = 0;
if (endval < 0) endval = 0;
if (begval > 255) begval = 255;
if (endval > 255) endval = 255;

vals[0] = begval;
vals[1] = endval;

return method;
}

// applymethod - create a color pixel in the array c given
//                the method (read "color") and vals (read
//                "intensity")
void applymethod(int c[],        // the color of current pixel
                                 // c[0] - red saturation
                                 // c[1] - green saturation
                                 // c[2] - blue saturation
                                 // c[3] - intensity
                 int method,     // the color we're building
                 int step,       // the offset of the pixel
                 int total,      // the number of pixels
                 int vals[]) {   // the range of intensity
if (method == NOOP)
    return;

// calculate the intensity by taking the max - min and
// multiplying that by how close they are to the beginning
// or end of the row/column (e.g., if we are in the middle
// of a row, give this pixel an intensity that is halfway
// between the maximum and minimum intensity)
int val = ((total < 2)
        ? vals[0]
        : vals[0] + ((vals[1] - vals[0])
                                    * step / (total - 1)));
```

(continued)

```
// now apply this intensity to the color specified by the
// method; leave the other colors alone
switch (method) {
case RED:
    c[0] = val;
    break;
case GREEN:
    c[1] = val;
    break;
case BLUE:
    c[2] = val;
    break;
case ALPHA:
    c[3] = val;
    break;
case SATURATION:
    int max = Math.max(Math.max(c[0], c[1]), c[2]);
    int min = max * (255 - val) / 255;
    if (c[0] == 0) c[0] = min;
    if (c[1] == 0) c[1] = min;
    if (c[2] == 0) c[2] = min;
    break;
}
}

// run - calculate the pixel array and then use it to create
//       the image
public void run() {
Thread me = Thread.currentThread();
me.setPriority(4);

// get the dimensions of the image to produce
int width = canvas.size().width;
int height = canvas.size().height;

// read the range and color selection from the horizontal
// and vertical controls
int xvals[] = new int[2];
int yvals[] = new int[2];
int xmethod = XControls.getParams(xvals);
int ymethod = YControls.getParams(yvals);

// allocate a pixel array big enough for the canvas
int pixels[] = new int[width * height];

// create the pixel array for the image
int c[] = new int[4];
int index = 0;
for (int j = 0; j < height; j++) {
```

```
        for (int i = 0; i < width; i++) {
        // start with a pixel that has full intensity but no
        // colors (the colors will be added by applymethod)
        c[0] = c[1] = c[2] = 0;
        c[3] = 255;

        // calculate the color of each pixel
        if (xmethod < ymethod) {
            applymethod(c, xmethod, i, width, xvals);
            applymethod(c, ymethod, j, height, yvals);
        } else {
            applymethod(c, ymethod, j, height, yvals);
            applymethod(c, xmethod, i, width, xvals);
        }

        // now pack the color array into a single 32-bit value
        // the way MemoryImageSource expects it
        pixels[index++] = ((c[3] << 24) |   // intensity
                    (c[0] << 16) |          // red
                    (c[1] << 8) |           // green
                    (c[2] << 0));           // blue
        if (kicker != me) {
            return;
        }
        }
    }

// create an image out of the resulting pixel array
newImage(me, width, height, pixels);
}

// newImage - create an image out of the pixel array by
//            using the MemoryImageSource class
synchronized void newImage(Thread me,
                        int width, int height,
                        int pixels[]) {
if (kicker != me) {
    return;
}
Image img;
img = createImage(new MemoryImageSource(width, height,
                ColorModel.getRGBdefault(),
                pixels, 0, width));
canvas.setImage(img);
kicker = null;
}
}
```

(continued)

```java
// DitherCanvas provides the canvas into which the calculated
// image is displayed
class DitherCanvas extends Canvas {
    Image img;
    static String calcString = "Calculating...";

    public void paint(Graphics g) {
    int w = size().width;
    int h = size().height;
    if (img == null) {
        super.paint(g);
        g.setColor(Color.black);
        FontMetrics fm = g.getFontMetrics();
        int x = (w - fm.stringWidth(calcString))/2;
        int y = h/2;
        g.drawString(calcString, x, y);
    } else {
        g.drawImage(img, 0, 0, w, h, this);
    }
    }

    public Dimension minimumSize() {
    return new Dimension(20, 20);
    }

    public Dimension preferredSize() {
    return new Dimension(200, 200);
    }

    public Image getImage() {
    return img;
    }

    public void setImage(Image img) {
    this.img = img;
    repaint();
    }
}

// DitherControls provides the x and y control widgets that
// the user can use to select what colors to vary and by how
// much (from what to what)
class DitherControls extends Panel {
    TextField start;
    TextField end;
    Button button;
    Choice choice;
    DitherTest applet;
```

```
static LayoutManager dcLayout = new
                        FlowLayout(FlowLayout.CENTER, 10, 5);

public DitherControls(DitherTest app,
    int s, int e, int type, // initial start, end, and color
    boolean vertical) {      // vertical or horizontal control
applet = app;
setLayout(dcLayout);
add(new Label(vertical ? "Vertical" : "Horizontal"));

// a choice is a drop-down menu
add(choice = new Choice());
choice.addItem("Noop");
choice.addItem("Red");
choice.addItem("Green");
choice.addItem("Blue");
choice.addItem("Alpha");
choice.addItem("Saturation");

// now set the controls to their initial value
choice.select(type);
add(start = new TextField(Integer.toString(s), 4));
add(end = new TextField(Integer.toString(e), 4));
}

// addRenderButton - called to add the New Image button to
//                   one of the controls (you don't need it
//                   twice)
public void addRenderButton() {
add(button = new Button("New Image"));
}

// getParams - read the control widget. store the min
//             and max color range in vals[] and return
//             the item selected as an integer offset.
public int getParams(int vals[]) {
vals[0] = Integer.parseInt(start.getText());
vals[1] = Integer.parseInt(end.getText());
return choice.getSelectedIndex();
}

// action - when the user clicks the "New Image" button
//          tell the applet to restart. the applet will
//          read the widgets using the getParams method.
public boolean action(Event ev, Object arg) {
if (ev.target instanceof Button) {
    applet.restart();
```

(continued)

```
        return true;
    }

    return false;
    }
}
```

As always, DitherTest begins with the *init* method, which starts by reading the default values out of the HTML page. It then creates the horizontal *DitherControls* objects along the top of the window and the vertical *Dither-Controls* objects along the bottom. The *DitherCanvas* object that will contain the image is placed in the middle.

start and *stop* create and kill a separate thread in which the actual image calculation is performed. *main* is provided to allow DitherTest to execute as either an application or an applet, as explained in the previous section on the CardTest applet.

The actual work is performed in *run*. This method first reads the settings for horizontal and vertical colors. It then creates a pixel array large enough to handle each pixel in the image to be created. *run* then calculates the color of each pixel in the image. That done, *run* calls *newImage* to convert the pixel array into an image.

The remaining elements in the program are relatively self-explanatory. The *DitherCanvas* object provides the canvas into which the image is painted. The *DitherControls* objects provide the control widgets that allow the user to set the color and intensity range for both the horizontal and vertical directions.

The default DitherTest window is shown in Figure B-5.

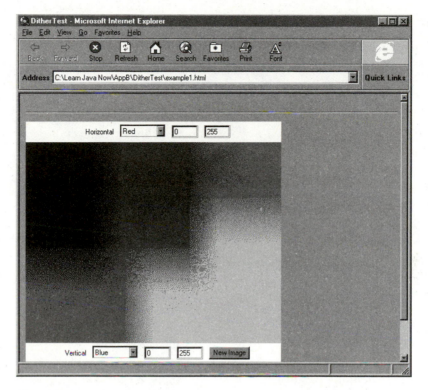

Figure B-5. *The DitherTest display is awash with color.*

Conclusion

A number of educational applets accompany the Sun JDK—far more than I can cover here. Play with them and figure them out for yourself. You can learn a lot by looking at applets created by others. And don't stop there. There are many good sources for applets on the Web. One of the best is //www.gamelan.com.

Index

B

Uniform Resource Locator (URL), 181, 288
uninstalling Visual J++, 340
unnamed package, 132
unsigned right shift operator (>>>), 15, 18
update, 258–59, 261–68, 276–77
uppercase, converting to, 140
URL, 181, 288
utility
    classes, 136
    ftp, 180

V

values, data types, 11
variables
    addresses, 67–68
    declaring, 11–14
    names, 12
    storage size, 12
    types, 11 (*See also* data, types)
Vector, 218
virtual machine, Java (JVM), 6–7, 351
Visual J++
    installing, 337–40
    uninstalling, 340
void return type, 33

W

.wav file format, 296
Web. *See* World Wide Web
while loop, 22–24
white space, 9
width
    fonts, 210
    image, 288
windowing, java.awt, 136
windows. *See also* display; screen
    Abstract Window Toolkit, 136, 299–336
    applet, 184–87, 202, 315
    AppletWizard summary, 192–93
    AWT, 136, 299–336

windows, *continued*
    drawing, 322–36
    layout policy, 307–14
    moving, 315
    panel, 349–50
    project, 193
    repainting, 207–8, 225–26
    resizing, 309–12, 315
    ResourceWizard, 322–36
Windows 95, multiprocessing, 238
Windows Explorer, folders, 193
Windows NT, multiprocessing, 238
WinMain, 185
Wizards. *See* AppletWizard; ResourceWizard
World Wide Web, 176–77
    browsers, 176
    executing applets, 6–7, 179–81
    game applets, 373
    HTML commands, 182–84
    java.applet, 136
    programs, 4
    URLs, 181, 288
wrappers, class, 73, 140
writeFloat, 170
writeInt, 170
write location, characters, 221, 222, 226
writeShort, 170
writing files, 170

X

x location, mouse, 203–10, 213–14
x offset, 186, 354

Y

y location, mouse, 203–10, 213–14
y offset, 186, 354

About the Author

Stephen R. "Randy" Davis is a programmer and writer who specializes in object-oriented languages such as C++ and Java. He counts eight books and numerous technical articles to his credit. Randy works as a software process specialist for E-Systems in Greenville, Texas, where he lives with his wife, Jenny; one son, Kinsey; two dogs; three cats; and a pot-bellied pig. He can be contacted at srdavis@ACM.org.

The manuscript for this book was prepared and submitted to Microsoft Press in electronic form. Text files were prepared using Microsoft Word 7.0 for Windows. Pages were composed by Microsoft Press using Adobe PageMaker 6.01 for Windows, with text in Melior and display type in Frutiger Condensed. Composed pages were delivered to the printer as electronic prepress files.

Cover Designers
Gregory Erickson
Robin Hjellen

Cover Illustrator
Philip Howe

Interior Graphic Designer
Kim Eggleston

Interior Graphic Artist
Travis Beaven

Principal Compositor
Peggy Herman

Indexer
Patti Schiendelman

To **challenge** the World Wide Web's most **innovative** sites with **ultra**-cool ones of your own, **read this.**

To build the smartest, most visually compelling Web sites you've ever seen, just take the techniques in HTML IN ACTION to the limits of your imagination. Bruce Morris, publisher of *NCT Web Magazine, The Web Developer's Journal,* and *Wacky HTML,* offers a powerhouse collection of the techniques and tricks you need to get the most from HTML. You'll review HTML basics; examine the use of graphics, multimedia, and animation; explore Java and HotJava; and deploy vanguard technologies such as CGI scripts and ActiveX™ tools. In short, HTML IN ACTION pushes the limits of what can be done with HTML—so you can push them even further.

U.S.A.	$29.95
U.K.	£27.99 [V.A.T. included]
Canada	$39.95
ISBN 1-55615-948-X	

The HTML IN ACTION companion CD includes:

- TrueType® fonts
- Internet Explorer
- Internet Control Pack
- Starter set of ActiveX controls

Microsoft Press